THE ILLUSTRATED
★ Guide to ★
TEXAS
H★LD'EM

Making Winners out of
Beginners *and* Advanced Players!

DISCARD

DENNIS PURDY

SOURCEBOOKS, INC.
NAPERVILLE, ILLINOIS

795.412
PUR

Published by Sourcebooks, Inc.
P.O. Box 4410, Naperville, Illinois 60567-4410
(630) 961-3900
FAX: (630) 961-2168
www.sourcebooks.com

Library of Congress Cataloging-in-Publication Data

Purdy, Dennis.
  The illustrated guide to Texas hold'em / Dennis Purdy.
     p. cm.
   ISBN 1-4022-0605-4 (alk. paper)
1. Poker. I. Title.

GV1251.P87 2005
795.412--dc22

                                    2005008914

Printed and bound in the United States of America
VHG 10 9 8 7 6 5 4 3

Contents

Acknowledgments

Thanking those who have helped us attain a long-desired goal can be perilous, for we risk offending someone if we forget to include them on a page such as this. Nevertheless, I'll give it a try and hope I haven't overlooked someone.

First, I'd like to thank two men whose names I don't even know, although one goes by the name of Smokestack Jack. It was on my second day of playing Texas Hold'em that Smokestack Jack hit the bad beat jackpot at the Muckleshoot Casino in Auburn, Washington. I only got a player's share, but it was almost $2,000! I was hooked on Hold'em.

Second, I'd like to thank Dan Hilger, owner of the former Luciano's Restaurant & Casino in Tacoma, Washington, and his poker room staff. It was here that I spent much of my playing time in the first three years of my Hold'em career. He and his fine poker room employees played a large part in the genesis of this book. It was his special-made playing cards that I used to create the illustrations for this book. Sadly, the casino is closed now, and I'll never again dine on the best chicken fettuccini in the world, but the memories of many great games and friends will last forever.

Of all the Luciano's poker room employees, the one I think I'll miss the most is Dawn Kappesser, a genuine professional Hold'em dealer and a great player in her own right. Dawn never failed to harpoon me when I made a bad play and she always made the game fun. I'll miss the way she always stole food off my plate, shared her Junior Mints with me, telegraphed when she was betting pocket Kings, and reminded me in a unique way when it was my big blind.

Most of all, I'd like to thank Robert "Doug" West, a true professional poker player who helped immensely with the material in this book. For more than a dozen years, Doug has been perfecting his craft of playing poker. For three of those years he took me under his wing and helped me understand the complexities of Hold'em in a way that no book ever did. He almost single-handedly turned the Luciano's poker room from a veritable graveyard into a bustling card room that oftentimes had to turn players away from the nightly tournaments. Most importantly, Doug turned me into a winner.

I'd like to thank my two youngest children, Dennika and Dakota, for being so supportive and understanding of the long hours I spent over the last several years perfecting my poker skills and writing this book.

I must mention my superagent, Evelyn Fazio, who helped see this idea through to fruition. Her many hours of help (mostly late at night) in the early stages of this project will always be appreciated by her Secret Weapon.

Finally, I'd like to thank Kathy, my personal muse. If she were a poker hand, she'd be a Royal Flush.

What This Book Is...and Isn't

So, you want to play Texas Hold'em, huh? All right, then, let's play it together and let's play it to win.

If you're like most beginning players, you've probably read (or skimmed) at least a book or two on Hold'em. You've undoubtedly watched the pros and celebrities on television with a combination of fascination, amusement, and even incredulity. And, if you're like I was when I first started studying Texas Hold'em, you're somewhat overwhelmed by the depth and complexity of the game. If you haven't played in an actual game yet, you're probably nervous about doing so. I know I was.

And you're probably really confused about a lot of the terminology. Don't worry, I've included probably the biggest Hold'em glossary ever published in a poker strategy book, so if you come across any words or phrases that are totally foreign to you, just go the glossary in the back of the book. There is no disputing the fact that everyone who plays this game must go through the pains of the Texas Hold'em learning curve. How quickly you adopt solid playing principles will determine how painfully you make your way through the curve.

It took me several years before I got to a point where I could throw away small pairs in early position, Ace-6/7/8/9 unsuited in any position, and pocket Kings with an Ace on the board. After playing such hands thousands of times during my early years, I finally got it into my hard head that I was just "pissing against the wind" by playing such hands.

Many—if not most—of my Hold'em losses the first several years were the result of my own bad play. It took me at least three years to fully catch on to the complexities and intricacies of Texas Hold'em before I got to the point where I stopped making naïve mistakes and became a force in the low limit games I regularly played in.

It is the pursuit of conveying to beginners how to win at low limit Texas Hold'em in spite of those complexities and intricacies that was the inspiration behind this book. An examination of the playing out of a typical Hold'em hand reveals subtleties that will, at various times, leave you amazed, jubilant, frustrated, satisfied, dismayed, or even furious, depending on how the cards fall. It is my intent, through this book, to help you to experience more good moments than bad, and to make you a winning player through thoughtful hand analysis that will lead to good playing habits and decisions.

So, with all the poker books on the market, why this one? Simple. Because it's different from all the others. It teaches in more of a visual way rather than just textual. It's been said that people remember 10 percent of what they hear or read, 20 percent of what they see, and 70 percent of what they do. That principle alone makes this a better book from which to learn.

Most of the other poker books take a chapter-by-chapter approach to learning. The author will teach you about one certain phase of the game in each chapter. Then, in the next chapter, the author will discuss another topic. In this book, strategy is discussed and illustrated, hand-by-hand, in situation format, as it is needed, as it develops, because Hold'em situations fluctuate, like an ebb and flow, when each new card is turned up on the board. You can start with pocket Aces, flop a 10-6-4 rainbow, turn a 6, and river an Ace that makes for three cards of the same suit on the board, and who knows what the heck has happened. That's why you need to be able to think quickly and correctly about what has happened at each betting level and how you should proceed. Should you check or bet? Raise or fold?

And Hold'em situations don't change just because of the cards that are dealt. They change from moment to moment based on your position in the hand, what other players do before you, what others are likely to do after you, how many players are still in the hand, and on and on. Because of all these aforementioned complexities and intricacies of Hold'em, this book has been designed to allow you to more easily grasp the points of strategy being made.

Another benefit of this book is that it focuses on low limit Hold'em and how it is actually being played in the casinos and card rooms across the country. This is not a complicated book of poker theory targeted toward sophisticated and knowledgeable players like so many of the other books on the market. It is aimed at beginners and players who are at the early stages of their Hold'em careers but who desire more success than they've achieved up to this point.

This book is also reader/player friendly. Frankly, most of the poker books I read in my early Hold'em playing days were very hard to fathom. Most of the material went right over my head. I was flooded with terms I'd never heard before. The poker theory these books espoused made me dizzy. The game made much more sense once I started playing it, but it was costly too, because I didn't possess the basics I'm going to give you in this book.

I wanted to write a book that would figuratively take a new player by the hand and walk him safely through the Hold'em jungles; something I wish had been available to me when I first started playing.

Chapter 1

The Basics of Texas Hold'em

This book makes the assumption that you're either a beginning player or a fairly new player to the game of Texas Hold'em and that you wish to learn how to play or how to play better. You've seen all the thrills and chills of Texas Hold'em tournaments on ESPN, FOX, Bravo, the Travel Channel, and other networks and figure it can't be all that difficult given some of the whacky characters you've witnessed. Now you're ready to take the plunge for yourself. Well, if you're not careful, that's exactly what you're going to do—PLUNGE!

So, before getting into the meat of this book—the 150 illustrated situational hands that will help you to easily visualize many basic Texas Hold'em strategies and help to make you a winner—I'll briefly go over the basics of Texas Hold'em for the unwashed among you.

Texas Hold'em is far and away the most popular poker game in America today. Forget about the Five Card Draw you saw Bret Maverick play in the old TV series, or the Five Card Stud Steve McQueen and Edward G. Robinson played to a brutal (at least for McQueen) climax in the movie *The Cincinnati Kid*. Those games are as old as the series and movie themselves. Today in poker rooms across the street, across the country, or around the world, it's Texas Hold'em, baby! Oh, you might occasionally find a game of Seven Card Stud (played mostly by old geezers 'cuz that's what they grew up with, and when they die, so will the game!), or Omaha Hi-Low Split, but you'll have to search for it. If you want to play poker outside your dining room table, it'll have to be Texas Hold'em.

Limit Vs. No Limit Hold'em

While there are a few slight variations played at some establishments, there are basically two kinds of Texas Hold'em that you can play: limit and no limit. No limit is the crazy version you typically see played on television. You know, the kind that first caught your attention and somehow made you think you'd like this game; the kind that led you to buy this book (a *very* good move on your part!). No limit Hold'em is the kind where one whacky character will push his whole stack of chips into the middle of the table, announce, "All in," and be called by another whacky character who also pushes his whole stack of chips into the pot until there is a pot of over a million dollars on the table.

Finally, no matter which wacky character wins the pot, everyone in the room will rise from their seat, hoot and holler a bit, turn to the person next to them and slap them on the back before letting out a collective deep breath. Then, everyone will sit back down, take another swig of beer, and the network will go to a commercial break. That, my friend, is no limit Texas Hold'em, and not the kind of poker we're talking about in this book.

What we're talking about in this book is limit Texas Hold'em. While 99 percent of the poker you see on television is no limit Texas Hold'em, 99 percent of what you'll be able to play in most poker rooms is limit Texas Hold'em. The two games are similar in some respects, but starkly different in others and it is important for you to know the difference.

Limit Texas Hold'em

"Limit" means that the betting levels are structured at certain limits. Limit Texas Hold'em can be further broken down into low, mid, and high limit. Low limit means the betting levels are at low limits, typically anything under $20 betting increments. Mid limit would be the $20 to $40 range, and high limit typically means anything more than that. The most common form of Texas Hold'em played in poker rooms today by far is low limit.

There are four betting rounds in each hand of limit Texas Hold'em. The first and second rounds are at one betting level, and the third and fourth rounds are at exactly double the betting level of the first two rounds. So, in a basic low-limit 4-8 game, this means that the betting level for the first two betting rounds is in $4 increments while the last two rounds are in $8 increments. Hence the name 4-8 Texas Hold'em.

There is no variance allowed in the amount of the bet. You *must* bet in $4 increments before and after the flop, and in $8 increments after the turn and river cards. Most establishments allow a bet and three raises before each betting round must end, but some poker rooms allow for a bet and four or even five raises, so make sure you know the house rules.

$4-$8, or 4-8 as you'll more commonly see it written on poker room sign-up boards, is only one level of low-limit Hold'em. Other common low-limit games are: 1-2, 2-4, 3-6 (the most commonly played, along with 4-8), 5-10, 6-12, and 10-20. Higher-limit games such as 15-30, 20-40, 30-60, 60-120, 100-200, and higher are typically played by professionals. So, for the sake of conformity, and because it is the most commonly played low-limit game, 4-8 is what we'll use for discussion in this book.

As mentioned earlier, the betting in limit Hold'em is structured. You are *not* allowed to vary the betting amounts. So, for example, if a player at the table bets $4 after receiving his two pocket cards, and it's your turn to bet, you must either fold your hand, call his $4 bet with $4 of your own, or raise the bet to $8. You can't bet $5, or $11, or anything other than $4 or $8. If you do raise the bet to $8, then any other player who wishes to raise the bet again *must* bet $12. There is no option to the amount of the bet in low-limit Hold'em. After the turn and river cards, the bets must be in $8 increments. So, for example, the first person to bet must bet $8. If another player wishes to raise, he must bet $16. A further raise would mean a $24 bet, and so on until the maximum number of raises has been reached. A bet and three raises after the river card, then, would mean you'd have to put $32 into the pot if you decide to stay in the hand.

So even though this is what is called low-limit Hold'em, you can see that the amount of money put into one hand could actually be fairly substantial for small bettors. A bet and three raises on each of the four betting rounds would require you to put in $96–on one hand!

The average professional Hold'em dealer deals about thirty to thirty-five hands an hour. If you find yourself in a loose game with several players who like to raise and reraise constantly, be CAREFUL! The amount of money going through your hands could be substantial, so you need to have an adequate bankroll and you'd better be winning your share of the pots.

Playing the Game

It takes two to tango, as they say, and two is the minimum number of players you need to play Hold'em. Even though the casino provides a house dealer, Texas Hold'em is not a game in which you can play one-on-one against the house, such as blackjack. You need other players as opponents. The typical Hold'em table will seat somewhere between nine and eleven players besides the house dealer, with ten being the most common.

The player positions at the table are referred to by seat number. The player to the immediate left of the dealer is "Seat 1." To his left is Seat 2, to his left Seat 3, and so on until you circle the table to Seat 10, the seat to the immediate right of the dealer. For the instructional purposes of this book, we're going to assume that each of the illustrated situations used begins with a ten-handed game (i.e., there is a player in each of the ten seats at the table at the beginning of the hand since this is the position you will find yourself in during most actual poker room games). These numbered seat positions will be used throughout the main portion of this book, so be sure you understand them.

While some poker games, including many dining-room-table games, are played for a high/low split of the pot, Texas Hold'em is played for high hand only. The only time a Hold'em pot is split is when two players have the same hand, which occurs a fair amount of the time due to the five community cards that are dealt on the table which all players may make use of. There are no wild cards in Texas Hold'em. It's strictly the best five-card hand made from the seven cards comprised from your two pocket cards and the five community cards.

Before the house dealer deals the hand, two things must happen. First, the dealer will place a "dealer button" in front of one player. This button, (normally white) which is about three inches in diameter and usually has the word "dealer" stamped on it, represents the player the dealer is dealing in place of, since the players can't actually deal the cards in a poker room game.

The second thing that must happen is that two players, on a rotating basis, are required to put money into the pot as "seed" money, or money which is used to generate betting action on each hand. These two players are known as the small blind and the big blind. They are, in effect, putting money "blindly" into the pot before they see their cards. It also lends a bit of mystery to the hand, since these two players have money invested in the pot without seeing their hands. The other players who choose to play their hands do so on the knowledge of their two pocket cards.

The two blinds are always the first two players to the immediate left of the dealer button. The first player to the left of the dealer button is the small blind; the player to his left is the big blind. The amount of the blinds is dependent on the level of limit Hold'em you are playing. The big blind must put in the equivalent of one full small bet. The small blind usually must put in the equivalent of one-half of a small bet. This means, therefore, that in a 4-8 game, the small bet level is $4. The big blind has to put in $4 and the small blind half of that, or $2.

The dealer then deals the cards, starting with the player to the immediate left of the player with the dealer button (the small blind). At the completion of the hand, the dealer will then move the dealer button clockwise, one position to the left. This moving of the dealer button is constant, allowing for all players to act equally as the dealer without actually dealing the cards. It also allows for all players to play the same positions an equal number of times, i.e., first to bet, second to bet, last to bet, and so on.

The eight players who are not in the blinds have the opportunity to look at their two pocket cards before deciding whether or not to place a bet on the hand. Since you have the opportunity to see your starting hand free of charge 80 percent of the time, and since far more two-card starting hands will be better thrown away than kept, *this is a critical part of winning at low limit Texas Hold'em!* This will be discussed in more depth in each of the 150 situations presented.

Once the blinds are in place, the dealer deals two cards face down to all players at the table. These two hole cards are known as your pocket cards. The first player to bet, or act, after the pocket cards are dealt, is the player to the immediate left of the big blind. He has to decide then and there whether or not he is going to play the hand. If he chooses not to play, he simply tosses (mucks) his cards into the middle of the table and it costs him nothing. This action is called "mucking his hand."

If he chooses to play the hand, then he either places a $4 bet in front of him to call the big blind bet, or he may raise the bet to $8. These are his only three options: fold, call the bet, or raise the bet. After he acts, the player to his immediate left acts, either calling the current bet level, raising, or folding. This continues around the table, in turn, until all players have acted on their hands. If no one has raised by the time the betting action gets to the small blind, he may either fold his hand and lose his $2 blind bet, call the bet (which requires that he put $2 more into the pot), or he can raise to $8, which means he must put in another $6.

Also, since the two blind hands were forced to put their money into the pot before the start of play, they have the option of raising themselves. For example, if no one raises before it gets back to the big blind, the big blind can make the raise. The dealer will address the big blind with, "Option?" This is the dealer's way of asking the big blind player if he wants to raise or not. If he wants to raise, he announces, "Raise." If not, many times you will hear the player say, "Big enough." This means that he is declining to raise; his $4 bet is big enough.

The dealer then burns the top card (places it face down on the table into the muck pile) before dealing three cards face up in the middle of the table where all players can see them. This three-card deal is called the flop. All players may make use of any or all of these same three exact cards in their hands. Players will, in fact, have to use at least three of the five board cards in their final hand because they each only get two starting cards and you have to have at least five cards to make a final poker hand.

After the flop is dealt, another round of betting takes place, but this time it doesn't start where it did after the pocket cards were dealt (the player to the left of the big blind). This time, and for the next two betting rounds as well, the betting starts with the first player to the immediate left of the dealer button who is still in the game. The first player to act has the option of "checking" (not betting), betting, or folding, although if no one has bet before him a player will not usually fold, but it does happen. This is called "checking out." All other players still interested in remaining in the hand will then bet or check accordingly and in turn until the betting round is over. Once one player bets, however, all other players are required to either call the bet, raise the bet, or fold their hands. There is no checking once a bet has been made. (In the same manner, there can be no checking before the flop is dealt because the two blind hands are actually bets.)

Once all bets are completed after the flop, the dealer again burns the top card and then deals one more card face up on the board next to the three flopped cards. This fourth face-up card is called the turn card, or the turn. It is also referred to as fourth street. Another round of betting takes place just as it did after the flop, but this time at the higher betting level ($8 increments instead of $4).

Once all interested players have completed their betting action, the dealer burns the top card again and deals one final card face up next to the other four cards. This fifth and last face-up card is called the river. It is also known as fifth street. One final round of betting takes place and, at the completion of the last bet, all players interested in contesting for the pot then turn over their cards and the high hand wins. It is up to the house dealer to make the determination of which player holds the winning hand. Once the winner is determined, the dealer will push all the chips in the pot to the winning player. If there is a tie for high hand, the dealer will divide the chips into two, or sometimes three, equal stacks and give each player his share.

During the play of the hand, as the pot is building, you will notice the dealer taking several chips out of the pot and placing them into one or two slots in the tabletop. This rake, as it is known, is the house's share for running the game. Out of this rake they pay the expenses, such as dealer and other employee salaries, supplies such as new cards and chips, taxes, utilities, and all the other incidentals. What's left is their profit. The typical rake of a low-limit game is 10 percent up to a $3 or $4 maximum plus another $1 that is used for house jackpots. So if the pot reaches, for example, $90, the house still only takes out $3 or $4. There could be a slight variance from poker room to poker room.

Once the winner has been paid and the rake has been dropped, the dealer will move the dealer button to the next player, announce, "Blinds, please," if the appropriate players haven't already placed them out, shuffle up the cards, and deal the next hand. And so it goes about thirty times an hour, hour after hour, day after day, at Texas Hold'em tables all around the world.

Chapter 2

Pregame Preparation

Okay, you've decided that you've watched this game on television and read about it in books long enough and you're ready to try it for yourself. Where do you go? That depends on where you live.

Some states have legalized casino gambling. Some casinos, but not all, offer Texas Hold'em. The nice thing about playing in legal casinos is that you can, for the most part, rest assured that the game is on the up and up. The lights are bright and there are security guards aplenty. Gambling commission officials make regular visits to keep tabs on everything. No one gets ripped off. My first recommendation is to play Hold'em in such a setting.

For those states without casino gambling, there are often large card rooms. Sometimes these are stand-alone establishments that offer nothing but poker, but bill themselves as "casinos." They are typically bright, well-staffed, and policed. This sort of establishment would be my second choice.

Sometimes legally licensed card rooms are located inside bowling alleys or taverns in a small room off by themselves. Oftentimes the lighting isn't as bright. They also tend to be lacking in security, both inside and outside in their often-dark parking lots. The professionalism of their staff and facilities can leave something to be desired. For these obvious reasons, these sorts of establishments would be my third choice.

A fairly new phenomenon which is growing in popularity across America is the private game. I've heard numerous stories of people renting apartments and converting them into Texas Hold'em card rooms. Some of these are in states where it is legal and some where it's not. The attraction of these private games, besides the poker itself, is that they are unregulated, meaning no taxes and no (or little) house rake. The drawbacks to such establishments (if you can call them that) should be obvious: no legitimate police or security personnel on duty for personal safety and no assurance of a fair game. These two facts alone would keep me from playing in such a game unless I personally knew all the participants.

Online Poker

Another fairly new alternative is playing Texas Hold'em online. Many new casino and card-room patrons first got their feet wet on the Internet in one of the many growing number of poker websites, such as PartyPoker.com, PokerRoom.com, and others. What you do, essentially, is open an account with the poker site by providing funds in advance. As long as you have money on account, you can play. You can fund your account in a number of ways, depending on the site. You can mail a cashier's check to the site's physical address, use a credit card, or do a funds transfer through any of a number of electronic funds transfer companies such as PayPal, Neteller, etc.

Most of the Internet poker sites allow you to open a "free" account, in which you're given play money to use in their play-money games, with the eventual hope that you'll like the experience and want to start a real money account. While this is good up to a point, the playing experience you're getting for free is skewed because so many of the players in the play-money games don't play the same way as if they were playing for real money. Players in play-money games get wild and crazy, making bets, calls, and raises they would never do in a game if it cost them real money. PokerRoom.com even allows players in play money games to lodge complaints against other players they feel are abusing the "spirit" of the game. The play you'll experience in a play-money game won't be anything at all like what you'll experience in real-money games, so in that vein they're a waste of time.

If you decide to play online poker for real money, one very important thing to keep in mind is the difference in the number of hands played per hour and how that can hurt you. For example, in most live casino games, the dealers can deal an average of about thirty hands an hour. Online games are dealt at a staggering pace, sometimes seventy-five to one hundred hands an hour! You'd better know your stuff if you're going to play online, because the play is FAST, and if you play too many weak hands, make too many bad calls, etc., your losses can mount up in a hurry as compared to a live game.

There are other pitfalls of online poker as well. Sometimes your connection gets disrupted and by the time you log back on, you discover you've lost several blind bets while you were off-line. Also, I've heard stories of several players teaming up together in the same online game or at the same tournament table, and, communicating by telephone, letting each other know what their pocket cards were. Then, only the conspirator with the best hand would stay in on the hand. At the end of the night the conspirators would work a split of the money they'd chiseled out of the honest players.

Certainly online poker has a place and an appeal; you can play twenty-four hours a day in your bathrobe if you want to; you don't have to be around a bunch of smokers if you don't want to; it's quick and easy to get into a game; if you're like me, you can do other things while you're waiting for the next hand to be dealt, especially if you're playing in a tournament where the play can be slower for a variety of reasons that don't need to be explained here. Whatever the appeal, online poker is here to stay. My recommendation is that you don't play online for money until you're very proficient at the game because of how quickly you can lose, and lose big. Learn the game in a live casino setting first, where the play is much slower paced and you have a chance to absorb what is happening.

All right, you've picked your preferred legal and safe establishment to try your hand at Hold'em. What next? You need to make sure that you take everything with you that you might need while playing poker. What, you might ask, could you possibly need besides money? Plenty.

What to Bring, What to Wear

I keep a separate coat for playing poker. One, because I don't smoke and, since the casinos I go to allow smoking, I don't want my good coat to stink like cigarette smoke. Two, because it has a large "possibles" pocket. A possibles pocket is a pocket that holds everything I could possibly need while playing poker. Some of these items include: a silver dollar I put on top of my pocket cards to protect them during play; aspirin (the kind I like); nasal spray (the heavy smoke sometimes clogs me up); Q-tips; a tiny toothbrush and floss sticks (some playing sessions can run ten to fifteen hours and it's nice to be able to brush your teeth in the restroom); any prescription medicines I might be taking at the time; a small notebook and pen in case I need to make any notes for later reference; Visine (the smoke again); cough drops and/or lozenges; my small set of poker percentage reference cards I designed for my own play; an extra handkerchief; a change of shirt, left in my vehicle (mostly in case I wear a sweater and the room is too warm, or if I wear a short-sleeved shirt and the room is too cool). In short, you should take anything with you that you might need and which you don't want to be wishing you hadn't forgotten when you're in the middle of a long and productive session from which you don't want to leave.

You need to take a proper bankroll for the game you're going to be playing. If you're going to be sitting in a $3-$6 or $4-$8 game, I would recommend taking at least $250 with you. This allows for a $200 buy-in and $50 for food, drink, and miscellaneous purchases. I've seen many, many beginning players buy in for $30, $40, or $50. This just isn't enough. If you catch a good hand and there's a lot of betting and raising, you want to be able to bet the whole way. Small buy-ins like these often come back to haunt you when you have to announce "all in" and you're only halfway through a hand you end up winning. If you're going to play, come to the game with enough money to play it properly. A lot of players will buy in for $100, but I don't think that's enough, either. I've put that much into one hand many times over the years.

Another important thing to bring to the game with you is a proper mindset. Don't play if you're tired, upset about something, angry, hungry, distracted, or when you've been drinking. Come happy. Come to enjoy. Don't come with a chip on your shoulder. Don't come with anything to prove to anyone except yourself, the fact that you can play winning Hold'em. If you can't play with a relaxed, positive attitude, stay home. Following this rule alone will save you a lot of money.

Getting into the Game

Once you've arrived at your preferred establishment with a proper bankroll and with a proper attitude, what's next? Take a few minutes to look the place over to get at ease. See who is playing at all the tables. Is there anyone you'd feel comfortable playing with? Or uncomfortable with? Who are the obviously good players? Who has lots of chips in front of them and who has but a few? Is there anyone playing so loosely he/she is being foolish? You may not have a choice as to which table you play at, but at least you can get a heads up on some of the players if and when you get into a game with them.

Two things you must do in order to become a winning Hold'em player are to keep your eyes open and your mouth shut. If you're going to play this game to win, especially when you're a beginner, your mind should be like a sponge, always absorbing. You should be filing away information on players and their tendencies and habits. You can do a lot of this while waiting to get into a game.

Once you're ready to play, you'll need to check in with the floor person or board person, whoever is in charge of keeping the player sign-up board current. Virtually all establishments keep some sort of waiting list, usually a board on one wall, with the names of players waiting to play. If the establishment offers more than one game, or more than one level of game, these will be broken down on the sign-up board.

For example, the board may have columns for players waiting to play in a $4-$8 game, a $10-$20, game, an Omaha game, etc. Just ask the person running the sign-up board to enter your name on any or all games you are willing to play. You'll notice that some players will be listed in several different columns. This means that they are willing to play in whichever game comes open first. Once they are placed in a game, their name will be removed from all the games they were listed under.

This same board is also where the names are kept of players who are seeking a seat change, either in their current game or in another game. If, for example, you like Seat 1, but are currently in Seat 5, you need to notify the board person of your desired seat position change. If your name is on the board and the desired seat comes open, your request will take precedence over another player who may ask for that seat when it is vacated, but who failed to sign up for it properly like you did.

If you don't get into a game right away, use your time wisely. Quietly and unobtrusively study the other players. Knowledge of how each of them plays can be powerful when you get into the game with them. And best of all, it won't cost you anything while you're waiting to get into the game.

Chapter 3

Let the Game Begin

Once it's your turn to be seated in a game, the floor person will either let you know or call out your name, depending on how large the casino's poker room is. He or she will advise you which table you'll be seated at and will ask you how much you'd like to buy in for. Depending on the establishment, you'll either pick up your own chips at the cage area or the floor person will bring them to you at the table. You may or may not pay the dealer for your buy-in, depending on the house policy.

Once seated, depending on where the dealer button is, the dealer will ask you if you want to post or wait for the big blind. What this means is that if you're not coming into the big blind already, you'll have to wait for the big blind to get to you, unless you want to "post" the amount of one full small bet to get in the action early. It's best to wait for the big blind, otherwise you'll essentially be paying two big blinds in one round just to get in on the action.

Since I went over the basics of how a hand is played in chapter 2, I won't repeat it here, but there are a few other tips worth passing along for beginning the playing session. As I mentioned earlier, I always buy in for $200 in a low-limit game, and it's not just because I feel it's the proper playing bankroll for a $3-$6 or $4-$8 game. I also buy in for $200 because most other players *don't* buy in for this much.

The theory (which has turned into reality, at least at my games) is that many players get intimidated by a player with large stacks of chips in front of him. Players come and go throughout the course of a long play-ing session. They don't all know what you bought in for. Some will con-clude that you won those chips. What's even better is when you start with $200 in chips and build your stack to $600, $700, or more. On a half dozen occasions my stack has even reached $1,000-$1,100, and let me tell you, that's a LOT of $1 chips!

On a regular basis I hear opposing players talk about my chip stack. Sometimes they'll say something to me directly such as, "I see you're building your castles again, Dennis." Sometimes I'll overhear quiet com-ments between two players at the other end of the table, such as, "Holy shit, would you look at that stack of chips. I don't know how he does it all the time." The other player will reply with something like, "He's such a tough player. He's the only one I never can figure out at the table." Whether or not these statements are always the case every night, the fact remains that the players I play against routinely are, if not intimidated by me, at least wary of me—and a lot of it has to do with the size of my chip stack. Even when I've had an unproductive or losing night, I might hear someone say, "Not building any castles tonight, Dennis?" That tells me someone is at least still thinking about my often-large stacks of chips.

Ideally you'd like to start out on a winning note. Wait for a good hand to jump in on. Also, you should typically play fewer hands at the start of a session if you're sitting down with a bunch of players you are unfamil-iar with. Study their habits. Catalog their betting tendencies. Observe and make note of which players are tight, conservative bettors and which ones are loose and free with their betting. And even if you're not in on a particular hand, pay attention to it all the way to the end. That way you can learn what types of hands your opponents are willing to play to the river. You can see who's willing to bluff, who's willing to play underpairs, who's willing to chase cards. In short, you can utilize your non-playing time at the table to figure out which players are the spiders and which ones are the flies.

When you're a new devotee to something, such as Hold'em poker, you will undoubtedly hear many terms and witness many things that you don't understand. You just can't possibly learn everything there is to learn before you sit down to play. So, when you hear or see something you don't fully understand, and if it doesn't affect you personally, I would make a mental note of it and research it after your playing session. "But," you might say, "why not just ask the dealer or another player what was meant or what happened?" Simple. Because it paints a big sign on your forehead: "Beginner. Take my money." This is another reason I recommend that you keep your mouth shut while playing poker, especially in the beginning. If you don't open your mouth, you can't say anything that will give you away as a naïve beginner. Sure, talk about the ballgame on the TV monitor, or the weather, or whatever else you want to, but don't talk poker with the other players. It will only give your opponents ammunition to use against you later.

Even at this stage of my playing career, I rarely speak when playing. Sometimes the other players think of me as aloof or even unfriendly, but I'm always watching, always cataloging, always filing away in my memory how each player plays. As a former card-counting blackjack professional, I have the ability to remember a lot of what happens on the poker table from hand to hand, day to day, and even month to month. You, too, probably have this same ability within you, but it's hard to do when you're talking.

When you finally do get a seat in the game, remember a few rules of poker etiquette and common sense.

- Be polite. Don't call other players names or comment on how badly they play. There are enough hammerheads at the table who will do this. Don't be one of them.
- Take your chips out of the rack and stack them in front of you. Players who play out of racks slow the game down.
- When you muck (discard) your hand, do it respectfully. Don't flick or toss your cards aggressively toward the dealer. Sometimes this will result in your cards hitting another player's unprotected pocket cards, and he'll be forced to muck his hand. (And he won't be very happy with you!) Besides, the dealer doesn't need to be treated disrespectfully. The Golden Rule applies at the poker table, too.
- Don't expose your hole cards when discarding your hand, either to the player next to you or to the whole table. This is just plain poor sportsmanship.
- Keep your burning cigarettes off the poker table. The ashes soil the felt surface and get onto the cards.
- Keep food and drinks off the table for the same reasons.

- Remember to tip the dealer when you win a hand. They virtually all work for minimum wage and tips. Without the dealers, there would be no game.
- Keep your profanities to yourself. No one wants to listen to a profanity-laced game.
- If you smoke, make sure the smoke isn't going directly into anyone's face.
- If you have to take a break to eat or use the restroom, don't do it when it's your blind or when you're on the button. It makes for a confusing, irritating situation for the other players and the dealer when the blind posting structure has to be altered to account for your leaving the table.
- Don't turn over another player's mucked cards. I did this once on the first day I played, not realizing what a big no-no it was. When the other player mucked his hand, he flicked them with his finger, but instead of landing in the middle of the table, they landed directly in front of me. I innocently turned them over and looked at them and the furor was on.
- Don't abuse the dealers. All they do is deal the cards. They don't tell lousy players to stay in until the river to hit a runner-runner suck out hand to beat you.
- Be honorable in your play. Don't use sneaky, underhanded tricks or tactics in order to win.
- And finally, don't educate the competition. If another player wants to improve his game, let him go out and buy his own books. (In which case you can recommend this one.)

Chapter 4

The Rules of Good Basic Strategy

There are almost as many strategies for playing Texas Hold'em as there are books about the game itself. One thing is clear, however; low limit Texas Hold'em is a vastly different game than the no-limit version you see on television. Low limit is even different than high limit, because there tends to be many, many more bad players at low limit Hold'em. Let's face it, it's much easier for most players to make a dumb call for $4 than for $200.

Some of the information contained in this book differs somewhat from conventional Hold'em wisdom. But a low-limit game filled with a lot of bad players is a different game than a higher-limit game with better players who understand the game, and there's no disputing that. For example, there is one low-limit game at a certain casino I've played in three times. The first two times I got creamed until I figured out what was going on. The third time around I got all of my money back and then some, but I had to understand the game before I was able to do so.

What was happening was that five or six of the players in the game were truly horrible players who would bet and raise on absolutely nothing, such as Jack-2 offsuit in the pocket, and then stay in until the river no matter what. Now, if you are playing against one such player, you will normally kick his can all over the place. But when five or six players are all doing the same thing every hand, one of them will invariably draw out on you much of the time. So, I had to tighten up, playing only the best starting hands and continuing on with the hand only if I got a strong flop. In this way, the "gang of six" wasn't often able to overcome my strong starting hand and flop.

The first rule of good basic strategy for most Hold'em games is to play only good starting hands. At the end of this chapter, you'll find a Relative Win Rate chart that ranks all 169 starting pocket hands *by their win rate, not by their hand rank.* Most of the time I play only the top twenty-five to thirty hands on this chart. There are exceptions, of course, but they are situational.

The second rule of good basic strategy is that the flop must both hit and help your hand or you fold if someone bets. After the flop, you have 71.4 percent of the cards you're going to get for your hand. The flop will go a long ways towards telling you if you should play any further.

The third rule of good basic strategy is that if you play a drawing hand, such as a flush or straight draw, you need to have hit four of the five cards you need by the flop. Three of one suit after the flop is not considered a legitimate flush draw. Nor are three cards towards a straight. You should hold four to a straight, preferably an open-ended one, or four cards of the same suit to continue on with these draws. And most of the time you should have at least three or four players still in the hand with you to continue on with these draws in order to get enough money into the pot to make it worthwhile. This is known as pot odds, which I'll go into in depth in the 150 situations section.

Rule four of good basic strategy says if you're not on a drawing hand, then to continue after the flop, in most cases you should hold at least top pair with a big kicker, or an overpair to the flop. An overpair to the flop would be a pocket pair that is higher than the rank of any card on the flop. And this assumes that the flop didn't come up three of one suit that you don't hold, or three consecutive ranks that don't fit your hand but could easily fit someone else's hand for a straight or flush draw.

The fifth rule of good basic strategy is to keep your eyes open for danger. What is the highest possible hand anyone could be holding? How likely is it that an opponent would be holding such a hand? You need to always be on the lookout for danger. Every time a new card is brought, reassess the board and its potential perils to your hand.

Rule six says when you have the best hand, make your opponents pay. No free cards.

The seventh rule of good basic strategy is that you should fold your hand when it's obvious that you are beaten. Don't call a river bet "just to see" if the other player really had the hand he was betting. Once you've played for a while, it will become easier to recognize when you're beaten, which then allows you to fold earlier in the hand. It's just as important to minimize the amount you lose on your losing hands as it is to maximize the amount you win on your winning hands.

Rule eight is that you must take your position into consideration when deciding whether or not to play a particular hand. For example, if you were dealt Ace-7 suited in first position, you would fold. But if you received these same cards in the small blind and there were no raises before you, then you would call the bet and play to see the flop.

Actual Odds Vs. Pot Odds

The ninth rule of good basic strategy is to learn and understand the concepts of actual odds and pot odds. "Actual odds" means the actual mathematical odds of something occurring. "Pot odds" means the relationship of the money in the pot to the actual odds of something occurring to give you that pot.

For example, let's consider that you and I were to engage in a quarter flipping contest. If I asked you to call the coin flip, heads or tails, you would understand that the actual odds of you guessing correctly (or, getting the call you wanted) would be 50 percent, or even, or put in the way we calculate poker hand probabilities, 1-to-1.

Now, what if I said that every time you guessed right I would give you a dollar and every time you guessed wrong you'd give me three dollars? You wouldn't do it, of course, and rightfully so. If you translate this simple exercise to poker, the 1-to-1 actual odds of heads versus tails represents the actual odds of getting the card(s) you need to win the hand. The 3-to-1 money odds represent the pot odds being laid in this proposition. It is, of course, a bad bet for you to lay 3-to-1 odds against you to get a 1-to-1 return on your money.

A typical example in Hold'em would be if you flopped four cards to an inside straight draw, such as 7-8-10-Jack. The odds of you getting a 9 for a straight by the river are approximately 5-to-1 against you. So, if you are alone in the hand with one other player, depending on how much money was put into the pot before the flop it probably will not be correct to play to the river in an effort to hit the straight since you will only be getting even money the rest of the way in an effort to hit a hand that the odds are 5-to-1 against you. If, on the other hand, there were seven players in the hand, then you would be getting 6-to-1 money (or pot) odds on a 5-to-1 proposition. Then it would be correct to play for a 9.

While I will go into the pot odds formula in greater detail in the 150 situations section, I will give an example here of the kind of mathematical calculating you'll have to do when you play Texas Hold'em to win. Let's say you hold a pocket hand of Jack and Queen of Hearts. This is a hand that you would play under most circumstances, as its 44.2 percent win rate would suggest. Now, let's say that five players stayed in the hand for one bet of $4. That means the pot contains $20. The flop then comes up 3-8-9, with two of the cards being Hearts. You now hold four cards to a Heart flush as well as a gut shot straight draw (i.e., 8-9-Jack-Queen, needing a 10 in the middle, or gut, for a straight). What you now need to do is calculate your chances for making a made hand, which would be either a straight or a flush, both of which could win the hand for you. Since there are two Hearts in your hand and two on the board, you only need one more Heart to make a Queen-high flush, a very good hand. There are thirteen Hearts in the suit, so that means there are potentially nine more Hearts available to come out.

These nine possible Hearts are known as outs, so you would be said to have nine outs to make your flush. But you're not done yet. If a 10 comes on the board on the turn or river, you'll make a Queen-high straight, also a very good hand. Since there are no 10s showing either in your hand or on the board, all four 10s have to be considered possible outs as well. If you add the nine Heart outs to the four 10 outs, you have thirteen outs. You do, however, have to subtract one from this because the 10 of Hearts is only one card but has been counted twice (as a Heart and a 10). That means you have exactly twelve possible outs for making a Queen-high straight or a Queen-high flush, both of which are very good hands and could win you the pot.

The next thing you need to do is calculate how many unseen cards there are. Since you know a deck has fifty-two cards and you can see five of them (your two pocket cards and the three cards that came on the flop), that means there are forty-seven unseen cards that contain the twelve you need. Granted, some of the cards you need might be (and likely are) in the hands of your opponents, but there is no way of knowing. All you can do is calculate the possibilities. If you subtract the twelve out cards from the forty-seven unseen cards, you are left with thirty-five cards that do not give you the straight or flush. This ratio of 35-to-12 reduces to about 3-to-1. That means that your actual odds of getting a card you need to make your hand are about 3-to-1.

Now, let's compare this ratio to the money, or pot odds, and see how we need to apply it in this situation. You know that the pot contains $20 in preflop money. After the flop, let's say you are the last player to act, the other four players deciding before you. We'll say that the first player to act bets $4 and is called by the next three players. It's now your turn to decide what to do. The pot has now grown to $36 with the additional four bets after the flop. What you have to decide, in effect, is whether or not you should call the $4 bet being asked of you. If you divide the $36 currently in the pot by the $4 bet you're being asked to make, the ratio of money in the pot (your potential winnings) to what you're being asked to risk to win it (the $4) is 9-to-1, which is expressed by the following simple equation:

$$36 \div 4 = 9$$

Put another way (in Hold'em terms), you're being asked to make a bet in which the odds against you are 3-to-1, but for which you'll be paid a return of 9-to-1 if you win the bet. This is a huge positive betting situation for you and one which you would absolutely take every time.

Consider, if you will, what would happen if you had this exact situation one hundred times in a row. About seventy-five times you would lose the bet and twenty-five times you would win the bet (at the 3-to-1 actual odds ratio). For each of the seventy-five times you lost this bet it would cost you $4, or a total of $300. For each of the twenty-five times you hit your hand and won the bet you would win $40, or $1,000 total (at the 9-to-1 money odds ratio). This, in simple terms, is what is known as pot odds. When the pot odds are in your favor, you should almost always make the bet. When they are against you, you should almost always fold. To be a consistent winner at Texas Hold'em, you need to be able to calculate pot odds and make the correct play. It's really not as difficult as it might seem. I've included a number of pot odds examples in the 150 Situations section of the book that will help you make this part of your game second nature.

Texas Hold'em Relative Win Rates for All 169 Pocket Hands

The following chart shows the win rate of each hand when randomly played against any other hand. This does not mean, for example, that a pair of pocket Aces wins 86.1 percent of the times played in a regular game, since in a normal game there is almost always more than one player in a hand and each player holding the Aces and the other hands will play them differently. This chart is only intended to give you, the reader, an idea of the relative strength of each starting hand as compared to all other hands.

These figures were calculated from a computer simulation of one million dealt hands.

(s = suited, un = unsuited)

#	Hand	Rate	#	Hand	Rate	#	Hand	Rate
1.	A-A pair	86.1%	17.	Q-J s	44.2%	33.	A-3 s	21.3%
2.	K-K pair	74.6%	18.	A-8 s	41.5%	34.	5-5 pair	20.7%
3.	A-K s	68.6%	19.	K-10 s	40.9%	35.	K-J un	20.5%
4.	Q-Q pair	68.5%	20.	A-9 s	40.5%	36.	A-2 s	20.0%
5.	A-K un	67.0%	21.	J-10 s	40.0%	37.	K-9 s	20.0%
6.	A-Q s	64.9%	22.	Q-10 s	39.4%	38.	Q-9 s	19.1%
7.	J-J pair	64.4%	23.	K-Q un	39.2%	39.	A-9 un	17.4%
8.	10-10 pair	60.8%	24.	10-9 s	38.3%	40.	Q-J un	16.8%
9.	A-Q un	60.5%	25.	A-10 un	34.4%	41.	A-7 un	10.2%
10.	A-J s	58.6%	26.	A-7 s	33.9%	42.	A-8 un	10.0%
11.	9-9 pair	55.4%	27.	A-4 s	30.6%	43.	A-6 un	9.9%
12.	K-Q s	54.6%	28.	A-5 s	29.7%	44.	9-8 s	9.8%
13.	8-8 pair	51.8%	29.	A-6 s	29.6%	45.	J-8 s	9.8%
14.	A-10 s	50.7%	30.	7-7 pair	28.6%	46.	A-4 un	9.6%
15.	A-J un	48.9%	31.	J-9 s	27.9%	47.	K-8 s	9.5%
16.	K-J s	45.3%	32.	6-6 pair	26.2%	48.	10-8 s	9.5%

49.	A-5 un	9.4%	94.	K-8 un	3.4%	139.	7-2 un	0.4%
50.	J-10 un	9.4%	95.	9-7 un	3.4%	140.	J-5 un	0.4%
51.	Q-10 un	9.3%	96.	J-4 s	3.3%	141.	J-3 un	0.4%
52.	K-10 un	9.1%	97.	8-4 s	3.3%	142.	10-4 un	0.4%
53.	Q-9 un	8.8%	98.	10-5 s	3.2%	143.	9-2 s	0.4%
54.	A-2 un	8.8%	99.	9-6 s	3.2%	144.	9-5 un	0.4%
55.	10-9 un	8.8%	100.	K-6 un	3.1%	145.	9-3 un	0.4%
56.	K-7 s	8.6%	101.	Q-2 s	3.1%	146.	8-3 s	0.4%
57.	A-3 un	8.5%	102.	J-6 s	3.1%	147.	8-3 un	0.4%
58.	K-6 s	8.4%	103.	Q-3 s	3.0%	148.	7-3 un	0.4%
59.	J-9 un	8.4%	104.	Q-4 s	3.0%	149.	5-4 un	0.4%
60.	10-7 s	8.4%	105.	K-7 un	2.8%	150.	4-2 un	0.4%
61.	4-4 pair	8.3%	106.	6-3 s	2.4%	151.	Q-2 un	0.3%
62.	K-9 un	8.2%	107.	7-3 s	2.1%	152.	10-6 un	0.3%
63.	8-7 s	8.0%	108.	K-2 un	1.6%	153.	9-3 s	0.3%
64.	7-6 s	7.2%	109.	Q-4 un	1.6%	154.	9-4 un	0.3%
65.	9-7 s	5.8%	110.	4-3 s	1.6%	155.	8-6 un	0.3%
66.	3-3 pair	4.5%	111.	K-4 un	1.5%	156.	8-2 un	0.3%
67.	Q-5 s	4.4%	112.	K-3 un	1.5%	157.	7-2 s	0.3%
68.	K-5 s	4.3%	113.	Q-6 un	1.5%	158.	7-5 un	0.3%
69.	Q-8 s	4.2%	114.	Q-7 un	1.4%	159.	6-2 s	0.3%
70.	6-5 s	4.2%	115.	Q-5 un	1.4%	160.	5-2 un	0.3%
71.	J-8 un	4.1%	116.	J-2 s	1.4%	161.	4-3 un	0.3%
72.	2-2 pair	4.0%	117.	K-5 un	1.3%	162.	10-2 un	0.3%
73.	K-3 s	4.0%	118.	10-4 s	1.3%	163.	8-2 s	0.3%
74.	10-6 s	3.9%	119.	10-3 s	1.3%	164.	6-5 un	0.3%
75.	K-4 s	3.9%	120.	3-2 s	0.7%	165.	5-3 un	0.3%
76.	10-8 un	3.9%	121.	9-4 s	0.7%	166.	3-2 un	0.3%
77.	8-5 s	3.9%	122.	7-6 un	0.7%	167.	6-4 un	0.2%
78.	7-4 s	3.9%	123.	5-2 s	0.6%	168.	6-3 un	0.2%
79.	9-5 s	3.8%	124.	10-2 s	0.5%	169.	6-2 un	0.2%
80.	Q-7 s	3.8%	125.	4-2 s	0.5%			
81.	J-7 s	3.8%	126.	J-6 un	0.5%			
82.	J-3 s	3.8%	127.	J-4 un	0.5%			
83.	9-8 un	3.8%	128.	J-2 un	0.5%			
84.	8-7 un	3.8%	129.	9-6 un	0.5%			
85.	5-3 s	3.7%	130.	8-5 un	0.5%			
86.	8-6 s	3.6%	131.	Q-3 un	0.4%			
87.	7-5 s	3.6%	132.	J-7 un	0.4%			
88.	6-4 s	3.6%	133.	10-7 un	0.4%			
89.	K-2 s	3.6%	134.	10-5 un	0.4%			
90.	5-4 s	3.6%	135.	10-3 un	0.4%			
91.	Q-8 un	3.5%	136.	9-2 un	0.4%			
92.	Q-6 s	3.5%	137.	8-4 un	0.4%			
93.	J-5 s	3.5%	138.	7-4 un	0.4%			

Texas Hold'em Hand Rank Chart

The following chart ranks the hands of poker from high to low and includes the exact odds of getting each hand in just five dealt cards.

Hand	Explanation	Odds
Royal Flush	A/K/Q/J/10, all of the same suit (e.g., all Clubs or all Hearts). It is not possible for two players to hold Royal Flushes in the same Hold'em hand.	649,739 to 1
Straight Flush	Five consecutively ranked cards of the same suit (e.g., the Q/J/10/9/8 of Diamonds). If two players hold straight flushes on the same hand, the one with the highest card in his hand is the winner.	64,973 to 1
Four of a Kind	Four cards of the same rank, such as four Kings or four 10s. If two players each hold four of a kind, the one with the higher ranked cards is the winner.	4,164 to 1
Full House	Three cards of one rank and two of another rank (e.g., three Jacks and two 7s). If two players hold full houses on the same hand, the one holding the higher three-card group is the winner. If this is a tie, than the one holding the higher pair is the winner. If this is a tie as well, then the pot is split.	693 to 1
Flush	Five cards of the same suit, but not in consecutive order (e.g., all Clubs or all Spades). If two players hold flushes on the same hand, the one with the higher ranked card of the flush suit is the winner.	508 to 1

Hand	Explanation	Odds
Straight	Five cards in consecutive rank, but not in the same suit (e.g., J/10/9/8/7 of different suits). If two players each hold straights, the one with the higher ranked card in his straight hand is the winner.	254 to 1
Three of a Kind	Three cards of one rank and no other pairs (e.g., three Queens or three 6s). If two players each hold three-of-a-kind hands, the one with the higher ranked cards is the winner. If this is a tie, then the player with the highest card remaining in his hand is the winner. If this is also a tie, then the player with the next highest card is the winner. If this, too, is a tie, then the pot is split.	46 to 1
Two Pair	Two cards of one rank and two cards of another rank (e.g., two Aces and two 4s). If two players both have two pair, then the one with the highest pair is the winner. If this is a tie, then the one with the next highest pair is the winner. If this is also a tie, then whoever has the highest "kicker" (remaining card) is the winner. If this is also a tie, then the pot is split.	20 to 1
One Pair	Two cards of the same rank with no other pairs (e.g., two Kings or two 9s). If two players each hold one pair, the player holding the higher ranked pair is the winner. If this is a tie, then the player holding the next highest ranked card in their hand is the winner. If this is a tie, then whichever player holds the next highest "fourth" card is the winner. If this is also a tie, then whoever holds the highest "fifth" card in their hand is the winner. If this is also a tie, then the pot is split.	1.25 to 1
No Pair	Five cards of different ranks and not of the same suit or in consecutive order (e.g., K/Q/10/8/6 of mixed suits). If two players go to showdown and neither has a pair, then whichever player holds the highest card in their hole is the winner. If this is a tie, then whichever player holds the second highest card in the hole is the winner. If this is also a tie, then the pot is split.	1 to 1

Chapter 5

Practice Situations

The time has come for the main event: the 150 practice situations. There are many things that can happen during the course of one poker hand. The situation—as well as your response and your fortunes—can change dramatically with the turn of a card or the action of another player. Some changes are but subtle, while others are profound. What you need to do in order to become a winning Hold'em player is recognize what is happening from card to card, bet to bet, and player to player.

The 150 situations are quite self-explanatory. I present you with a situation on the left-hand page, ask you what you should do, and then provide the correct/best answer on the right-hand page, always with the rationale behind the decision. Within these 150 situations, you will experience a wide range of thought-provoking Texas Hold'em problems. Within the 150 answers, I hope the lightbulb will go off as you experience the enlightenment of unraveling these situational problems as well as the joy of learning how to become a winning Texas Hold'em player.

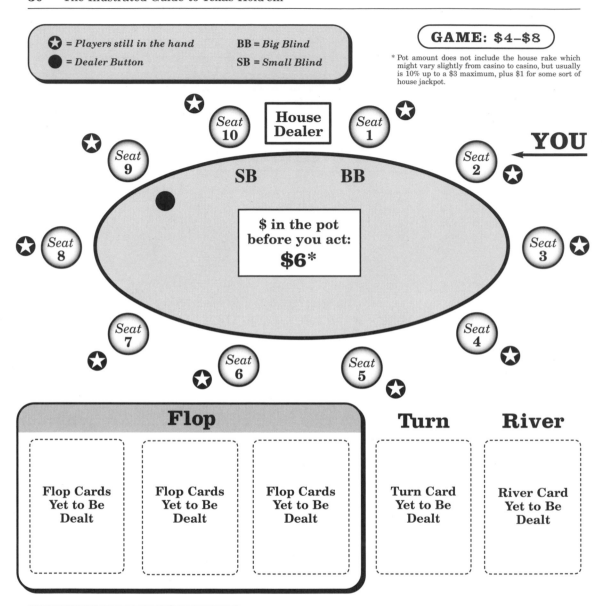

= *Players still in the hand*   BB = *Big Blind*

= *Dealer Button*   SB = *Small Blind*

GAME: $4–$8

* Pot amount does not include the house rake which might vary slightly from casino to casino, but usually is 10% up to a $3 maximum, plus $1 for some sort of house jackpot.

House Dealer

YOU

Seat 10
Seat 1
Seat 2
Seat 9
Seat 8
Seat 3
Seat 7
Seat 4
Seat 6
Seat 5

SB   BB

$ in the pot before you act:
$6*

Flop

| Flop Cards Yet to Be Dealt | Flop Cards Yet to Be Dealt | Flop Cards Yet to Be Dealt |

Turn

Turn Card Yet to Be Dealt

River

River Card Yet to Be Dealt

Pocket

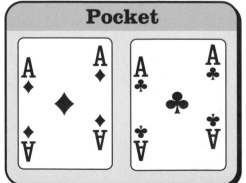

Situation #1

You have been dealt a pair of Aces in your pocket. You are the first to act with the other nine players to decide on their hands, in order, after you. The only money in the pot is the $6 from the two blind hands. Should you fold, call the $4 bet, or raise to $8, and why?

Starting Hand (Pocket): **A♣ A♦**

This Pocket's Win Rate: **86.1%**

Win Rate Rank: **1 of 169 possible**

Situation #1: Answer

We begin your study of Texas Hold'em with the best pocket hand you could hold—two Aces. Without question, and under any circumstances, you always play pocket Aces before the flop. The only question is whether to call or raise. In this situation, you are the first to act. Your choices are to call the $4 big blind bet or raise to $8. There are two schools of thought on this hand. You might want to just call. The reason for calling instead of raising is to keep as many players in the hand as possible, thereby making a bigger pot. However, you must be aware that if there are more callers in the pot, there is a greater chance another player will draw out on a hand that will beat your two Aces.

Which brings us to the second school of thought, which says to raise the bet to $8. By raising in first position, you are projecting to other players that you have a strong hand. If these other players believe that you do have the strong hand you project and are not bluffing, many of them will fold rather than call with a marginal hand. This means that there will be less money in the pot for you to win, but you will stand a greater chance of winning the hand because there will be less players in the pot who have a chance of drawing out a better hand. Personally, I always call with this hand in this position because I like to play for bigger pots and trap opponents when I can.

GAME: $4–$8

* Pot amount does not include the house rake which might vary slightly from casino to casino, but usually is 10% up to a $3 maximum, plus $1 for some sort of house jackpot.

Seat 10   House Dealer   Seat 1

Seat 9   Seat 2

SB   BB

$ in the pot before you act:
$14*

Seat 8   Seat 3

YOU →

Seat 7   Seat 4

Seat 6   Seat 5

Flop

| Flop Cards Yet to Be Dealt | Flop Cards Yet to Be Dealt | Flop Cards Yet to Be Dealt |

Turn
Turn Card Yet to Be Dealt

River
River Card Yet to Be Dealt

Pocket

7♠   2♥

Situation #2

You have been dealt 7-2 unsuited in your pocket. Seats 3 and 6 have both called the $4 bet. It is your turn to act, with seats 8, 9, 10, and 1 yet to act after you. Should you fold, call the $4 bet, or raise to $8, and why?

> Starting Hand (Pocket): **7♠ 2♥**
>
> This Pocket's Win Rate: **0.4%**
>
> Win Rate Rank: **139 of 169 possible**

Situation #2: Answer

Just as Situation #1 was an easy decision, so too is this situation. While the pocket Aces in the previous situation represented the highest pocket hand you could have, this hand's 7-2 unsuited is considered by many poker experts to be the worst possible hand you could catch in the pocket. Technically there are several other hands that actually rank lower (e.g., any nonpair with a high card of 6 or lower), and there are other hands that have a lower win rate (this hand ranks 139 in win rate). Still, this is an awful hand that is universally recognized as being the worst hand to draw to. Even a 3-2 hand has a better chance of hitting a straight than 7-2. So, under *almost* all circumstances, you should fold 7-2 unsuited, regardless of what position you are in.

There is one exception to this. If you hold this hand in the big blind and all the other players left in the hand before you only called and did not raise, you would obviously check the bet and stay in to see the flop. Then, if you catch a miracle flop, like two more 7s or two more 2s or another 7-2 for two pair, you can come out of nowhere and maybe win a nice pot. But by and large, the main purpose of this situation is to help you recognize that 7-2 is universally considered to be the worst hand in Hold'em.

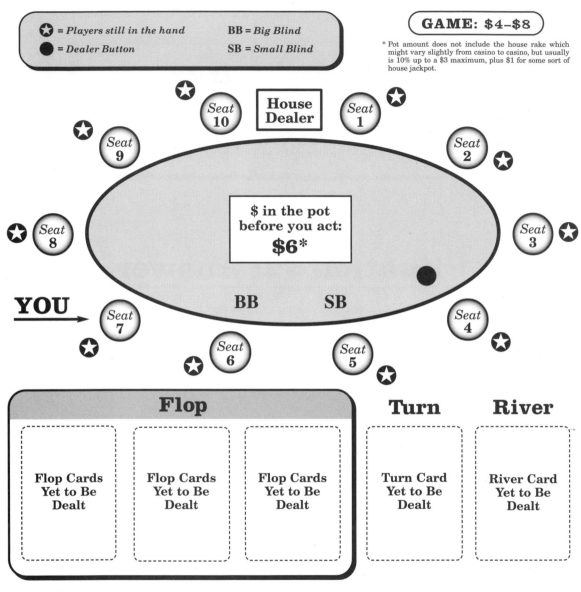

★ = *Players still in the hand*   BB = *Big Blind*

● = *Dealer Button*   SB = *Small Blind*

GAME: $4–$8

* Pot amount does not include the house rake which might vary slightly from casino to casino, but usually is 10% up to a $3 maximum, plus $1 for some sort of house jackpot.

Seat 10   **House Dealer**   Seat 1

Seat 9   Seat 2

Seat 8   **$ in the pot before you act: $6***   Seat 3

YOU →   Seat 7   BB   SB   Seat 4

Seat 6   Seat 5

Flop

| Flop Cards Yet to Be Dealt | Flop Cards Yet to Be Dealt | Flop Cards Yet to Be Dealt |

Turn
Turn Card Yet to Be Dealt

River
River Card Yet to Be Dealt

Pocket

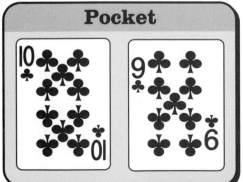

Situation #3

You have been dealt 10-9 suited. The only money in the pot is the $6 from the two blinds. You are first to act with all nine other players to act after you. Should you fold, call the $4 big blind bet, or raise to $8, and why?

Starting Hand (Pocket): **10♣ 9♣**

This Pocket's Win Rate: **38.3%**

Win Rate Rank: **24 of 169 possible**

Situation #3: Answer

This is actually a decent hand, ranking 24 out of 169 possible pocket hands in the win rate chart with a healthy win rate of 38.3 percent. But you should fold the hand. Why? Because of your *position*. While catching good starting hands in the pocket is important, there is more to consider when attempting to play winning Texas Hold'em, and one primary consideration is your position.

This situation was chosen specifically to illustrate the importance of position. Yes, it's a decent starting hand, but what you don't know, because you're the first to act, is what the other players are going to do after you. What if another player raises, he gets reraised, and still another player raises after that, capping the betting at the maximum level? Will you still like your hand as much, knowing now that you might be going up against pocket Aces, Kings, Queens, or even A-K suited or unsuited or other high pairs? Or what if only one player raises you and everyone else folds? You're heads up against a strong hand with a weak one. That's not a good position to be in. So when the betting gets back to you, you are now faced with putting another $12 into the pot (for a total of $16) and going against a number of probable better hands than yours, or now folding and losing $4 unnecessarily.

A hand of 10-9 suited is better played against a number of players as cheaply as possible because it's a drawing hand. The odds are against you, so you have to be getting the proper money odds (**pot odds**) to do so. The moral of this story is if you're going to bet in first position, you better have a hand that you're willing to put more than one bet into the pot for before ever seeing the flop.

⭐ = *Players still in the hand*   BB = *Big Blind*

⬤ = *Dealer Button*   SB = *Small Blind*

GAME: $4–$8

* Pot amount does not include the house rake which might vary slightly from casino to casino, but usually is 10% up to a $3 maximum, plus $1 for some sort of house jackpot.

YOU → ⭐

Seat 10   **House Dealer**   Seat 1

Seat 9   Seat 2

SB

$ in the pot before you act:
$98*

⭐ Seat 8   Seat 3 ⭐

BB

Seat 7   Seat 4

⭐   ⭐

Seat 6   Seat 5

Flop

8♣ 8♣

9♣ 6♣

J♦ J♦

Turn

10♥ 10♥

River

River Card Yet to Be Dealt

Pocket

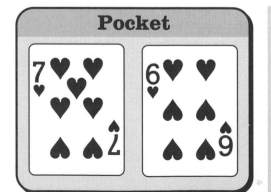

7♥ 7♥

6♥ 6♥

Situation #4

You received 7-6 suited in your pocket and called along with four other players before you. After the flop, Seat 3 bet $4, and the other three players called the bet, as did you. After the turn (which gave you a 10-high straight), Seat 3 bet $8, Seat 4 called, but then Seat 7 raised to $16. Seat 8 followed by raising again to $24. Do you fold, call the $24, or raise to $32, thereby capping the betting, and why?

Starting Hand (Pocket): **6♥ 7♥**

This Pocket's Win Rate: **7.2%**

Win Rate Rank: **64 of 169 possible**

Situation #4: Answer

This has turned into a large pot with the very real prospect that it's going to get much larger, and you already have a straight. But you should fold the hand. Why? Because you're most likely already beaten and not just by one player. So, how can you tell? Let's take a look.

When the 10 came on the turn, it gave you your straight. But it gave you the low, or **idiot end** of the straight. As you can see, the board already has four cards to a straight displayed, the 8-9-10-J. Any player holding a Queen now also has a straight, but they have the high end of the straight, which beats your straight. Further, because Seat 8 reraised Seat 7's raise, he might even have K-Q in his pocket for the **nut** straight, meaning the highest possible straight. Further still, with two Clubs on the board, you have to worry about the possibility of someone (especially Seat 4) having two Clubs in his pocket and who is calling in the hopes of catching a fifth Club and beating everyone's straights.

This is a dangerous hand you hold given the betting activity. It's not likely that three or possibly four players are trying to bluff. Somebody has something strong and it's definitely better than what you hold. You should be glad you were in last betting position because it didn't cost you anything further after the turn card to gain the information of your opponents' power or projected power. And, there's virtually nothing that could come on the river that will improve your position. Cut your losses (which are small up to this point) and fold the hand.

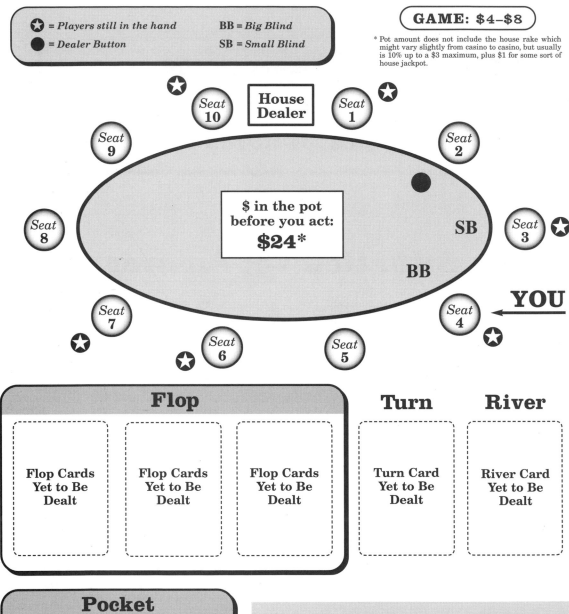

= Players still in the hand   BB = Big Blind

= Dealer Button   SB = Small Blind

GAME: $4–$8

* Pot amount does not include the house rake which might vary slightly from casino to casino, but usually is 10% up to a $3 maximum, plus $1 for some sort of house jackpot.

Seat 10   House Dealer   Seat 1

Seat 9   Seat 2

$ in the pot before you act: **$24***

SB

Seat 8   Seat 3

BB

YOU

Seat 7   Seat 4

Seat 6   Seat 5

Flop

| Flop Cards Yet to Be Dealt | Flop Cards Yet to Be Dealt | Flop Cards Yet to Be Dealt |

Turn

Turn Card Yet to Be Dealt

River

River Card Yet to Be Dealt

Pocket

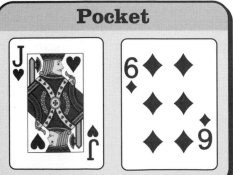

Situation #5

You have been dealt J-6 unsuited while in the big blind position. Five players, including the small blind, have all called the bet for $4. With your big blind money, there is a total of $24 in the pot. Should you fold, check, or raise the bet to $8, and why?

Starting Hand (Pocket): **J♥ 6♦**

This Pocket's Win Rate: **0.5%**

Win Rate Rank: **126 of 169 possible**

Situation #5: Answer

This is a very poor hand as you can see from the box above. This hand has less than a 1 percent chance of winning. Even so, you're going to play this hand at this point because you're already in a full bet of $4 because you were in the big blind position. It won't cost you any more to play, as you are the last to act before the flop so no one can raise after you. When the betting gets around to you, the dealer will either say, "Option," or "Big enough?" Both of these are ways of asking you if you want to raise the bet. You will just say, "Check," or tap the table in front of you with your hand which is another way of indicating that you wish to check.

The real key for you in this hand now is the flop. The flop needs to hit this hand very strongly or you've got to get out. As it stands now, you have almost no chance for a straight and only an outside chance for a flush, and if it's not a Heart flush, then you probably don't want it anyway. This realistically leaves pairs or three of a kind as to what you're hoping for. And these are no good against someone else's straight and flush possibilities if they played workable hands, which your J-6 isn't.

Unless you catch two Jacks or two 6s, or one of each on the flop for two pair, or something like a 4-5-7, or Q-10-9 (something that gives you two more shots at a straight that's not the idiot end), or three Hearts, then you need to fold after the flop. This hand is a real uphill battle.

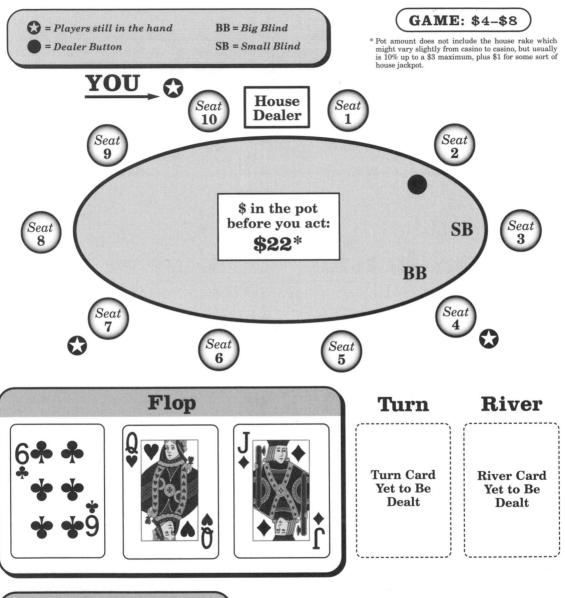

GAME: $4–$8

*Pot amount does not include the house rake which might vary slightly from casino to casino, but usually is 10% up to a $3 maximum, plus $1 for some sort of house jackpot.

YOU →

Seat 10   **House Dealer**   Seat 1

Seat 9   Seat 2

$ in the pot before you act:
$22*

SB   Seat 3

Seat 8

BB

Seat 7   Seat 4

Seat 6   Seat 5

Flop

6♣   Q♥   J♦

Turn

Turn Card Yet to Be Dealt

River

River Card Yet to Be Dealt

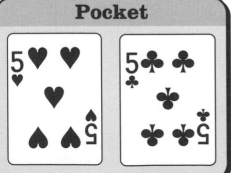

Pocket

5♥   5♣

Situation #6

You have been dealt a pair of 5s in your pocket. Before the flop, there were four callers including you. You are the last player to act after the flop. Seat 4 checks. Seat 7 bets $4 and Seat 8 folds. Should you fold, call the $4 bet, or raise the bet to $8, and why?

Starting Hand (Pocket): **5♥ 5♣**

This Pocket's Win Rate: **20.7%**

Win Rate Rank: **34 of 169 possible**

Situation #6: Answer

You began with pocket 5s, a modest hand at best, but playable. But when the flop came you got no help at all. In fact, you got hurt because every card on the board is higher than your 5s. These are called **overcards**. Any opponent holding either a 6, Jack, or Queen has you beat. And if, perchance, none of them held any of these three cards in their pockets, they might already be holding a pocket pair higher than your 5s. If they don't hold a pocket pair already, then the turn and river cards are yet to come which could pair them up, and they likely are holding cards higher than a 5, which beats you, too.

Your only realistic hope with this hand was to catch another 5 without having to put any more money into the pot than what you did before the flop. You **missed** on the flop.

So let's assume that Seat 7 has either the Jack or the Queen and has you beaten. Is it worth it to try and hit another 5 to overtake him? Let's figure it out. Since (realistically) the only cards that are going to help you are the other two 5s, you have two chances (or **outs**) to catch what you need. There are forty-seven unseen cards (fifty-two minus the two in your pocket and three on the board). This means your chances of catching another 5 are 45-to-2, or, 22½-to-1. If the player to act after you folds, then you are being asked to lay even money (your bets against the bets of Seat 7) the rest of the way in order to hit a 22½-to-1 long shot. You won't survive long in Hold'em by making these kinds of calls. Throw the hand away and save your money.

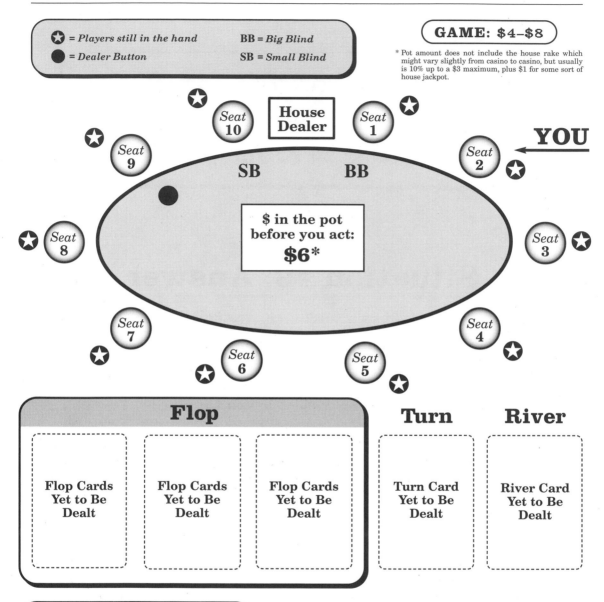

GAME: $4–$8

* Pot amount does not include the house rake which might vary slightly from casino to casino, but usually is 10% up to a $3 maximum, plus $1 for some sort of house jackpot.

Seat 10 House Dealer Seat 1 **YOU**

Seat 9

SB   BB

$ in the pot before you act: **$6***

Seat 8   Seat 3

Seat 7   Seat 4

Seat 6   Seat 5

Flop

| Flop Cards Yet to Be Dealt | Flop Cards Yet to Be Dealt | Flop Cards Yet to Be Dealt |

Turn

Turn Card Yet to Be Dealt

River

River Card Yet to Be Dealt

Pocket

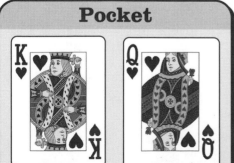

Situation #7

You have been dealt a pocket hand of K-Q suited. You are **under the gun**, meaning the first to act. The only money in the pot is the $6 from the two blinds. Should you fold, call the $4 bet, or raise to $8, and why?

Starting Hand (Pocket): **K♥ Q♥**

This Pocket's Win Rate: **54.6%**

Win Rate Rank: **12 of 169 possible**

Situation #7: Answer

As you can see in the above chart, this is a very good starting hand. But don't get carried away yet. While a suited King-Queen might be pretty to see staring back at you when you peek at your pocket cards, it has a ways to go before it's worth taking home to meet your mom, especially when you're in first position. At this point you have no idea what the other nine players are holding or how they're going to bet. Let's face it, unless you catch a couple of hearts on the flop, or two more cards to your straight draw (preferably an open-ended straight draw), or a King or Queen *without an Ace* appearing on the board, then you've got next to nothing except a pretty pocket hand. Even a pair of 2s beats you at this stage of the hand.

Certainly the hand is worth playing and you don't want to fold it, but at this point you need to be cautious. Once the other players act on their hands, you'll have more information about what their projected strength (or lack thereof) is. It's conceivable that the next eight players could all fold to the big blind, leaving you heads up against Seat 1. It's also conceivable that the next three players to act after you will all raise and reraise. This hand in this position is no more than a calling hand. So call the $4 and see what happens.

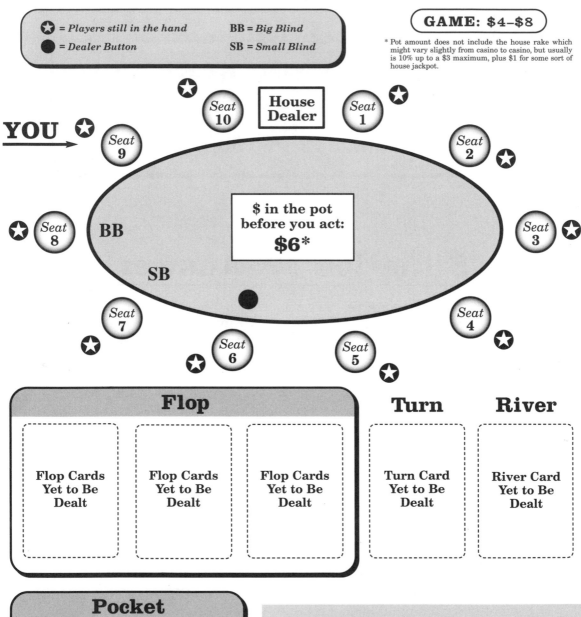

★ = *Players still in the hand*   BB = *Big Blind*

● = *Dealer Button*   SB = *Small Blind*

GAME: $4–$8

* Pot amount does not include the house rake which might vary slightly from casino to casino, but usually is 10% up to a $3 maximum, plus $1 for some sort of house jackpot.

Seat 10 | House Dealer | Seat 1

YOU → Seat 9

Seat 2

Seat 8   BB

$ in the pot before you act:
$6*

Seat 3

SB

Seat 7

Seat 4

Seat 6   Seat 5

Flop

| Flop Cards Yet to Be Dealt | Flop Cards Yet to Be Dealt | Flop Cards Yet to Be Dealt |

Turn

Turn Card Yet to Be Dealt

River

River Card Yet to Be Dealt

Pocket

K♣ J♦

Situation #8

You have been dealt a pocket hand of K-J unsuited. Once again, you are under the gun. The only money in the pot is the $6 from the two blinds. Should you fold, call the $4 bet, or raise to $8, and why?

Starting Hand (Pocket): **K♣ J♦**

This Pocket's Win Rate: **20.5%**

Win Rate Rank: **35 of 169 possible**

Situation #8: Answer

A pocket of King-Jack unsuited is really a much weaker hand than it might first appear, especially to a beginning player. And when you are first to act it's even weaker. First of all, you already lose to any pair or any Ace-high hand, both of which are commonly played by many players in low limit Hold'em. So to beat everybody at the table you have to at least catch a King or Jack on the board, have no Ace appear, and hope that everything else works out just right for you (i.e., no player holds a pocket of King-Queen). That's a tall order, particularly when you're in first position and don't know how anyone's going to act when it's their turn. You might call this bet and run into a raise and reraise before the flop.

King-Jack offsuit is worth playing in some cases, but not when you're under the gun. The few times you will hit this hand just right on the flop and end up a winner will not offset the total of all the small losses you'll take over the long run by playing this hand *in this position* until the flop. Fold the hand now before you get yourself into some expensive trouble later on in the hand.

★ = *Players still in the hand*   BB = *Big Blind*

● = *Dealer Button*   SB = *Small Blind*

GAME: $4–$8

* Pot amount does not include the house rake which might vary slightly from casino to casino, but usually is 10% up to a $3 maximum, plus $1 for some sort of house jackpot.

Seat 10

House Dealer

Seat 1

Seat 9

YOU ←

Seat 2 ★

SB

BB

$ in the pot before you act:

$18*

Seat 8

Seat 3

Seat 7 ★

Seat 4

Seat 6

Seat 5

Flop

Q♠ 7♦ K♠

Turn

Turn Card Yet to Be Dealt

River

River Card Yet to Be Dealt

Pocket

A♠ 9♠

Situation #9

You received the Ace and 9 of Spades in your pocket. Seat 7 raised before the flop and you called from the big blind position, while everyone else folded, putting you **heads up** against Seat 7. You are first to act. Do you check to see what Seat 7 does, or do you bet $4, and why?

Starting Hand (Pocket): **A♠ 9♠**

This Pocket's Win Rate: **40.5%**

Win Rate Rank: **20 of 169 possible**

Situation #9: Answer

This started off as a decent hand and improved with the flop. But you're not quite there yet, and that is going to play into your betting strategy on this hand. Technically you have only an Ace-high hand and it stands the realistic chance of not getting any better with the turn and river cards. You have to find out what your opponent thinks of his hand. He did, after all, raise before the flop, and this probably indicates some power, at least in his mind.

You have to believe, since he raised before the flop, that if you check he's going to bet. In that case you'll have to call because you hold the nut flush draw (the four spades, Ace high). This gives him control of the hand. You might consider check-raising him too. Now, had you hit three spades on the flop you could have checked, confident in the knowledge that you hold the highest possible hand at that point. But with only four Spades and no pair, not only are you vulnerable, at this point you're probably already beaten.

So, the correct move to make at this point is to bet first and see what Seat 7 decides to do. If he reraises you, you'll have to decide if he truly has a big pocket pair (or even three Kings now) or is on some kind of draw, and whether or not you want to continue to contest the hand. If he just calls, then you can be somewhat sure that the flop didn't help him and maybe (in his mind) even hurt him (he had pocket Jacks or 10s, or something like that). And he might even just fold if you bet, which wouldn't be the worst thing that could happen for you since you only hold an Ace-high hand anyway. If he calls your bet, then you see what the turn card is before going through the assessment process all over again.

⭐ = *Players still in the hand*   BB = *Big Blind*

⚫ = *Dealer Button*   SB = *Small Blind*

GAME: $4–$8

* Pot amount does not include the house rake which might vary slightly from casino to casino, but usually is 10% up to a $3 maximum, plus $1 for some sort of house jackpot.

Seat 10

House Dealer

Seat 1

YOU

Seat 9

Seat 2

BB

$ in the pot before you act:
$10*

Seat 8

SB

Seat 3

Seat 7

Seat 4

Seat 6

Seat 5

Flop

| Flop Cards Yet to Be Dealt | Flop Cards Yet to Be Dealt | Flop Cards Yet to Be Dealt |

Turn

Turn Card Yet to Be Dealt

River

River Card Yet to Be Dealt

Pocket

Q♦ 2♦

Situation #10

You have been dealt a pocket hand of Q-2 suited. You are the second player to act. Seat 10 calls the $4 big blind bet. With eight more players to act after you, should you fold, call the $4 bet, or raise to $8, and why?

Starting Hand (Pocket): **Q♦ 2♦**

This Pocket's Win Rate: **3.1%**

Win Rate Rank: **101 of 169 possible**

Situation #10: Answer

Many, many beginning and intermediate Hold'em players will play a hand like this in any position in spite of its poor winning rate. And this hand is especially poor considering your early position in the betting. With eight players yet to act behind you, you may not get into this pot for just $4.

Consider, if you will, what you must catch on the board in order to realistically win this hand. If the flop comes A-Q-9, for example, you have paired your Queen, but the Ace is probably going to pair one or more of your opponents, leaving you dead. Even if the flop comes up something like Q-J-8 and pairs your Queen, if anyone else has a Queen their **kicker** (second pocket card) will undoubtedly beat your 2. The turn and river could also bring a King or an Ace, thereby making your Queen almost certainly worthless, particularly if there are four or five players still in the hand.

Another possibility for you is the flush, but you better hit at least two Diamonds on the flop or you're facing a real uphill battle. Even if two Diamonds come on the flop, the odds are still against you of a fifth one coming on the turn or river. And should a fifth Diamond come, you're still only Queen high. Another player might have two Diamonds in the pocket just like you, either Ace high or King high.

There are a whole lot of ways to lose with this starting hand and only a few ways to win with it. Throw this hand away and don't lose a moment's peace over it.

★ = *Players still in the hand*   BB = *Big Blind*

● = *Dealer Button*   SB = *Small Blind*

GAME: $4–$8

* Pot amount does not include the house rake which might vary slightly from casino to casino, but usually is 10% up to a $3 maximum, plus $1 for some sort of house jackpot.

Seat 10

House Dealer

Seat 1

Seat 9

Seat 2

SB

Seat 8

$ in the pot before you act:

$36*

BB

Seat 3

Seat 7

Seat 4

Seat 6

Seat 5

YOU

Flop

K♣   Q♦   3♥

Turn

Turn Card Yet to Be Dealt

River

River Card Yet to Be Dealt

Pocket

A♣   4♣

Situation #11

You received the Ace and 4 of Clubs in your pocket. Six players, including you, called before the flop. After the flop, Seat 2 bet and Seats 3 and 4 called. Do you fold, call the $4 bet, or raise to $8, and why?

Starting Hand (Pocket): **A♣ 4♣**

This Pocket's Win Rate: **30.6%**

Win Rate Rank: **27 of 169 possible**

Situation #11: Answer

An Ace-4 suited in the pocket is a generally playable hand, although it typically shouldn't be played in early position unless the game you're in happens to be a **loose-passive game** (meaning lots of action, but little raising). But the flop missed you. Your only real shot at winning this hand now is to catch two more Clubs, but the odds of that happening are about 15-to-1 at this point. If you catch an Ace on the turn for a pair of Aces, you're also probably beaten because with six players still in the hand, you've got to figure that someone besides you (and maybe even two players) stayed with an Ace and has a better kicker than your 4.

With five opponents still in the hand, there is just too much opposition and you have too far to go to continue to contest the hand. Fold it.

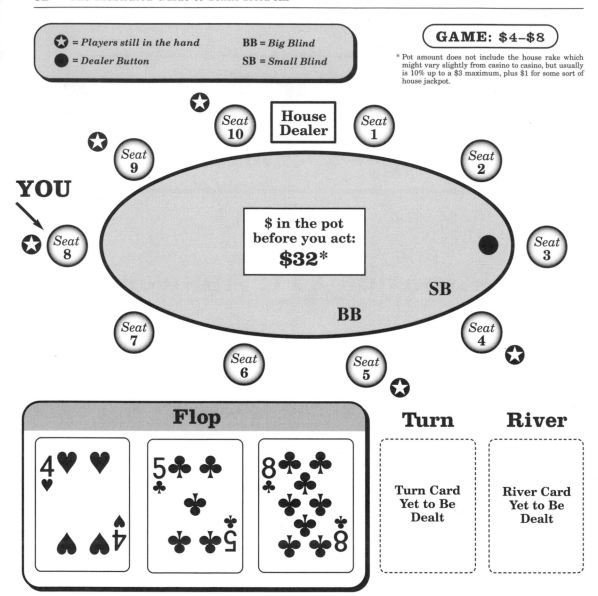

= *Players still in the hand*   BB = *Big Blind*

= *Dealer Button*   SB = *Small Blind*

GAME: $4–$8

* Pot amount does not include the house rake which might vary slightly from casino to casino, but usually is 10% up to a $3 maximum, plus $1 for some sort of house jackpot.

Seat 10

House Dealer

Seat 1

Seat 9

Seat 2

YOU

Seat 8

$ in the pot before you act:
$32*

Seat 3

SB

Seat 7

BB

Seat 4

Seat 6

Seat 5

Flop

4♥   5♣   8♣

Turn

Turn Card Yet to Be Dealt

River

River Card Yet to Be Dealt

Pocket

7♦   7♠

Situation #12

You were dealt a pair of 7s in your pocket. The game has been very loose and passive. (Lots of action, little raising.) Before the flop, you called along with four other players, including both blinds. After the flop, Seat 4 bet $4 and Seat 5 then raised to $8. It is now your turn to act. Do you fold, call the $8 bet, or raise to $12, and why?

Starting Hand (Pocket): **7♦ 7♠**

This Pocket's Win Rate: **28.6%**

Win Rate Rank: **30 of 169 possible**

Situation #12: Answer

A pair of 7s in the pocket was worth the call. This flop has now given you a **gut shot** straight draw. But there's plenty of trouble on the horizon. First of all, you have to hit a 6 on the turn or the river for a straight. The odds against you are stiff (over 5-to-1). In addition, with two Clubs on the board there is a real chance of someone hitting a flush draw, which will beat your straight even if you do hit it. In fact, the odds of someone holding two Clubs hitting their flush on the turn or river is better than your odds of hitting your straight on the turn or river. And flushes beat straights every time.

Third, even if the flush drawers don't hit their needed Club(s), if you don't hit your straight you're still probably beaten. Think about it: The small and big blinds got into the pot without having to project any strength. (The big blind was in for the $4 anyway, so you got no indication of his hand. The small blind only had to call $2 to be in the hand and in low limit Hold'em, many players will toss in $2 on almost any hand just to see what flops. For $2 they might just catch their miracle cards.) This bet and raise after the flop translates into probable big pairs, or maybe a pair of 8s (**top pair**) with a decent kicker. Or maybe even a flush draw that is trying to scare everyone out of the pot.

Now, after the flop, the small blind has bet and the big blind has raised. This indicates some sort of power on their parts. You also don't know what the two players behind you are going to do when their turn comes.

Since the odds of you catching the needed 6 are against you, and since you might lose even if you do catch that 6, you should fold this hand.

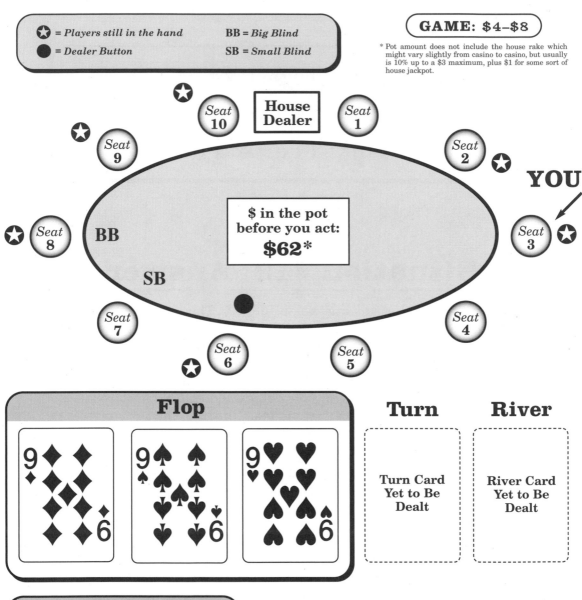

GAME: $4–$8

* Pot amount does not include the house rake which might vary slightly from casino to casino, but usually is 10% up to a $3 maximum, plus $1 for some sort of house jackpot.

Seat 10 | House Dealer | Seat 1

Seat 9

Seat 2

YOU

$ in the pot before you act: **$62***

BB

Seat 3

Seat 8

SB

Seat 7

Seat 4

Seat 6

Seat 5

Flop

9♦ 9♠ 9♥

Turn

Turn Card Yet to Be Dealt

River

River Card Yet to Be Dealt

Pocket

A♥ K♣

Situation #13

You were dealt A-K unsuited (**big slick**) in your pocket. Before the flop, Seat 9 raised to $8 after which five players, including you, all called. After the flop, Seat 8 checks, Seat 9 bets $4, and Seats 10 and 2 call. It is now your turn to act. Do you fold, call the $4, or raise to $8, and why?

Starting Hand (Pocket): **A♥ K♣**

This Pocket's Win Rate: **67.0%**

Win Rate Rank: **5 of 169 possible**

Situation #13: Answer

You started off with a great pocket but the flop now forces you to take pause. While there is still a remote chance of a straight flush coming (not for you), in all likelihood four 9s will be the best possible hand followed by a full house, 9s over some pair. And right now, you don't have either. Before the flop Seat 9 raised under the gun. This means, most of the time, he has some real power, such as a pocket pair (probably big) or an Ace with a good kicker (just like you), possibly even suited (not like you). When five other players (including you) all called the raise, you were all indicating some sort of good hand, otherwise you wouldn't be calling in the first place.

After the monster flop, Seat 9 bet again and Seats 10 and 2 called. This is good information for you. It should tell you that not one of the three players who acted in front of you is afraid of the 9-9-9 flop. And you don't know yet what Seat 6 is going to do. It's entirely likely that Seat 9 doesn't have the fourth 9 and is betting only for information and maybe the hope that other players will drop out. If he doesn't have the fourth 9 or any big pair in his pocket, he's going to be a bit uneasy that he received two callers already. It's also entirely possible that one of the other players in this hand has the fourth 9 and is just slow playing it trying to keep as many players in the hand as possible in order to build a bigger pot.

Finally, you need to consider the odds of hitting either an Ace or King on the turn or river to give you even a modest shot at winning this hand. With forty-seven unseen cards, of which six are either Aces or Kings, your odds are 41-to-6, or about 7-to-1, divided by two chances, equals 3.5-to-1. Fold.

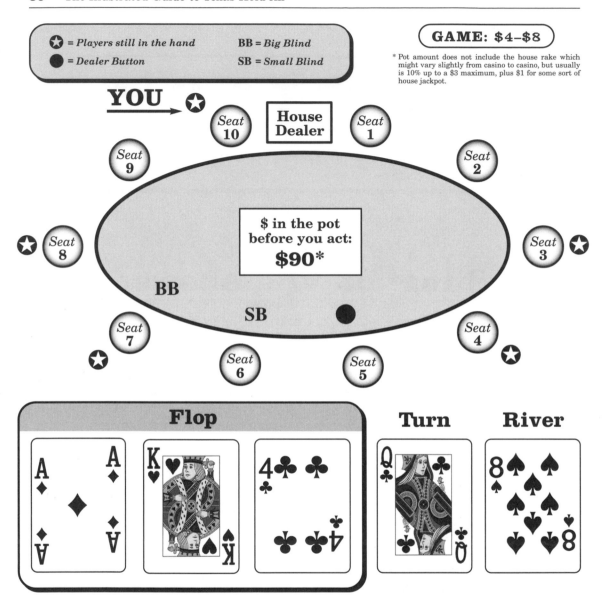

YOU

= Players still in the hand   BB = Big Blind
= Dealer Button   SB = Small Blind

GAME: $4–$8

* Pot amount does not include the house rake which might vary slightly from casino to casino, but usually is 10% up to a $3 maximum, plus $1 for some sort of house jackpot.

House Dealer

Seat 10
Seat 1
Seat 9
Seat 2
Seat 8
Seat 3
Seat 7
Seat 4
Seat 6
Seat 5

$ in the pot before you act:
$90*

BB

SB

Flop

Turn   **River**

Pocket

Situation #14

The flop, turn, and river cards have revealed the five cards shown. There were five callers before the flop; Seats 3, 4, 7, 8, and 10 (you), and everyone stayed until the end. There was a bet and four callers after both the flop and turn. After the river, Seat 7 checked, but Seat 8 bet $8. Should you fold, call the $8 bet, or raise to $16, and why?

Starting Hand (Pocket): **J♦ 10♥**

This Pocket's Win Rate: **9.4%**

Win Rate Rank: **50 of 169 possible**

Situation #14: Answer

These are the kind of boards and pots you like to see in low limit Texas Hold'em. Once the Q♣ came on the turn, you made an Ace-high straight—the nuts. Once the Spade came on the river, you were home free. The most anyone else could do on this hand is tie you for the pot, and the only way they could do that is if they held a Jack and a 10 just like you. So, the correct play here is to raise and keep on raising if someone reraises you, because you're going to rake in the chips when the dust settles!

⭐ = *Players still in the hand*   BB = *Big Blind*

⬤ = *Dealer Button*   SB = *Small Blind*

GAME: $4–$8

* Pot amount does not include the house rake which might vary slightly from casino to casino, but usually is 10% up to a $3 maximum, plus $1 for some sort of house jackpot.

Seat 10 | House Dealer | Seat 1

Seat 9

Seat 2

Seat 8 ⭐

$ in the pot before you act:

$20*

SB · Seat 3

BB

Seat 7

Seat 4 · ◀ **YOU**

⭐

Seat 6

Seat 5

Flop

J♦ K♥ A♥

Turn

2♥

River

River Card Yet to Be Dealt

Pocket

Q♣ 9♣

Situation #15

The flop and turn have revealed the four cards shown. There were three callers before the flop; Seats 3, 4 (you), and 8, after which everyone checked. After the turn, Seat 3 and you both checked, but Seat 8 bet $8. Seat 3 folded, leaving you alone in the hand with Seat 8. Should you fold, call the $8 bet, or raise to $16, and why?

Starting Hand (Pocket): **Q♣ 9♣**

This Pocket's Win Rate: **19.1%**

Win Rate Rank: **38 of 169 possible**

Situation #15: Answer

This is a hand where pot odds clearly come into play. Your only realistic chance of winning this hand is for a 10 to come on the river and you might have to have it be a suit other than Hearts, since a fourth Heart on the board could lead to a flush for your opponent in Seat 8 (if he doesn't have one already), which beats your straight.

Back to the pot odds. After Seat 8 made his $8 bet, the pot stood at $20. If you call this bet, you need to put in $8. Effectively, then, you are risking $8 in an effort to win $20. This is a return of 2.5 to 1. The odds of catching a 10 are 42-to-4 (forty-six cards you haven't seen, four of them 10s, means 42-4) which reduces to 10.5-to-1. Getting 2.5-to-1 on a 10.5-to-1 proposition is poor pot odds, therefore a horrible bet. Fold the hand, pure and simple. If there were $105 or more in the pot and you were faced with this bet, then it would be proper to call.

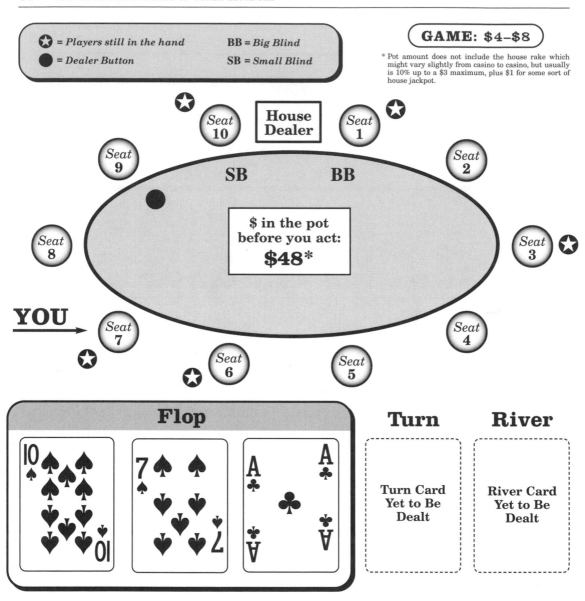

⭐ = *Players still in the hand*   BB = *Big Blind*

⬤ = *Dealer Button*   SB = *Small Blind*

GAME: $4–$8

* Pot amount does not include the house rake which might vary slightly from casino to casino, but usually is 10% up to a $3 maximum, plus $1 for some sort of house jackpot.

House Dealer

SB   BB

$ in the pot before you act:
$48*

YOU →

Seat 10
Seat 1
Seat 9
Seat 2
Seat 8
Seat 3
Seat 7
Seat 4
Seat 6
Seat 5

Flop

10♠ 7♠ A♣

Turn

Turn Card Yet to Be Dealt

River

River Card Yet to Be Dealt

Pocket

K♦ 10♦

Situation #16

The flop has revealed the three cards shown. There were five callers before the flop; Seats 1, 3, 6, 7 (you), and 10. The other four players all have to act before you do. Seat 10 bet $4, Seat 1 raised to $8, and Seats 3 and 6 called the raise. Should you fold, call the $8 raise as well, or reraise to $12, and why?

Starting Hand (Pocket): **K♦ 10♦**

This Pocket's Win Rate: **40.9%**

Win Rate Rank: **19 of 169 possible**

Situation #16: Answer

Your pocket cards were definitely worth playing before the flop. After the flop, you've paired your 10, but that's the only bit of good news for you on this board. If you're thinking that your King also sets you up for a possible straight—and technically it does—you're right, but it's a seductive trap. For you to get a straight you have to hit what is called **runner-runner**, or two cards, the turn and the river, *exactly* as needed. And even if you catch a Jack and a Queen for a straight (the odds of which are approximately 135-1), since the flop saw two Spades, if the turn and/or river cards are Spades, you could be in serious danger of another player having made a flush, which beats your straight. And their odds of catching a flush after this flop are better than your odds of catching a straight, and the flush is the higher hand.

Also, when four players in front of you on this hand bet and/or raise, then you can be almost sure one or two of them hold Aces, four cards to a Spade flush, or maybe even an open-ended straight draw (7-8-9-10). All of these very real possibilities on this hand after the flop dictate that you fold the hand.

Finally, before the flop you also had a chance for a King-high Diamond flush. Since no Diamonds came on the flop, that possibility is dead. As pretty as your pocket cards were, after the flop they turned *ugly* in a real hurry, and kept getting uglier as more callers stayed in the hand. Fold this hand, wait for the next one, and be thankful it only cost you $4.

★ = *Players still in the hand* BB = *Big Blind*

● = *Dealer Button* SB = *Small Blind*

GAME: $4–$8

* Pot amount does not include the house rake which might vary slightly from casino to casino, but usually is 10% up to a $3 maximum, plus $1 for some sort of house jackpot.

Seat 10

House Dealer

Seat 1

YOU

Seat 9

Seat 2

SB BB

$ in the pot before you act:
$6*

Seat 8

Seat 3

Seat 7

Seat 4

Seat 6

Seat 5

Flop

Flop Cards Yet to Be Dealt	Flop Cards Yet to Be Dealt	Flop Cards Yet to Be Dealt

Turn

Turn Card Yet to Be Dealt

River

River Card Yet to Be Dealt

Pocket

3♥ 3♣

Situation #17

You have been dealt a pair of 3s. You are the first to act with the other nine players to decide on their hands, in order, after you. The only money in the pot is the $6 from the two blind hands. Should you fold, call the $4 bet, or raise to $8, and why?

Starting Hand (Pocket): **3♣ 3♥**

This Pocket's Win Rate: **4.5%**

Win Rate Rank: **66 of 169 possible**

Situation #17: Answer

Don't be deceived by the fact that you have a pocket pair, because once the cards come on the flop, turn, and river, you are a virtual certainty to be dead meat. Every card in the deck (except 2s) beats your 3s if your opponent(s) pair up one of their pocket cards. Also, it's entirely possible that one or more players hold a pocket pair, just like you, but with a rank higher than 3.

Another aspect going against you is your poor position. Since you are the first to act, nine players will be acting behind you and you have no advance knowledge as to the relative strength or projected strength of their hands. If someone raises your bet, you'll be forced with putting even more money into a pot you're not likely to win. One thing is certain: almost everyone (95.5 percent, statistically) who calls or raises your bet will end up beating you. Without question you should fold the hand.

⭐ = *Players still in the hand*   BB = *Big Blind*

⚫ = *Dealer Button*   SB = *Small Blind*

GAME: $4–$8

* Pot amount does not include the house rake which might vary slightly from casino to casino, but usually is 10% up to a $3 maximum, plus $1 for some sort of house jackpot.

YOU ➝ ⭐

Seat 10   **House Dealer**   *Seat* 1   ⭐

⭐   *Seat* 9   *Seat* 2   ⭐

⭐   *Seat* 8   **BB**   **$ in the pot before you act:** **$10***   *Seat* 3   ⭐

SB

⭐   *Seat* 7   ⚫   *Seat* 4   ⭐

⭐   *Seat* 6   *Seat* 5   ⭐

Flop

Flop Cards Yet to Be Dealt	Flop Cards Yet to Be Dealt	Flop Cards Yet to Be Dealt

Turn

Turn Card Yet to Be Dealt

River

River Card Yet to Be Dealt

Pocket

4♠   5♠

Situation #18

You have been dealt 4-5 suited in your pocket. Occupying Seat 10, you are second to act. Seat 9 is under the gun and bets $4. Should you fold, call the $4 bet, or raise to $8, and why?

Starting Hand (Pocket): **4♠ 5♠**

This Pocket's Win Rate: **3.6%**

Win Rate Rank: **90 of 169 possible**

Situation #18: Answer

This is a very weak hand. Besides the low ranks of your two cards, you have the further disadvantage of poor position. Many beginning and intermediate Hold'em players will play almost any two suited cards, at least until the flop. This is a bad habit that should be avoided. Since Seat 9 bet in first position, he is indicating he has some sort of strong hand. If you call with your weak hand you still have to contend with the eight other players behind you, one or more of whom might raise, thereby costing you even more money. Don't fall into the trap of playing any two suited cards unless the cards are of decent rank and/or you are in proper betting position. Fold the hand.

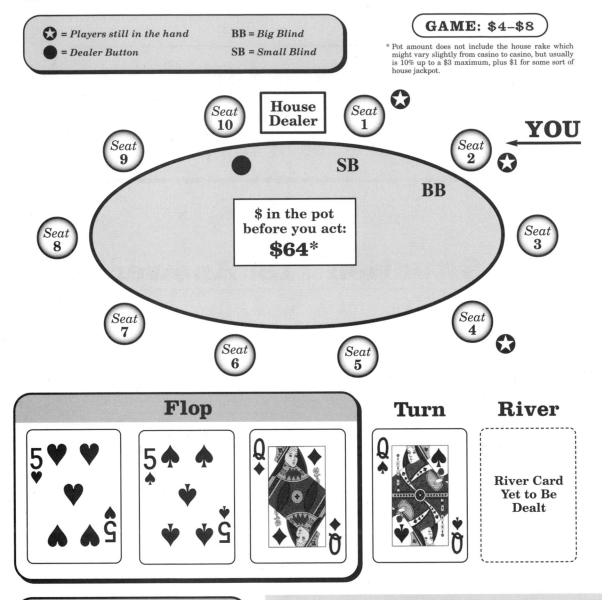

Seat 10 | House Dealer | Seat 1 | ⭐

Seat 9

Seat 2 ⭐ ← YOU

SB

BB

$ in the pot before you act: **$64***

Seat 8

Seat 3

Seat 7

Seat 4 ⭐

Seat 6

Seat 5

Flop

5♥ 5♠ Q♦

Turn

Q♠

River

River Card Yet to Be Dealt

Pocket

5♦ 9♦

Situation #19

You were dealt 9-5 suited in your pocket while in the big blind. The flop gave you three 5s and the turn a full house, 5s over Queens. There were five players in before the flop, but two dropped after the flop. Three of you remain. After the turn, Seat 1 checked, you bet $8, and Seat 4 called. Seat 1 then raised. Do you fold, call the check-raise for another $8, or reraise to $24, and why?

> ## Starting Hand (Pocket): **5♦ 9♦**
> ## This Pocket's Win Rate: **3.8%**
> ## Win Rate Rank: **79 of 169 possible**

Situation #19: Answer

Tough hand, this one. You can't throw away a full house at this point even though you might be beaten, because you could still catch a fourth 5 on the river. Also, the check-raiser in Seat 1 might also have a 5, like you, or maybe even a pair of Aces or Kings and wants you to think he has a Queen-high full house. He probably doesn't have pocket Queens because he would be scaring out potential money in the pot by check-raising on the turn. If he were going to do this with four Queens, he would do it on the river and not the turn, knowing that you're not going to throw you hand away at that point when it will only cost you one more bet.

At this stage it's correct to just call Seat 1's check-raise. Then if you don't catch another 5 on the river, you would just call a bet by Seat 1. And if he checks after the river, you should check, too, in case he's thinking of running another check-raise by you.

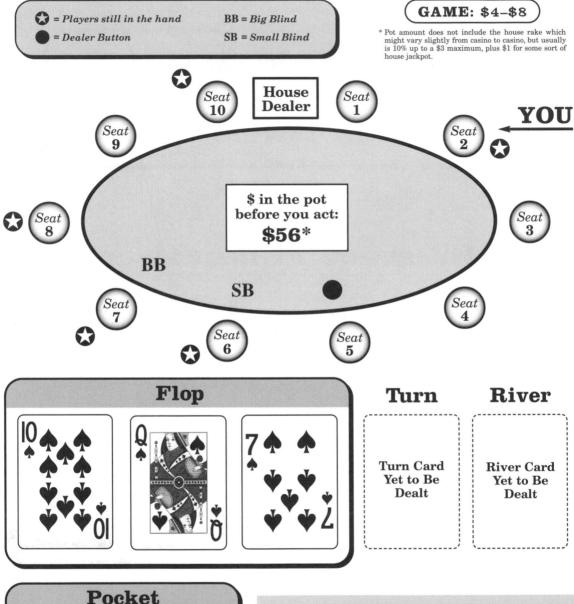

GAME: $4–$8

* Pot amount does not include the house rake which might vary slightly from casino to casino, but usually is 10% up to a $3 maximum, plus $1 for some sort of house jackpot.

Seat 10 — House Dealer — Seat 1

YOU

Seat 9   Seat 2

$ in the pot before you act: **$56***

Seat 8   Seat 3

BB

SB

Seat 7   Seat 4

Seat 6   Seat 5

Flop

10♠ Q♠ 7♠

Turn

Turn Card Yet to Be Dealt

River

River Card Yet to Be Dealt

Pocket

A♦ 10♣

Situation #20

You were dealt A-10 unsuited in your pocket. Seat 10 raised before the flop and there were four callers, including you. After the flop, Seat 6 checked, Seat 7 bet $4, and Seat 8 called. Seat 10 raised again, to $8. You're next to act. Should you fold, call the $8 raise, or reraise to $12, and why?

Starting Hand (Pocket): **A♦ 10♣**

This Pocket's Win Rate: **34.4%**

Win Rate Rank: **25 of 169 possible**

Situation #20: Answer

You should probably fold at this point. Seat 10 raised before the flop, so he indicates power. With three other callers besides yourself, you have plenty of opposition. After the flop, which gave you **middle pair**, Seat 7 bet and Seat 10 raised again. That almost assuredly means at least one big pair out there against you and maybe two. Plus now there's a Spade draw after the flop. There's also a lot of combinations for players to have straight draws, both open ended and gut shots. You, on the other hand, have no flush possibility and only a runner-runner straight possibility (King-Jack), which probably would give you only a **split pot** since the board would have K-Q-J-10 on it and anyone holding an Ace would tie you.

Also, anyone holding a Queen already has you beat. Realistically you need at least another 10 to come up and maybe more to beat the straights and flushes that could be lurking out there, or even three Queens if that's what Seat 10 was raising on from the beginning. There's just not a lot of upside to staying in this hand and a lot of downside. Fold the hand.

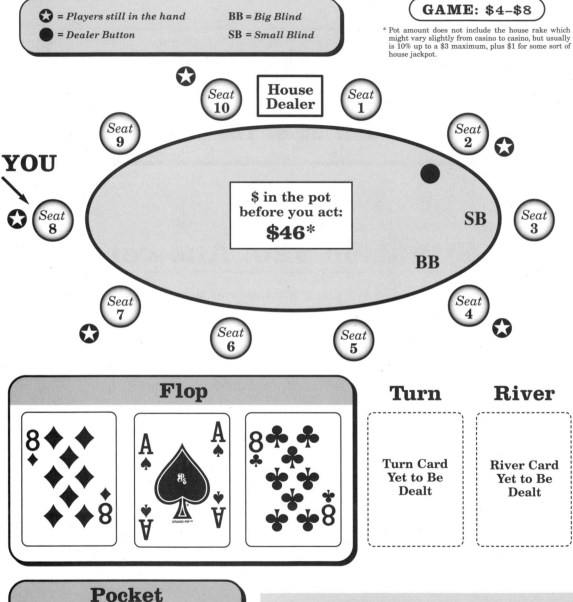

GAME: $4–$8

Pot amount does not include the house rake which might vary slightly from casino to casino, but usually is 10% up to a $3 maximum, plus $1 for some sort of house jackpot.

Seat 10
House Dealer
Seat 1
Seat 9
Seat 2
YOU
$ in the pot before you act:
$46*
SB
Seat 8
Seat 3
BB
Seat 7
Seat 4
Seat 6
Seat 5

Flop

Turn

Turn Card Yet to Be Dealt

River

River Card Yet to Be Dealt

Pocket

Situation #21

You received a pair of 8s in your pocket. Seat 7 raised before the flop and four others, including you with your pair of 8s, called the raise. After the flop, Seat 4 checked and Seat 7 bet $4. Should you fold, call the $4 bet, or raise to $8, and why?

> Starting Hand (Pocket): **8♥ 8♠**
>
> This Pocket's Win Rate: **51.8%**
>
> Win Rate Rank: **13 of 169 possible**

Situation #21: Answer

No doubt about it, you flopped a monster. It will take an incredible amount of bad luck for you to lose this hand so what you've got to figure out now is how to maximize the most money from this hand. Many times when an Ace and a pair come on the flop, the first bet will scare out most of the players since everyone's afraid of three 8s or a pair of Aces unless they hold one or the other themselves.

So, the player in Seat 7 actually did you a favor by betting first. This allows you to just call the bet, thereby putting the players in Seats 8, 10, and 2 a bit more at ease and helping you to set your trap. Had Seat 7 checked, you, too, should have checked so as not to scare out the other players, even to the point that if everyone checked after the flop, it would be all right. Then, no matter what comes on the turn, you could bet if Seat 7 doesn't, and call again or raise if he does bet.

There are three things to be aware of on this hand. First is if another Ace comes on the board. Hopefully it will give someone a full house, Aces over 8s, and they'll think they've got you beaten. But if they have pocket Aces, and catch two Aces on the board, then the incredible bad luck would have happened and you'll lose. But statistically this isn't too likely. Second is if the turn and river bring a pair higher than 8s which could conceivably match a pocket pair and give an opponent four of a kind. Third is the possibility of a straight flush. Other than those three statistical improbabilities, I'd bet this hand for all it was worth after the turn, even if a second Ace appeared on the board.

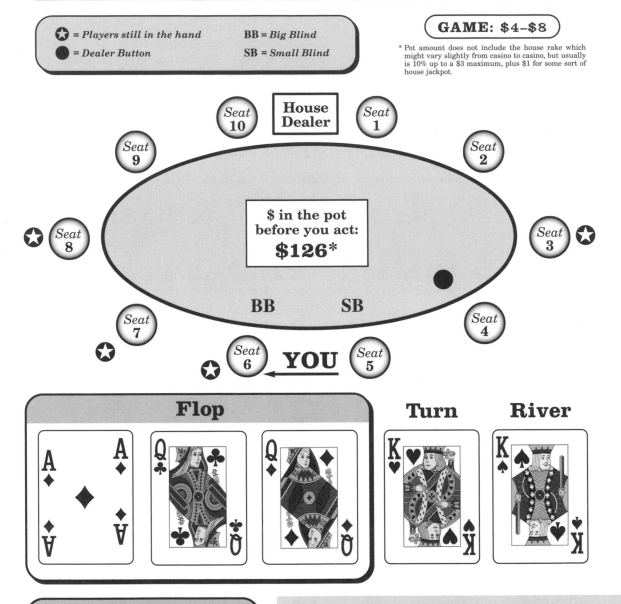

GAME: $4–$8

* Pot amount does not include the house rake which might vary slightly from casino to casino, but usually is 10% up to a $3 maximum, plus $1 for some sort of house jackpot.

⭐ = *Players still in the hand*   BB = *Big Blind*

⬤ = *Dealer Button*   SB = *Small Blind*

$ in the pot before you act:
$126*

Flop

Turn   **River**

Pocket

Situation #22

You were in the big blind when you received A-2 unsuited. There were five players in before the flop. You bet first from Seat 6 after the flop and received three callers. You also bet first after the turn and again received three callers. After the river card was dealt, you bet again and were called by Seat 7, but Seat 8 raised to $16 and Seat 3 reraised to $24. Do you fold, call the $24, or cap the betting at $32, and why?

Starting Hand (Pocket): **A♠ 2♥**

This Pocket's Win Rate: **8.8%**

Win Rate Rank: **54 of 169 possible**

Situation #22: Answer

Three pair, unfortunately, is not a hand you can play in Hold'em. It appears very likely from the betting after the river card that one or two players caught full houses. This should be obvious since two pair are on the board. It's not like the full house possibilities are hidden as when one pair is on the board. Rather than bet first after the river, you should have checked. There are too many players still in the hand, and it only takes one to have caught a full house. Because of the size of the pot, if you had checked on the river and there was only one bet back to you, you could consider calling. But once there was a raise and reraise, it was obvious you were beaten. By checking on the river instead of betting first, you could have saved yourself $8.

What will make this hand hard to fold for most beginning and intermediate players is the fact that your Ace gives you top pair. Too often such players will call the bet and then say, "I just want to see it." Since there were two raises on the river, you can be assured that at least one of them (and probably both) isn't bluffing. Fold your hand, with regrets, especially since it is a large pot that you were primarily responsible for building.

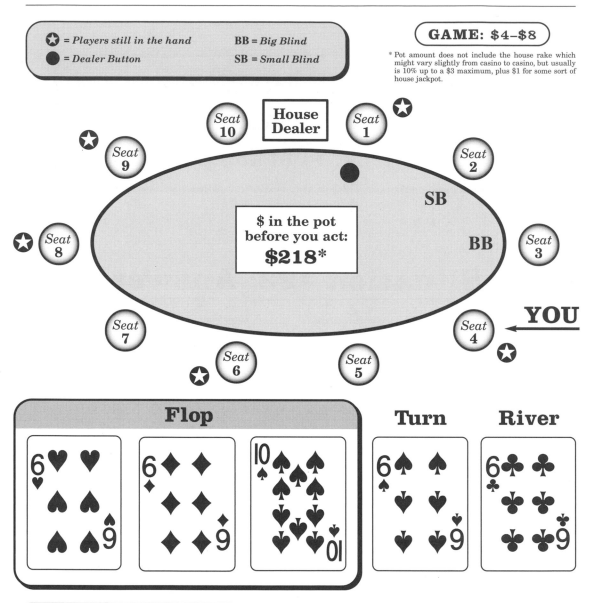

GAME: $4–$8

* Pot amount does not include the house rake which might vary slightly from casino to casino, but usually is 10% up to a $3 maximum, plus $1 for some sort of house jackpot.

Seat 10 | House Dealer | Seat 1

Seat 9

Seat 2

SB

$ in the pot before you act:

$218*

Seat 8

BB

Seat 3

Seat 7

Seat 4 ← YOU

Seat 6   Seat 5

Flop

6♥   6♦   10♠

Turn   **River**

6♠   6♣

Pocket

Q♣   Q♥

Situation #23

After receiving a pair of Queens in the pocket, you raised before the flop from Seat 4 and got four callers. After the flop and turn you again bet first and got four callers each time. After the river you bet $8, but this time Seat 6 raised to $16 and Seat 8 reraised to $24. Seat 9 then capped the betting at $32 and Seat 1 called. Do you call the $32 or fold, and why?

Starting Hand (Pocket): **Q♣ Q♥**

This Pocket's Win Rate: **68.5%**

Win Rate Rank: **4 of 169 possible**

Situation #23: Answer

The last six on the river killed you. Until then you had a good shot at winning a huge pot. Since no one had raised your bets before the flop, after the flop, or after the turn, you had to figure that no one had anything more than a pocket pair, or something with their 10 which paired the board for a full house, or an Ace with a decent kicker. Everyone was being cautious, waiting to see what would come on the turn and river.

When the last 6 came on the river, it effectively killed your pair of Queens since only one of them will now play with the four 6s. Since only one card of any player's hand will now play, it becomes a matter of high card in the hole. Since there were three raises after your bet on the river, you can assume that at least two if not all three of the players hold Aces, and if one doesn't, then he at least has a King. With this hand in this situation with the betting that has just taken place, your hand is worthless. Don't throw in another $24 just because it's a big pot or because you want to keep all three of your opponents "honest." Just as in Situation 22, you could have saved yourself $8 by checking on the river instead of betting. The bets and raises would have come anyway and you could have folded for $8 less. Fold your pair of Queens and become a more mature Texas Hold'em player: one with discipline who can discern the obvious.

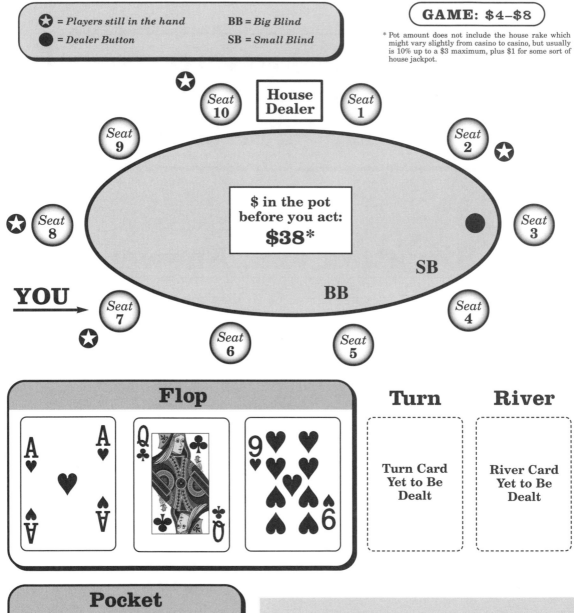

★ = *Players still in the hand*   BB = *Big Blind*

● = *Dealer Button*   SB = *Small Blind*

GAME: $4–$8

* Pot amount does not include the house rake which might vary slightly from casino to casino, but usually is 10% up to a $3 maximum, plus $1 for some sort of house jackpot.

Seat 10

House Dealer

Seat 1

Seat 9

Seat 2

$ in the pot before you act:
$38*

Seat 3

Seat 8

SB

YOU →

Seat 7

BB

Seat 4

Seat 6

Seat 5

Flop

A♥ A♥ ♥ A♥

Q♣ Q♣

9♥ ♥ 9♥

Turn

Turn Card Yet to Be Dealt

River

River Card Yet to Be Dealt

Pocket

10♦ 10♦

10♠ 10♠

Situation #24

You received a pair of 10s in your pocket. Five players, including you, stayed in for one bet to see the flop. After the flop, Seat 5 and you both checked. Seat 8 bet $4, Seat 10 called, and Seat 2 raised to $8. Seat 5 then folded. Do you fold as well, call the $8, or raise to $12, and why?

Starting Hand (Pocket): **10♦ 10♠**

This Pocket's Win Rate: **60.8%**

Win Rate Rank: **8 of 169 possible**

Situation #24: Answer

You started off with a solid pocket hand; a pair of 10s. Once the flop came, however, you received no help on the board. The two overcards (the Ace and Queen) effectively killed your hand since you also have no flush draw and only a slim runner-runner chance for a straight.

It's conceivable that you could win with a set of 10s, but the odds of catching a third 10 are slim (only two possible 10s left in the forty-seven unseen cards), and the pot isn't big enough or likely to get big enough to take a chance on a possible "iffy" winner. Fold the hand.

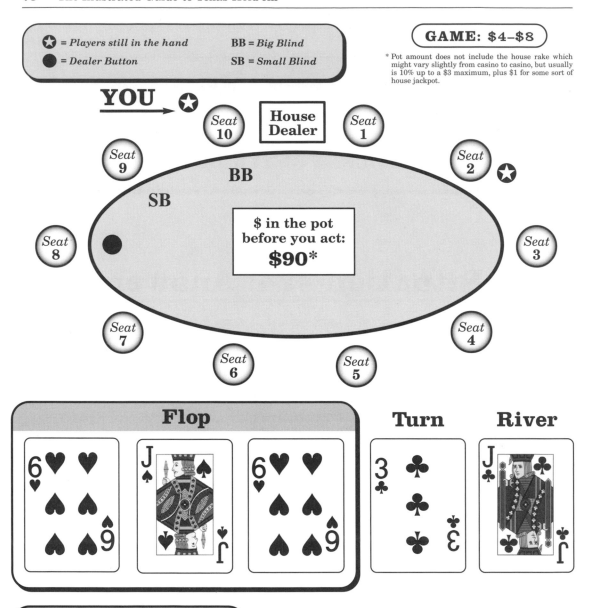

* Pot amount does not include the house rake which might vary slightly from casino to casino, but usually is 10% up to a $3 maximum, plus $1 for some sort of house jackpot.

GAME: $4–$8

= Players still in the hand   BB = Big Blind

= Dealer Button   SB = Small Blind

YOU

Seat 10   House Dealer   Seat 1

Seat 9   Seat 2

BB

SB

$ in the pot before you act: **$90***

Seat 8   Seat 3

Seat 7   Seat 4

Seat 6   Seat 5

Flop   **Turn**   **River**

Pocket

Situation #25

There have been only four players in this hand from the beginning and you are first to act. After the flop and turn, you bet and everyone called. After the river, you bet $8 on your full house, then Seat 2 raised to $16. Seats 3 and 4 folded. Do you fold, call the $16, or reraise to $24, and why?

Starting Hand (Pocket): **10♦ 6♦**

This Pocket's Win Rate: **3.9%**

Win Rate Rank: **74 of 169 possible**

Situation #25: Answer

You call the raise for an additional $8 even though you're probably going to lose to a higher full house—someone with a pocket Jack for Jacks over 6s. Occasionally a good player will seize upon an opportunity such as this kind of a river-card situation to check-raise in order to make you *think* they hit the higher full house, hoping you'll fold.

Another cardinal rule of Hold'em poker is that it's better to make a small mistake of calling a hand such as this rather than the larger mistake of folding and finding out you were bluffed out of a large pot.

GAME: $4–$8

* Pot amount does not include the house rake which might vary slightly from casino to casino, but usually is 10% up to a $3 maximum, plus $1 for some sort of house jackpot.

House Dealer

Seat 10

Seat 1

Seat 9

Seat 2

$ in the pot before you act:

$6*

Seat 8

Seat 3

YOU →

Seat 7

BB   SB

Seat 4

Seat 6

Seat 5

Flop

Flop Cards Yet to Be Dealt	Flop Cards Yet to Be Dealt	Flop Cards Yet to Be Dealt

Turn

Turn Card Yet to Be Dealt

River

River Card Yet to Be Dealt

Pocket

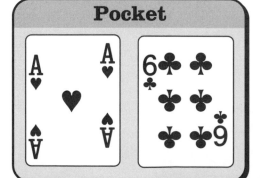

Situation #26

You have been dealt Ace-6 unsuited in your pocket. The only money in the pot is the $6 from the two blinds. You are first to act with all nine other players to act after you. Should you fold, call the $4 bet, or raise to $8, and why?

Starting Hand (Pocket): **A♥ 6♣**

This Pocket's Win Rate: **9.9%**

Win Rate Rank: **43 of 169 possible**

Situation #26: Answer

Ace-6 unsuited is not a good starting hand. You need four of the five board cards to hit just right to give you a flush or a straight, so those two possibilities are slim at best. You are already beaten by any pocket pair, so if they catch three of a kind on the flop you've almost no chance to win. If you catch an Ace on the flop for a pair, you don't have a good kicker to go with it. And, since many players in low limit Hold'em will play an Ace-Anything hand, you've got to figure that among the nine players yet to act after you, anyone with an Ace will be contesting you for the pot. If that's the case, at least you need to have a kicker going in, and you don't. Even if you catch a couple of 6s on the board at some point, you could still be easily beaten by someone holding a pocket pair higher than 6s who catches three of a kind on the board.

Simply put, there are just too many things that have to work just right for you to win this hand, and there are too many things already wrong with this hand (e.g., no kicker, poor position, etc.) to keep them from happening. Fold the hand and wait for a good one.

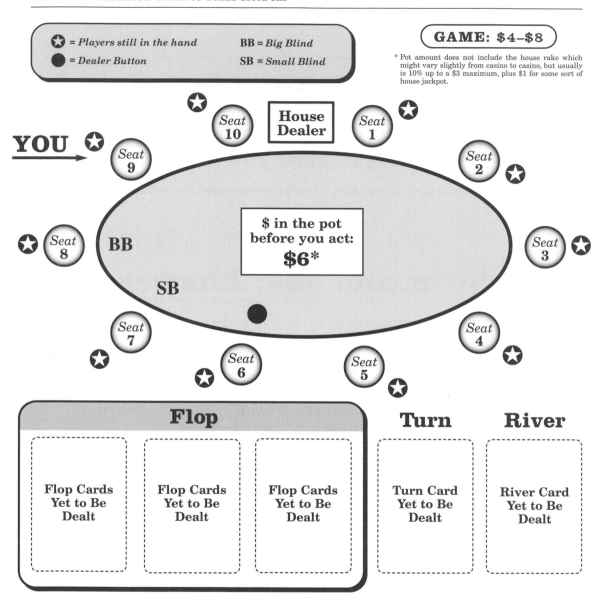

GAME: $4–$8

Seat 10

House Dealer

Seat 1

YOU →

Seat 9

Seat 2

$ in the pot before you act:
$6*

BB

Seat 8

Seat 3

SB

Seat 7

Seat 4

Seat 6

Seat 5

Flop

| Flop Cards Yet to Be Dealt | Flop Cards Yet to Be Dealt | Flop Cards Yet to Be Dealt |

Turn

Turn Card Yet to Be Dealt

River

River Card Yet to Be Dealt

Pocket

Situation #27

You have been dealt Jack-10 offsuit. The only money in the pot is the $6 from the two blinds. You are first to act with all nine other players to act after you. Should you fold, call the $4 bet, or raise to $8, and why?

Starting Hand (Pocket): **J♦ 10♣**

This Pocket's Win Rate: **9.4%**

Win Rate Rank: **50 of 169 possible**

Situation #27: Answer

Remember on the previous situation with the Ace-6 unsuited starting hand in first position I told you to wait for a better hand to play? Well, this ain't it. In fact, if you look at the win rate percentage and win rate rank for the two hands, you'll notice that it's actually lower for this hand than the Ace-6 unsuited in first position. This is another hand that many beginning Hold'em players can't help playing. "Hey," they tell themselves, "I've already got two connected cards for a straight." Well, yeah, but if you put that together with a buffalo nickel you still won't get a bubble bath—or a winning hand 9 times out of 10.

When you're in first position you need to have a strong hand in order to play because you don't know what's coming behind you. What if there's a raise and a reraise behind you with the other seven players folding? That means it's a **shorthanded game**, a game in which big cards do better and drawing hands such as this do worse because they don't get the proper pot odds to play such drawing hands.

Had you been in last position and there were five or six callers before you, then maybe you could play a hand like this. Once again, fold the hand and wait for a good one.

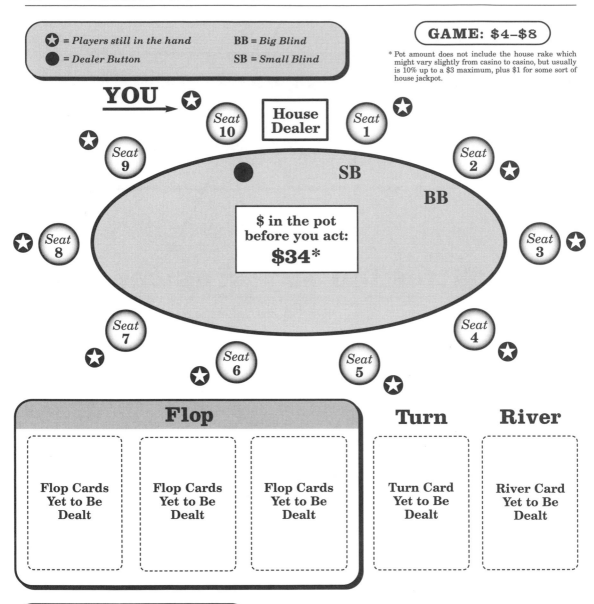

YOU ★

Seat 10   House Dealer   Seat 1   ★

★   Seat 9

● SB

BB

$ in the pot before you act:

$34*

★ Seat 8

Seat 2 ★

Seat 3 ★

Seat 7 ★   Seat 6 ★   Seat 5 ★

Seat 4 ★

Flop

| Flop Cards Yet to Be Dealt | Flop Cards Yet to Be Dealt | Flop Cards Yet to Be Dealt |

Turn

Turn Card Yet to Be Dealt

River

River Card Yet to Be Dealt

Pocket

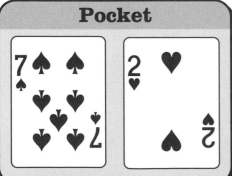

Situation #28

You have been dealt Texas Hold'em's worst starting hand, 7-2 unsuited while **on the button**. Every player in front of you has called for $4 and the small and big blinds have yet to act after you, so there will almost certainly be nine other players in the hand. Should you fold, call the $4 bet, or raise to $8, and why?

Starting Hand (Pocket): **7♠ 2♥**

This Pocket's Win Rate: **0.4%**

Win Rate Rank: **139 of 169 possible**

Situation #28: Answer

Even though the possibility of a huge pot is building, you need to fold this hand. With less than a half percent win rate, it wouldn't matter if there were twenty-five callers in the pot in front of you with no raises. Fold the hand and don't fall into the trap so many beginning players do in playing virtually anything when there are lots of callers.

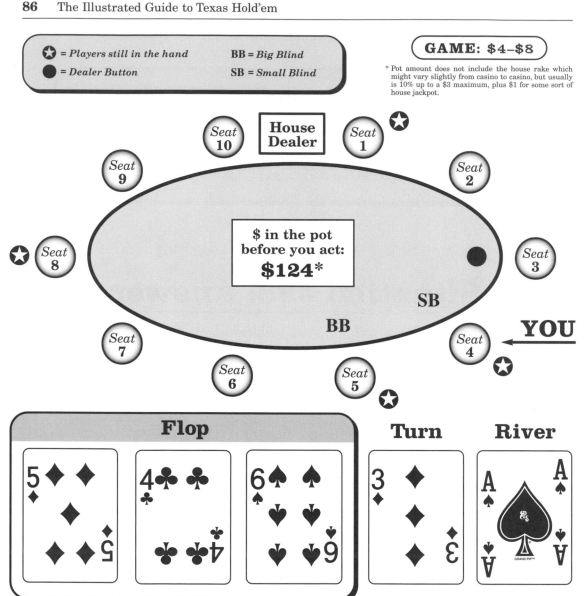

★ = *Players still in the hand*   BB = *Big Blind*

● = *Dealer Button*   SB = *Small Blind*

GAME: $4–$8

* Pot amount does not include the house rake which might vary slightly from casino to casino, but usually is 10% up to a $3 maximum, plus $1 for some sort of house jackpot.

Seat 10 — House Dealer — Seat 1 ★

Seat 9

Seat 2

★ Seat 8

$ in the pot before you act: $124*

Seat 3 ●

SB

Seat 7

BB

Seat 4 ← **YOU** ★

Seat 6

Seat 5 ★

Flop

5♦   4♣   6♠

Turn

3♦

River

A♠

Pocket

7♥   8♥

Situation #29

You were dealt 7-8 suited in your pocket while in the small blind. Five players, including you, called to see the flop, after which you bet first and three others called to see the turn. You again bet first after the turn and the other three players all called you again. After the river card, you bet $8. Seat 5 raised to $16 and both Seats 8 and 1 called. Should you fold, call the $16, or raise to $24, and why?

Starting Hand (Pocket): **7♥ 8♥**

This Pocket's Win Rate: **8.0%**

Win Rate Rank: **63 of 169 possible**

Situation #29: Answer

You should raise to $24 and call Seat 5 if he raises again after you because you have the highest possible hand for this board. There are no flush possibilities since there are only two Spades and two Diamonds on the board. There are no full house possibilities since there are no pairs on the board. Thus, the highest possible hand is a straight, and with this board your 7-8 hand is the nuts. Just keep quiet and keep on raising as long as they let you.

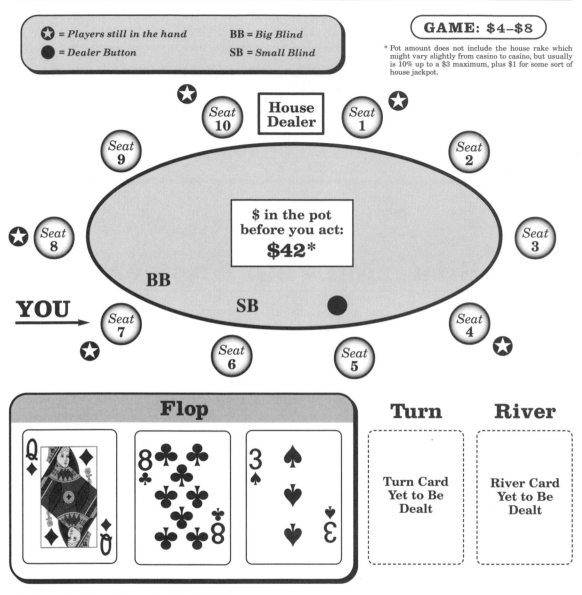

⭐ = *Players still in the hand*   **BB** = *Big Blind*

⚫ = *Dealer Button*   **SB** = *Small Blind*

GAME: $4–$8

* Pot amount does not include the house rake which might vary slightly from casino to casino, but usually is 10% up to a $3 maximum, plus $1 for some sort of house jackpot.

House Dealer

Seat 10   Seat 1   Seat 9   Seat 2   Seat 8   Seat 3

$ in the pot before you act:

$42*

BB

SB

YOU →

Seat 7   Seat 6   Seat 5   Seat 4

Flop

Turn

Turn Card Yet to Be Dealt

River

River Card Yet to Be Dealt

Pocket

Situation #30

You received a pair of Queens in your pocket. Before the flop, Seat 8 raised and four of you called the $8 bet. After the flop it's your turn to act first. Should you check or bet $4, and why?

Starting Hand (Pocket): **Q♥ Q♣**

This Pocket's Win Rate: **68.5%**

Win Rate Rank: **4 of 169 possible**

Situation #30: Answer

You should check. Any bet by you after the flop is likely to indicate to your opponents that you have either a Queen in your pocket or that you can beat two Queens (as in pocket Kings or Aces), or that you have at the very least a pocket of Ace-King. By checking you are not only disguising your hand but you are hoping that someone else bets so that you can call or raise, and if no one does, then you're hoping that someone catches a pair on the turn to give you more action in a pot that is now heavily in your favor after the flop.

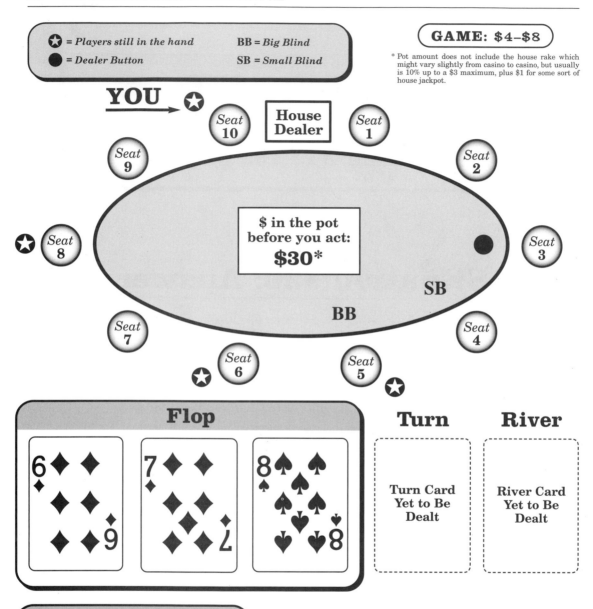

GAME: $4–$8

* Pot amount does not include the house rake which might vary slightly from casino to casino, but usually is 10% up to a $3 maximum, plus $1 for some sort of house jackpot.

YOU →

Seat 10   House Dealer   Seat 1

Seat 9   Seat 2

$ in the pot before you act: **$30***

Seat 8   Seat 3

SB

BB

Seat 7   Seat 4

Seat 6   Seat 5

Flop

6♦   7♦   8♠

Turn

Turn Card Yet to Be Dealt

River

River Card Yet to Be Dealt

Pocket

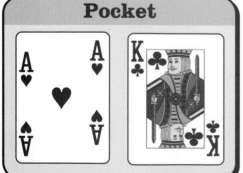

A♥   K♣

Situation #31

You have been dealt big slick, Ace-King unsuited. There were four of you in to see the flop and you are last to act. Seat 5 bets $4 and Seats 6 and 8 call the bet. Should you fold, call the $4 bet, or raise to $8, and why?

Starting Hand (Pocket): **A♥ K♣**

This Pocket's Win Rate: **67.0%**

Win Rate Rank: **5 of 169 possible**

Situation #31: Answer

You started off with one of the top pockets in Hold'em, Ace-King unsuited. Unfortunately, the flop totally missed you. With obvious straight and flush draws on the board—neither of which can hit your hand—and three callers in the pot in front of you, you have to let one of Hold'em's cardinal rules apply here.

CARDINAL RULE

In most cases, if the flop doesn't fit your hand, fold.

Even though it's tough to throw Ace-King into the muck, that advice is most appropriate for this hand.

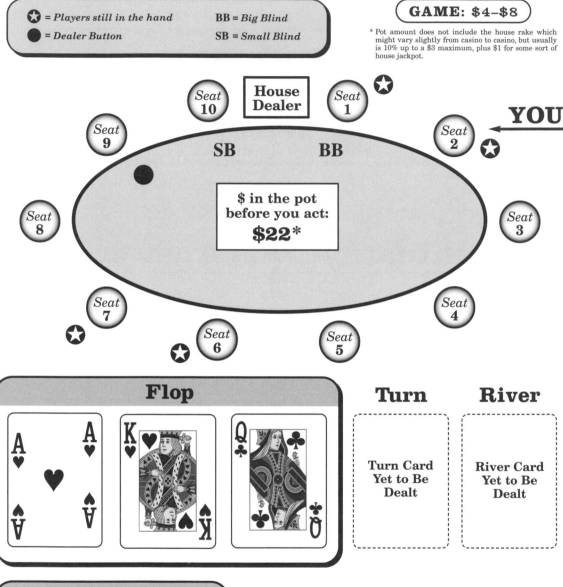

* Pot amount does not include the house rake which might vary slightly from casino to casino, but usually is 10% up to a $3 maximum, plus $1 for some sort of house jackpot.

GAME: $4–$8

⭐ = Players still in the hand   BB = Big Blind

⬤ = Dealer Button   SB = Small Blind

Seat 10   House Dealer   Seat 1   ⭐   **YOU**

Seat 9   Seat 2   ⭐

SB   BB

$ in the pot before you act: **$22***

Seat 8   Seat 3

Seat 7   Seat 4

⭐   Seat 6   Seat 5

⭐

Flop   **Turn**   **River**

Turn Card Yet to Be Dealt   River Card Yet to Be Dealt

Pocket

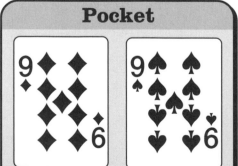

Situation #32

You have been dealt a pair of 9s in your pocket. There were four of you in to see the flop and you are the second player to act. Seat 1 bets $4. Do you fold, call the $4, or raise to $8 in an attempt to bluff everyone out, and why?

Starting Hand (Pocket): **9♦ 9♠**

This Pocket's Win Rate: **55.4%**

Win Rate Rank: **11 of 169 possible**

Situation #32: Answer

First of all, you can forget about raising to bluff everyone else out. Typically, most players will play Ace-Anything and since an Ace hit the board they're not going anywhere. Lots of Kings/Queens-Anything also get played so you're likely up against one or two of those as well. Bluffing should be used only on rare occasions in Hold'em, and usually only when going heads up against one other player; this isn't one of those occasions.

Now your choices are to fold or call. If you call this bet, you'll have to recognize that you're strictly chasing another 9. And with three over-cards already on the board against you as well as a Heart flush draw, hitting another 9 may not be enough anyway. This is another example of the flop missing your hand entirely. Not only did it miss your hand, it put three overcards on the board and probably made everyone else's. Your only choice here is to fold the hand.

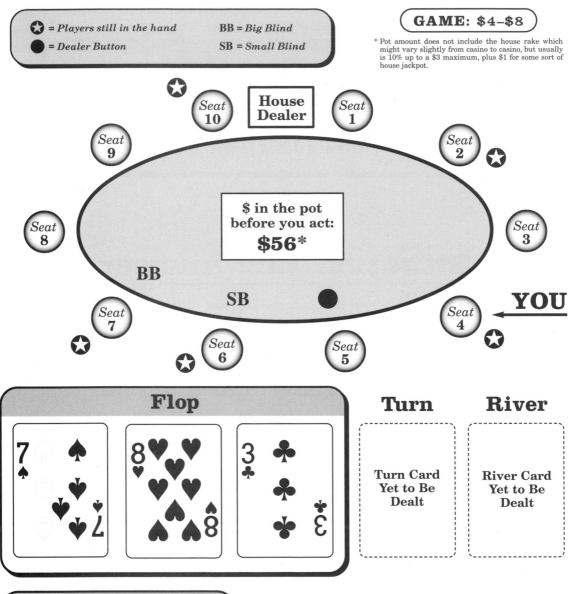

= *Players still in the hand*   BB = *Big Blind*

= *Dealer Button*   SB = *Small Blind*

GAME: $4–$8

* Pot amount does not include the house rake which might vary slightly from casino to casino, but usually is 10% up to a $3 maximum, plus $1 for some sort of house jackpot.

House Dealer

Seat 10

Seat 1

Seat 9

Seat 2

$ in the pot before you act: $56*

Seat 8

Seat 3

BB

SB

YOU

Seat 7

Seat 4

Seat 6

Seat 5

Flop

7♠   8♥   3♣

Turn

Turn Card Yet to Be Dealt

River

River Card Yet to Be Dealt

Pocket

8♦   8♣

Situation #33

You have been dealt a pair of 8s in your pocket. There were five of you in to see the flop for two bets (Seat 6 raised) and you are the last player to act. After the flop, Seat 6 bets $4. Seats 7, 10, and 2 all call the bet. Do you fold, call the $4, or raise to $8, and why?

Starting Hand (Pocket): **8♦ 8♣**

This Pocket's Win Rate: **51.8%**

Win Rate Rank: **13 of 169 possible**

Situation #33: Answer

You raise the bet to $8. Right now you have the highest possible hand with this board. There is no other possible hand that an opponent could hold that would either beat or tie your hand. Since you have the best hand, bet it strong and make them pay. Seat 6 likely has some sort of big cards since he raised before the flop and came out betting after the flop. The other three callers could have big cards or some portion of the flop, but they still can't beat you.

Also, it will take two more of one suit to make a flush, and at least one more card to make a straight, so nothing is there yet. The thing to watch out for on the turn and river are overcards (9s through Aces) that could defeat your three 8s, or runner-runner of one suit to make for a possible flush, or cards that could make a straight with what's already on the board.

CARDINAL RULE

When you know you have the best hand, make your opponents pay.

However, if the turn or river cards pair up with something already on the board, then you've just made a full house and will beat all the straights and flushes that come up.

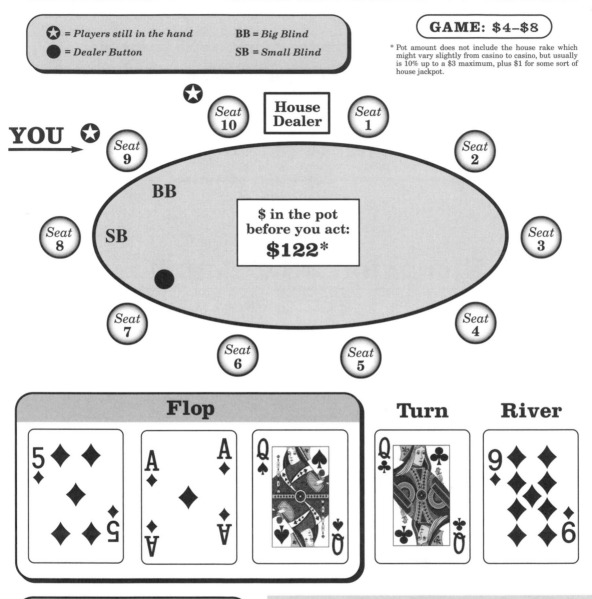

★ = *Players still in the hand*   BB = *Big Blind*

● = *Dealer Button*   SB = *Small Blind*

GAME: $4–$8

* Pot amount does not include the house rake which might vary slightly from casino to casino, but usually is 10% up to a $3 maximum, plus $1 for some sort of house jackpot.

YOU ★

Seat 10   **House Dealer**   Seat 1
Seat 9   Seat 2
BB
Seat 8   **SB**   Seat 3
$ in the pot before you act: **$122***
Seat 7   Seat 4
Seat 6   Seat 5

Flop

5♦   A♦ A♦   Q♠

Turn

Q♣

River

9♦ 6♦

Pocket

Q♥   5♣

Situation #34

You were dealt Q-5 unsuited in the big blind. Before the flop, Seat 10 bet and there were 5 callers, including you. After the flop, you were first to act and you bet $4. Seat 10 raised to $8 and everyone folded back to you. You reraised and he capped it at $16. After the turn, you bet $8, he raised to $16, you reraised, and he capped it at $32. After the river, should you check or bet $8, and why?

Starting Hand (Pocket): **Q♥ 5♣**

This Pocket's Win Rate: **1.4%**

Win Rate Rank: **115 of 169 possible**

Situation #34: Answer

After all the action on the flop and turn, it's time to start becoming uneasy about this hand and you should check. Remember, he bet before the flop when he was the first to act. This should indicate that he has some kind of a strong hand. Then, when you hit your two pair on the flop and bet, he followed this with a raise. This should indicate to you that he's not afraid of the Ace on the board. If he's not afraid of the Ace with a Queen and a 5 on the board, that should tell you he's at least got an Ace in his hand.

Now, a pair of Aces by themselves doesn't beat your two pair, and, in all candor, he can't be placing you on a Queen-5. He, too, must realize you have something strong since you reraised him after the flop. And, since he reraised you again to cap it after the flop, he's not afraid of your possible two pair (whatever they are) or your possible three of a kind (whatever they are).

After the turn, when you hit your full house, Queens over 5s, you bet, he raised, you reraised, and he reraised. Again, this should tell you something about his hand. With an Ace and two Queens on the board, he raised you twice after the turn. He either doesn't believe you have four Queens (or knows you don't) or doesn't believe you have a full house consisting of some combination of Aces and Queens (or knows you don't). After the river he's also not afraid of the flush draw, either, since he raised you again.

By now (if not a little earlier in the hand), I would be putting him on either pocket Aces or Ace-Queen. Either way I'd be getting the awful feeling that I'm beaten on this hand, so now I'm just going to call the $16 and see what he has. *(This exact hand actually happened to me, which is why it wound up in this book. The other guy had pocket Aces.)*

⭐ = *Players still in the hand*   BB = *Big Blind*

⚫ = *Dealer Button*   SB = *Small Blind*

Seat 10

House Dealer

Seat 1

Seat 9

Seat 2

SB

$ in the pot before you act: $50*

Seat 8

BB

Seat 3 ⭐

YOU ➡

Seat 7

⭐

Seat 4

Seat 6

Seat 5

⭐

Flop

9♣ 5♣ 6♣

Turn

8♠

River

River Card Yet to Be Dealt

Pocket

K♥ K♦

Situation #35

You have been dealt a pair of Kings in your pocket. There were three of you in to see the flop for two bets. Seat 3 bet first, Seat 5 called, you raised, and Seats 3 and 5 called your raise. After the flop, you all checked. After the turn, Seat 3 bet $8 and Seat 5 raised to $16. Do you fold, call the $16, or raise to $24, and why?

Starting Hand (Pocket): **K♥ K♦**

This Pocket's Win Rate: **74.6%**

Win Rate Rank: **2 of 169 possible**

Situation #35: Answer

You started off with the second best hand in Hold'em, two Kings. But after the flop and turn, you now probably don't even have the second best hand at the table. With only one card yet to come, the only hands you can hope for are two pair, three Kings, or a 7 for a straight on the board (which could still be beaten by an opponent's flush or higher straight).

Since there are now obvious straight and flush draws on the board, and betting action that indicates one or both players have hit either a straight or a flush, you need to fold this hand and save your chips to fight another day.

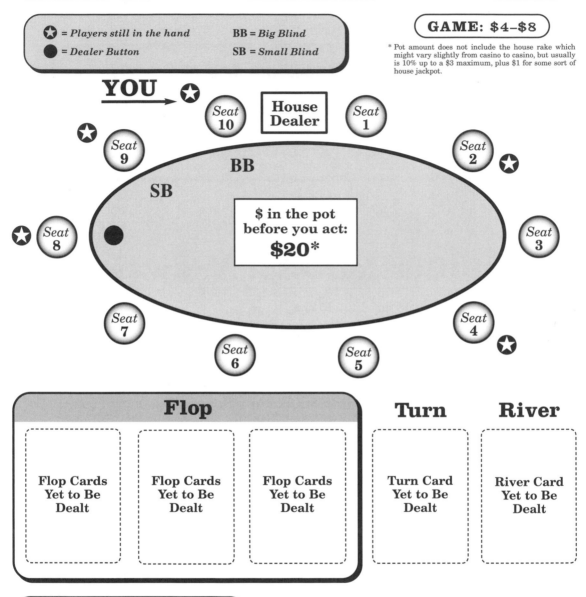

★ = *Players still in the hand*   BB = *Big Blind*
● = *Dealer Button*   SB = *Small Blind*

GAME: $4–$8

* Pot amount does not include the house rake which might vary slightly from casino to casino, but usually is 10% up to a $3 maximum, plus $1 for some sort of house jackpot.

YOU →

Seat 10   **House Dealer**   Seat 1

Seat 9   Seat 2

BB

SB

Seat 8

$ in the pot before you act:
$20*

Seat 3

Seat 7   Seat 4

Seat 6   Seat 5

Flop

| Flop Cards Yet to Be Dealt | Flop Cards Yet to Be Dealt | Flop Cards Yet to Be Dealt |

Turn

Turn Card Yet to Be Dealt

River

River Card Yet to Be Dealt

Pocket

Situation #36

You have been dealt Queen-7 offsuit in the big blind. There are four callers before you. Should you fold this hand now, check, or raise it to $8, and why?

Starting Hand (Pocket): **Q♦ 7♠**

This Pocket's Win Rate: **1.4%**

Win Rate Rank: **114 of 169 possible**

Situation #36: Answer

Queen-7 offsuit is a lousy hand, no two ways about it. But, since you are in the big blind and are forced to put in the $4 full bet, you can see the flop for free if you check, so that is the correct play at this point. Once the flop comes up you can determine whether or not it hit you well enough to stay in the hand after that. If you flop two Queens, two 7s, or one of each, you'll have a strong hand. Anything less than that and you'll have to be careful about continuing in the hand unless everyone checks around.

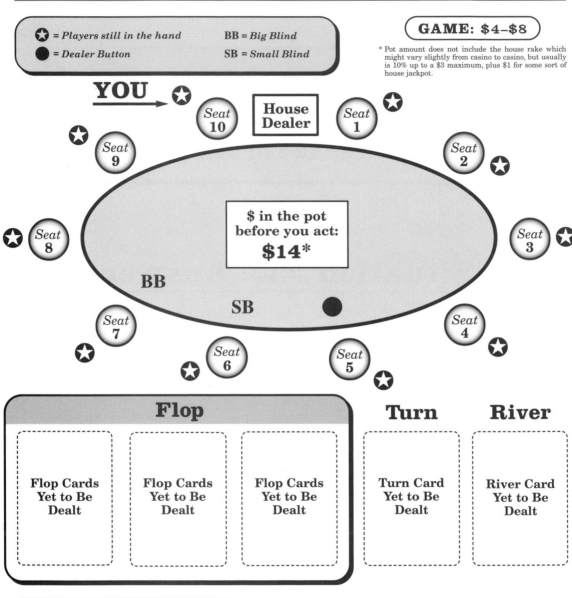

= Players still in the hand

= Dealer Button

BB = Big Blind

SB = Small Blind

GAME: $4–$8

* Pot amount does not include the house rake which might vary slightly from casino to casino, but usually is 10% up to a $3 maximum, plus $1 for some sort of house jackpot.

YOU

Seat 10

House Dealer

Seat 1

Seat 9

Seat 2

$ in the pot before you act:
$14*

Seat 8

Seat 3

BB

SB

Seat 7

Seat 4

Seat 6

Seat 5

Flop

| Flop Cards Yet to Be Dealt | Flop Cards Yet to Be Dealt | Flop Cards Yet to Be Dealt |

Turn

Turn Card Yet to Be Dealt

River

River Card Yet to Be Dealt

Pocket

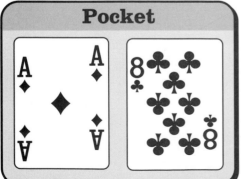

Situation #37

You have been dealt Ace-8 offsuit in the pocket. The first two players to act, Seats 8 and 9, both call the $4 bet. Should you fold this hand now, call the $4, or raise it to $8, and why?

Starting Hand (Pocket): **A♦ 8♣**

This Pocket's Win Rate: **10.0%**

Win Rate Rank: **42 of 169 possible**

Situation #37: Answer

Even though you hold an Ace with an 8 kicker, this is not a very strong hand. Your cards are unsuited, so an Ace-high flush will be harder to come by. Also, your cards are not conducive to making a straight, so that, too, shouldn't be a consideration. All you're basically left to fight with at this point is an Ace with a medium kicker. With two callers in already under the gun (which means they likely have some sort of strong hand) and seven more players to act after you, this is one hand you don't want any part of with these cards. Get out now while the getting's good (and doesn't cost you anything!).

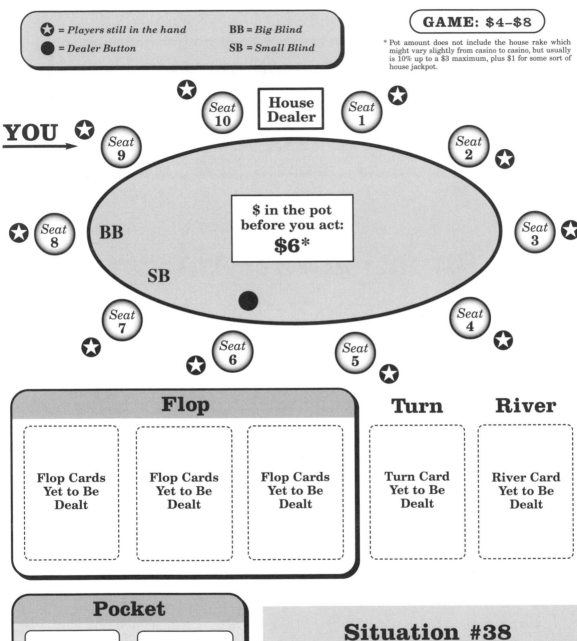

= *Players still in the hand*   BB = *Big Blind*

= *Dealer Button*   SB = *Small Blind*

GAME: $4–$8

* Pot amount does not include the house rake which might vary slightly from casino to casino, but usually is 10% up to a $3 maximum, plus $1 for some sort of house jackpot.

Seat 10   **House Dealer**   Seat 1

YOU →   Seat 9   Seat 2

BB   **$ in the pot before you act: $6***   Seat 3

Seat 8

SB

Seat 7   Seat 4

Seat 6   Seat 5

Flop

| Flop Cards Yet to Be Dealt | Flop Cards Yet to Be Dealt | Flop Cards Yet to Be Dealt |

Turn

Turn Card Yet to Be Dealt

River

River Card Yet to Be Dealt

Pocket

2♥   2♣

Situation #38

You have been dealt a pair of 2s in your pocket. You are the first to act. Do you fold, bet $4, or raise the big blind bet to $8, and why?

Starting Hand (Pocket): **2♥ 2♣**

This Pocket's Win Rate: **4.0%**

Win Rate Rank: **72 of 169 possible**

Situation #38: Answer

Yes, a pair of 2s beats A-K suited...technically. But once the five board cards are dealt, your 2s are a virtual certainty to lose. Even if a third 2 flops for you, anyone else with a pair who catches three of a kind will beat you. For all practical purposes, you only have two outs for your hand; the other two 2s. If you happen to catch a 3-4-5-6 on the board, then anyone else holding a 7 will beat you as well.

A pair of 2s in first position is a terrible hand. If you call the $4 bet in early position like this, you still have to contend with the other nine players acting behind you. There could be a raise or two, which means you either have to throw good money after bad, or fold after making the $4 bet. Save yourself the trouble that will almost certainly follow if you play this hand in this position. Fold it.

= *Players still in the hand*   BB = *Big Blind*

= *Dealer Button*   SB = *Small Blind*

GAME: $4–$8

* Pot amount does not include the house rake which might vary slightly from casino to casino, but usually is 10% up to a $3 maximum, plus $1 for some sort of house jackpot.

Seat 10

House Dealer

Seat 1

Seat 9

Seat 2

SB   BB

YOU

Seat 8

$ in the pot before you act:
$26*

Seat 3

Seat 7

Seat 4

Seat 6

Seat 5

Flop

| Flop Cards Yet to Be Dealt | Flop Cards Yet to Be Dealt | Flop Cards Yet to Be Dealt |

Turn

Turn Card Yet to Be Dealt

River

River Card Yet to Be Dealt

Pocket

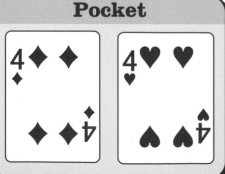

Situation #39

You have been dealt a pair of 4s in your pocket. You are the seventh to act. Three players before you are still in the hand. Seat 3 bet $4, Seat 4 raised to $8, and Seat 6 called. There are three more players to act after you, including the blinds. Do you fold, call the $8, or raise to $12, and why?

Starting Hand (Pocket): **4♦ 4♥**

This Pocket's Win Rate: **8.3%**

Win Rate Rank: **61 of 169 possible**

Situation #39: Answer

A pair of 4s in late position is a weak hand. There has already been a raise in front of you that has been called. This projects two strong hands, and you still have three players to act after you, plus Seat 3 again. Like the pair of 2s in the previous situation, this pair of 4s has, realistically, only two outs—the other 4s. There are times when you have to resist the temptation to play small pairs out of position. Late position after a raise with several callers against you and several more to act after you is one of those times. Fold the hand.

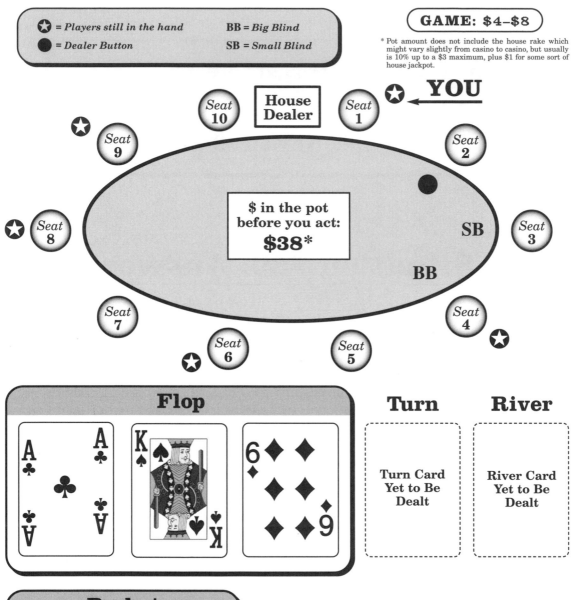

★ = *Players still in the hand*   BB = *Big Blind*

● = *Dealer Button*   SB = *Small Blind*

GAME: $4–$8

* Pot amount does not include the house rake which might vary slightly from casino to casino, but usually is 10% up to a $3 maximum, plus $1 for some sort of house jackpot.

Seat 10   **House Dealer**   Seat 1   **YOU**

Seat 9   Seat 2

$ in the pot before you act:
$38*

SB

Seat 8   Seat 3

BB

Seat 7   Seat 4

Seat 6   Seat 5

Flop

A♣   K♠   6♦

Turn

Turn Card Yet to Be Dealt

River

River Card Yet to Be Dealt

Pocket

6♥   6♠

Situation #40

You have been dealt a pair of 6s in your pocket. There were five of you in to see the flop for one bet and you are the last player to act. After the flop, Seat 4 bets $4. Seats 6, 8, and 9 all call the bet. Do you fold, call the $4, or raise to $8, and why?

Starting Hand (Pocket): **6♥ 6♠**

This Pocket's Win Rate: **26.2%**

Win Rate Rank: **32 of 169 possible**

Situation #40: Answer

You raise the bet to $8. Right now the only hands that can beat you are pocket Aces and pocket Kings. You received good information before the flop when no one raised the bet, which typically happens with pocket Aces and Kings. After the flop there was one bet and three callers. Again, no indication of pocket Aces or Kings. In all likelihood, the probable best hands against you now are either a pair of Aces, a pair of Kings, or another pocket pair that is less than Kings.

Your three 6s are well concealed because two of them are in the pocket. Your raise to $8 not only represents that you have what you think is the best hand, it gains you information about your opponents' hands. If they call your raise, then they probably have an Ace or a King in their pocket, but you still have them beat. If they fold, then they likely believe you have some combination of Aces/Kings in your pocket. If they reraise you, then you have to be careful and just call their raise. The good thing for you is that if the turn or river pairs any of the three board cards, you will have a full house.

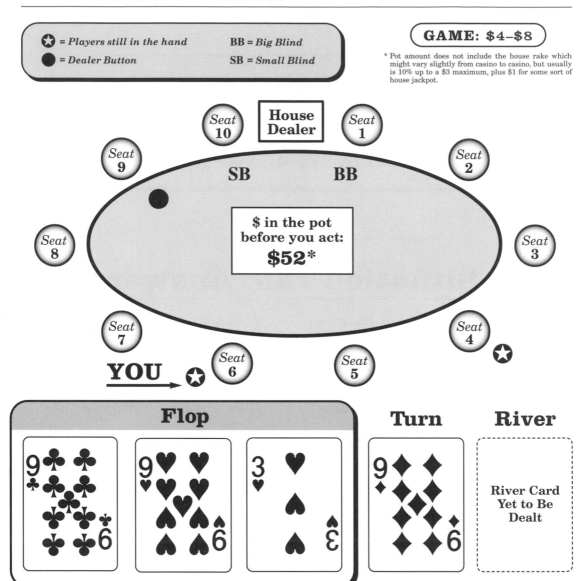

GAME: $4–$8

* Pot amount does not include the house rake which might vary slightly from casino to casino, but usually is 10% up to a $3 maximum, plus $1 for some sort of house jackpot.

⭐ = Players still in the hand   BB = Big Blind

⬤ = Dealer Button   SB = Small Blind

Seat 10 | House Dealer | Seat 1

Seat 9   Seat 2

SB   BB

Seat 8 $ in the pot before you act: **$52***   Seat 3

Seat 7   Seat 4

YOU →   Seat 6   Seat 5

Flop   **Turn**   **River**

9♣   9♥   3♥   9♦   River Card Yet to Be Dealt

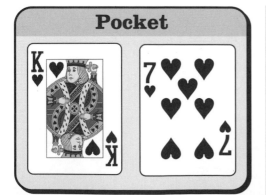

Pocket

K♥   7♥

Situation #41

You received King-7 suited in your pocket. Five players including the blinds stayed in for one bet to see the flop. After the flop, Seat 4 checked, you bet $4 on your flush draw, the other three players folded, and Seat 4 called your bet. After the turn, Seat 4 checked and you bet $8 as a bluff. Seat 4 then raised you to $16. Should you fold, call the check-raise of $16, or reraise to $24, and why?

Starting Hand (Pocket): **K♥ 7♥**

This Pocket's Win Rate: **8.6%**

Win Rate Rank: **56 of 169 possible**

Situation #41: Answer

Lick your wounds and fold your hand. When you bet your flush draw after the flop and three players folded, it was obvious that the pair of 9s on the board scared them off. Seat 4, however, didn't fold in the face of your bet and the two 9s. Seat 4's check-raise of you after the third 9 came on the turn should make it obvious that you're beaten, at least at this stage of the hand. At the very least you're probably facing a full house, at the worst four 9s.

Your only glimmer of hope on this hand is if another King comes on the river and your opponent has a pocket pair smaller than Kings, but the odds are long against you of catching the card you need (23-to-1), and the pot odds are not worth taking the chance ($52-to-$8, or 6.5-to-1).

This hand was a very weak one to begin with as the 8.6 percent win rate shown above indicates, which is why you shouldn't have played the hand in the first place. When you play starting hands that are not pairs, that give you no chance for a straight, and that have a weak kicker besides, you are just asking for trouble.

Playing this hand at all was not a good decision, but the reality of low limit Hold'em is that these kind of hands are played all the time. This situation will hopefully show you why you don't play hands like this.

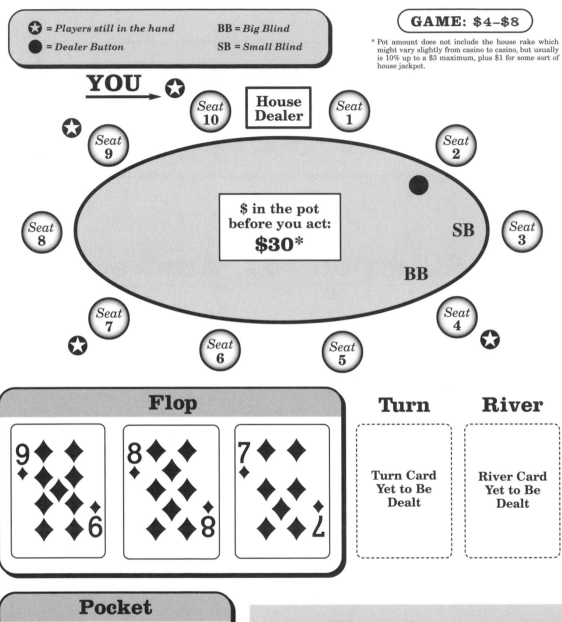

⭐ = *Players still in the hand*   BB = *Big Blind*

⚫ = *Dealer Button*   SB = *Small Blind*

YOU →

Seat 10 | House Dealer | Seat 1

Seat 9 | Seat 2

Seat 8 | Seat 3

Seat 7 | Seat 4

Seat 6 | Seat 5

$ in the pot before you act: **$30***

SB

BB

Flop

9♦ ... 6

8♦ ... 8

7♦ ... 7

Turn

Turn Card Yet to Be Dealt

River

River Card Yet to Be Dealt

Pocket

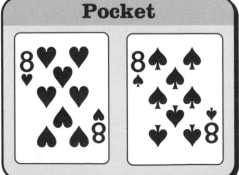

8♥ ... 8

8♠ ... 8

Situation #42

You have been dealt a pair of 8s in your pocket. There were four of you in to see the flop for one bet and you are the last player to act. After the flop, Seat 4 checks, Seat 7 bets $4, and Seat 9 raises to $8. Do you fold, call the $8, or raise to $12, and why?

Starting Hand (Pocket): **8♥ 8♠**

This Pocket's Win Rate: **51.8%**

Win Rate Rank: **13 of 169 possible**

Situation #42: Answer

You call the $8. You've got a very good hand at this point, but it is still very vulnerable to a straight or a Diamond flush. Seat 9's raise could be an indication of having caught a flush, but it is also likely he caught either a flush *draw* or a straight and he wants everyone else to *think* he caught the flush and is trying to drive them out with his raise. He might even have three 9s or three 7s, both of which are vulnerable to straights and flushes, just like your three 8s.

In any event, what you need is for the board to pair to give you a full house. If you do pair the board on the turn, then you have to consider what could possibly be out there to beat you. If a 9 comes, then pocket 9s beat you, as do the pocket hands 9-8 and 9-7. If an 8 comes on the turn, you're home free, unless one of your opponents has or hits a straight flush or holds pocket 9s and catches a 9 on the river. If a 7 comes on the turn, you're still in good shape unless your opponent holds pocket 9s or pocket 7s.

Now, on the river, if a...well, you get the idea. Until you have the nuts, you don't have the nuts. Try and look at each hand with an eye towards what could possibly be out there already to beat you, or what could potentially come up on the turn and river to beat you.

★ = Players still in the hand   BB = Big Blind

● = Dealer Button   SB = Small Blind

GAME: $4–$8

* Pot amount does not include the house rake which might vary slightly from casino to casino, but usually is 10% up to a $3 maximum, plus $1 for some sort of house jackpot.

Seat 10   House Dealer   Seat 1   **YOU**

Seat 9   Seat 2

BB

SB

Seat 8 $ in the pot before you act: **$22***   Seat 3

Seat 7   Seat 4

Seat 6   Seat 5

Flop

Turn
Turn Card Yet to Be Dealt

River
River Card Yet to Be Dealt

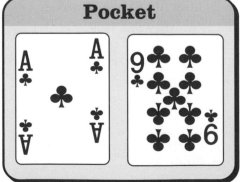

Pocket

Situation #43

You are in a loose-passive game. You have been dealt Ace-9 suited in your pocket. You were first to act after the deal and you raised the big blind bet to $8. Everyone folded to Seat 10 (the big blind) who called your raise. After the flop, Seat 10 was first to act and he bet $4. Do you fold, call the $4, or raise to $8, and why?

Starting Hand (Pocket): **A♣ 9♣**

This Pocket's Win Rate: **40.5%**

Win Rate Rank: **20 of 169 possible**

Situation #43: Answer

You started out with a decent but vulnerable hand (win rate of just over 40 percent) and your under-the-gun raise accomplished the desired effect of getting eight of your nine opponents in this loose-passive game to fold, with only the big blind staying in. The flop didn't help you very much, giving you only bottom pair. Worse still, three Hearts came on the board. When your sole opponent comes out betting after the flop, this should be an indication of projected power. He either has one or two Hearts in his hand, a straight or straight draw, a King, or maybe more. He could also be bluffing or just betting first for information.

No matter the reason for his bet, what you have to do is assess your own chances of coming up with a winning hand and deciding whether or not the money in the pot is worth the risk you're being asked to take (it's that pot odds thing again).

Okay, let's figure it out. If he has two Hearts you're almost drawing dead (meaning you can't win no matter what cards come up). If he already has a straight or flush, you're only hope is if two 9s come on the turn and river (or a Jack-10 if he has a straight). Anything else and you're dead. Long odds, that. Let's say the flop just gave him something as simple as a pair of Kings. To beat him, you need either an Ace or a 9 to come on the turn or river *without* another King coming. The odds of this occurring are:

41 ÷ (6 - 2) ÷ 2 = 5.13-to-1

To put this equation into English, there are forty-one cards that aren't Aces or 9s. There are six that are, but you need to deduct two from this for the two Kings that could come up that still beat you. You have two chances (turn and river) to get what you need. This makes the odds a little over 5-to-1 against you for an even money proposition. And that assumes he won't hit a flush or straight. Fold the hand.

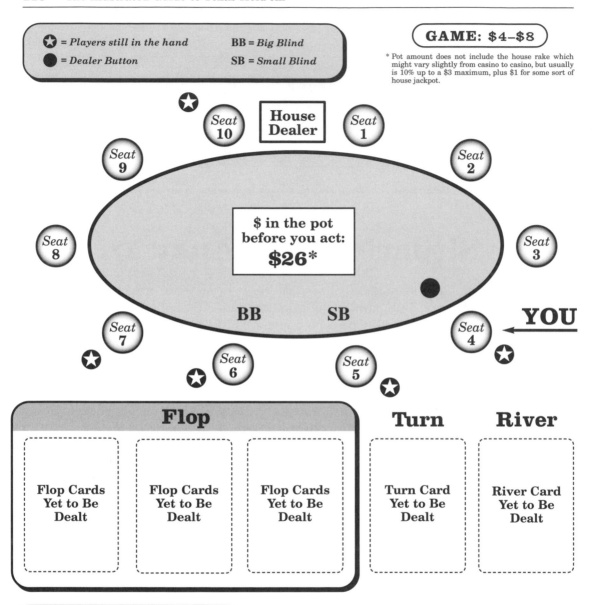

= Players still in the hand   BB = Big Blind

= Dealer Button   SB = Small Blind

GAME: $4–$8

* Pot amount does not include the house rake which might vary slightly from casino to casino, but usually is 10% up to a $3 maximum, plus $1 for some sort of house jackpot.

Seat 10

House Dealer

Seat 1

Seat 9

Seat 2

$ in the pot before you act:
$26*

Seat 8

Seat 3

BB   SB

Seat 7

Seat 4   **YOU**

Seat 6

Seat 5

Flop

| Flop Cards Yet to Be Dealt | Flop Cards Yet to Be Dealt | Flop Cards Yet to Be Dealt |

Turn

Turn Card Yet to Be Dealt

River

River Card Yet to Be Dealt

Pocket

10♥ 9♥

Situation #44

You have been dealt the suited connectors 10♥ 9♥ in your pocket. Seat 7, who is under the gun, raises to $8. Seats 8 and 9 fold. Seat 10 reraises to $12. Seats 1, 2, and 3 fold to you. With the two blinds still yet to act after you, do you fold as well, call the $12, or raise to $16, and why?

Starting Hand (Pocket): **10♥ 9♥**

This Pocket's Win Rate: **38.3%**

Win Rate Rank: **24 of 169 possible**

Situation #44: Answer

Your pocket hand is decent, about at the bottom end of playable hands for Texas Hold'em, ranking twenty-fourth on the win rate chart.

The problem for you here is that there is some real projected power at the table before you ever get the chance to act. When a player under the gun raises, he usually has a strong hand. He has to because there are nine players to act after him and he needs to be able to withstand their action. And when another player raises him, it's time for you to take serious stock of your hand.

Since (statistically speaking) the blinds are probably going to fold, if you stay in this hand there will only be three players, two of which have projected real power...and you. Since you paid good money for this book, it's my job to break the news to you...*10-9 suited is not real power* although many beginning Hold'em players like to think it is.

A hand like this needs a lot of callers tossing money into the pot because the pot odds against you winning are high. It needs to be financially worth it, and with only two other players, this hand isn't worth it. Fold the hand.

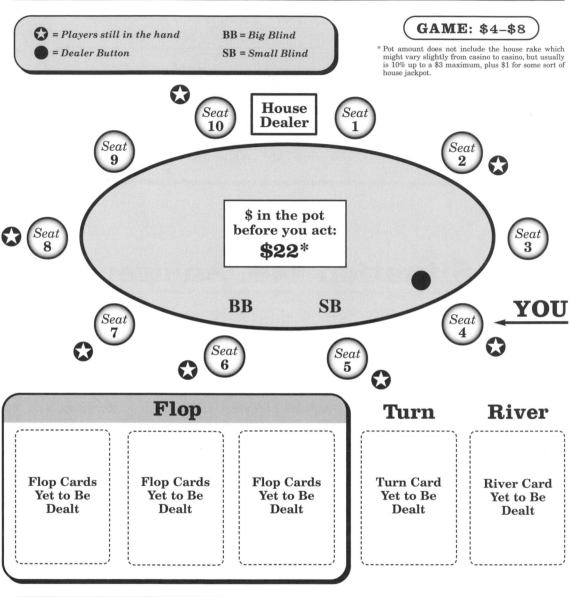

★ = Players still in the hand   BB = Big Blind

● = Dealer Button   SB = Small Blind

GAME: $4–$8

* Pot amount does not include the house rake which might vary slightly from casino to casino, but usually is 10% up to a $3 maximum, plus $1 for some sort of house jackpot.

House Dealer

Seat 10

Seat 1

Seat 9

Seat 2

$ in the pot before you act: **$22***

Seat 8

Seat 3

BB   SB

YOU

Seat 4

Seat 7

Seat 6

Seat 5

Flop

| Flop Cards Yet to Be Dealt | Flop Cards Yet to Be Dealt | Flop Cards Yet to Be Dealt |

Turn

Turn Card Yet to Be Dealt

River

River Card Yet to Be Dealt

Pocket

10♦   9♦

Situation #45

You have been dealt the suited connectors 10♦ 9♦ in your pocket. Seat 7, who is under the gun, bets $4. Seats 8, 10, and 2 all call the bet. With the two blinds still yet to act after you, do you fold, call the $4 bet, or raise to $8, and why?

Starting Hand (Pocket): **10♦ 9♦**

This Pocket's Win Rate: **38.3%**

Win Rate Rank: **24 of 169 possible**

Situation #45: Answer

"Wait a minute!" you say. Didn't we just do this hand? Well, yes and no. And that's the thing about Texas Hold'em—the same hand can and should be played differently in different situations, and this is a classic example.

In the previous situation, there were only two likely players against you with your 10-9 suited hand and they both projected real power. This time there are already four *callers* in front of you with the blinds to act after you. If you call, that will make five players in the hand. The big blind will certainly stay in the hand for six, and the small blind will most likely stay in because there are so many callers and the pot is large with no real strength yet projected. That makes for seven likely players, with no strength projected. *Now* you're in the ideal situation you want to be in with a hand like this—lots of callers and no strength projected. You're in cheap with a potentially large pot brewing.

Call the bet and see what the flop brings.

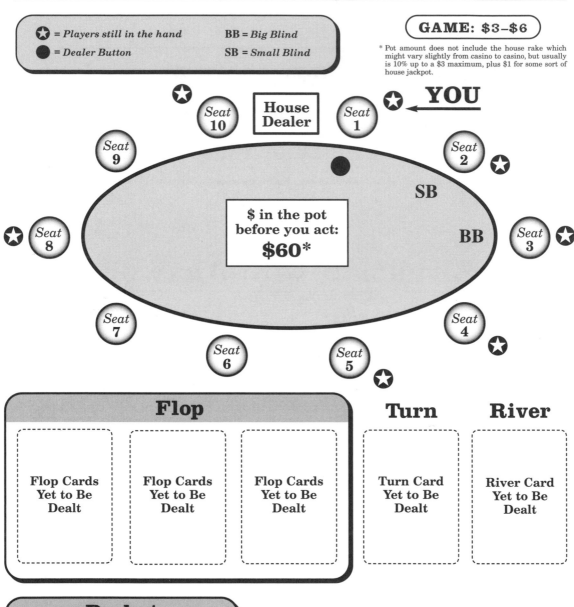

⭐ = Players still in the hand   BB = Big Blind

⚫ = Dealer Button   SB = Small Blind

GAME: $3–$6

* Pot amount does not include the house rake which might vary slightly from casino to casino, but usually is 10% up to a $3 maximum, plus $1 for some sort of house jackpot.

Seat 10   **House Dealer**   Seat 1   **YOU** ←

Seat 9   Seat 2   **SB**

Seat 8   **$ in the pot before you act:** **$60***   **BB**   Seat 3

Seat 7   Seat 4

Seat 6   Seat 5

Flop

| Flop Cards Yet to Be Dealt | Flop Cards Yet to Be Dealt | Flop Cards Yet to Be Dealt |

Turn

Turn Card Yet to Be Dealt

River

River Card Yet to Be Dealt

Pocket

6♣   3♣

Situation #46

Situations 46–49 all deal with the same hand at the four betting stages of a hand the author was actually involved in.

You're playing in a $3-$6 game and it is a **kill pot** (meaning the betting is double, or $6-$12). Seat 4, under the gun, raises to $12. Seats 5 and 8 call. Seat 10 raises to $18. It is your turn to act, with the two blinds after you. Do you fold, call the $18, or raise to $24, and why?

> Starting Hand (Pocket): **6♣ 3♣**
>
> This Pocket's Win Rate: **2.4%**
>
> Win Rate Rank: **106 of 169 possible**

Situation #46: Answer

As to whether you should fold, call, or raise, let's consider some things. Seat 4 raised to $12 under the gun, so he's projected power. Seats 5 and 8 called, so they weren't afraid of Seat 4's raise. Obviously Seat 10 wasn't either, because he raised to $18. Now it's your turn. Under normal circumstances you should fold this hand because it's not that good (only a 2.4 percent win rate). However, since four players are already in the pot and you have the blinds to act after you, there could be as many as six or seven players in on the hand if you stay.

A hand of 6-3 suited gives you a shot at a flush and a straight. Since a kill pot is expensive, most $3-$6 players won't stay in for double betting levels unless they have a good hand, which usually means big cards. With a raise, two callers, and a reraise in front of me (I was in Seat 1), I felt these four players all had some sort of big cards in their pockets. Further, since the pot was undoubtedly going to get much, much larger, I felt the pot odds were sufficient for me to at least call the bet and hope for a great flop. Since I decided that it was worth it to stay in, I decided to go ahead and reraise, capping the betting at $24, resolving to fold the hand if I didn't catch a strong flop.

I did this for several reasons. First, I felt another player was going to cap it anyway and I'd be staying in, so by capping the betting I was trying to mislead my opponents into thinking that I had big cards as well. Second, I was on the button and would have the advantage of being last to act on the last three betting rounds of the hand. Third, by capping the betting I felt sure that everyone else with any kind of a hand at all would call the bet simply because the pot was so huge. I was right, as the big blind called as well for a total of six players, with a pot of $146 *before the flop!*

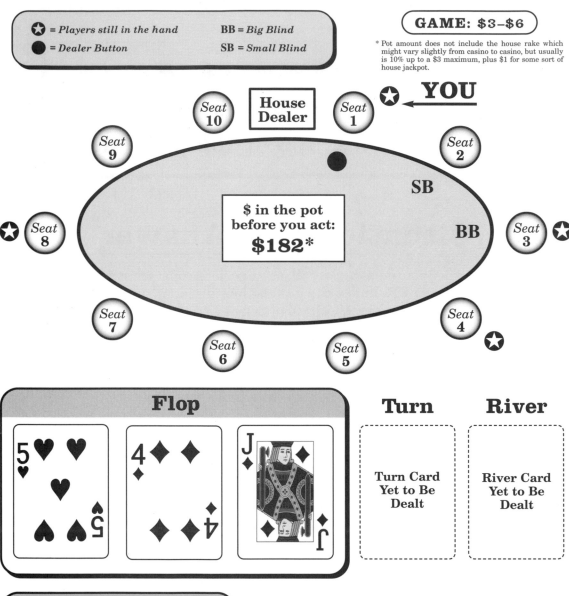

= Players still in the hand   BB = *Big Blind*

= Dealer Button   SB = *Small Blind*

GAME: $3–$6

Seat 10

House Dealer

Seat 1

← **YOU**

Seat 9

Seat 2

SB

$ in the pot before you act:

$182*

BB

Seat 8

Seat 3

Seat 7

Seat 4

Seat 6

Seat 5

Flop

5♥ ♥ ♥ ♥ ♠ ♠ ♠ 5

4♦ ♦ ♦ ♦ ♦ ♦ 4

J♦ ♦ ♦ J

Turn

Turn Card Yet to Be Dealt

River

River Card Yet to Be Dealt

Pocket

6♣ ♣ ♣ ♣ ♣ ♣ ♣ 9

3 ♣ ♣ ♣ ♣ 3

Situation #47

Situations 46–49 all deal with the same hand at the four betting stages of a hand the author was actually involved in.

After the flop, Seat 3 bet $6 and Seat 4 raised to $12. Seat 5 folded. Seat 8 raised to $18. Seat 10 folded. Do you fold, call the $18, or cap the betting at $24, and why?

Starting Hand (Pocket): **6♣ 3♣**

This Pocket's Win Rate: **2.4%**

Win Rate Rank: **106 of 169 possible**

Situation #47: Answer

As the old saying goes, in for a penny, in for a pound. After flopping an open-ended straight draw, there was no way I was going to drop out of this monster pot until I ran out of cards. I again capped the betting at $24 with the dual reasons of misleading my opponents as to my hand and figuring that the way the three other remaining players had bet after the flop they weren't going to fold now. I was right, and all three called the bet. There was now a whopping $242 in the pot before the turn card was dealt.

Because of the strong flop, I also now had correct pot odds to make the call or raise. Before my raise I was being asked to make an $18 bet for a chance to win a $182 pot, or about 10-to-1 odds for a bet that was less than 3-to-1 actual odds. By raising to $24 with the expectation that the other players would all call, I was still getting 10-to-1 pot odds ($242 pot for $24 bet).

I also figured that once the turn card came it would tell the story, at least for a couple of us, and that there was a chance the betting would slow down. If the turn card didn't help any of my opponents or me, they might all check to me because of my cap betting in the earlier two rounds rather than bet $12 and risk a raise to $24 or more. I figured my strong betting in last position (*which is one of the reasons that position is important*) in the first two rounds might get me a free river card if the turn card came a blank for everyone.

As an interesting aside, I suddenly found religion, silently telling the great poker god in the sky that if ever he (or she) felt like repaying me for some unspecified good deeds in my past, that all accounts could be settled right now with just one little ol' black 2 or 7.

★ = *Players still in the hand* BB = *Big Blind*

● = *Dealer Button* SB = *Small Blind*

GAME: $3–$6

* Pot amount does not include the house rake which might vary slightly from casino to casino, but usually is 10% up to a $3 maximum, plus $1 for some sort of house jackpot.

★ **YOU** ←

Seat 10

House Dealer

Seat 1

Seat 9

Seat 2

SB

$ in the pot before you act:

$278*

BB

Seat 3 ★

★ Seat 8

Seat 7

Seat 4 ★

Seat 6

Seat 5

Flop

5♥ 4♦ J♦

Turn

7♠

River

River Card Yet to Be Dealt

Pocket

6♣ 3♣

Situation #48

Situations 46–49 all deal with the same hand at the four betting stages of a hand the author was actually involved in.

After the turn card was dealt, Seat 3 bet $12. Seats 4 and 8 called the bet. Do you fold, call the $12 bet, or raise to $24, and why?

Starting Hand (Pocket): **6♣ 3♣**

This Pocket's Win Rate: **2.4%**

Win Rate Rank: **106 of 169 possible**

Situation #48: Answer

Don't you just love Texas Hold'em? Ask for a black 7 and get a black 7! Euphoria! The great poker god in the sky came through for me.

Now that I had a straight (although not the nut straight), I felt relatively sure that I had the best hand. The only hand that could be better than mine was an 8-high straight, and I couldn't imagine that any of the other three players still in the hand had bet and raised like they did early in the hand on an 8-6 pocket. I figured that the likely best hand against me was three Jacks. If it was, I knew that whoever held that hand wasn't going to fold it, so I just had to hope that statistics and odds (and Lady Luck!) stayed on my side for one more card and that the board didn't pair.

So my mission now was to make the other three players still in the hand pay as much as possible. Figuratively, now was the time to reach down their throats and tear their lungs out. It didn't matter to me now what any other player did because I was going to raise any bet I could.

I appreciated Seat 3's $12 bet because he was building *my* pot for me, I told myself. On the one hand, I was a bit disappointed that Seats 4 and 8 only called, but, on the other hand, at least a sense of weakness had now shown up at the table. I raised the bet to $24 and the other three players all called. The pot was just too big for any of them to drop out.

Now it was all coming down to the river. I said another silent prayer to the great poker god in the sky: "Don't pair the board, don't bring a Diamond, and don't bring a 6. That's all I ask."

⭐ = *Players still in the hand*   **BB** = *Big Blind*

⬤ = *Dealer Button*   **SB** = *Small Blind*

GAME: $3–$6

* Pot amount does not include the house rake which might vary slightly from casino to casino, but usually is 10% up to a $3 maximum, plus $1 for some sort of house jackpot.

⭐ **YOU**

Seat 10

House Dealer

Seat 1

Seat 9

Seat 2

SB

Seat 8 ⭐

$ in the pot before you act:

$338*

BB

Seat 3 ⭐

Seat 7

Seat 4 ⭐

Seat 6

Seat 5

Flop

5♥ 4♦ J♦

Turn

7♠

River

6♦

Pocket

6♣ 3♣

Situation #49

Situations 46–49 all deal with the same hand at the four betting stages of a hand the author was actually involved in.

After the river card was dealt, Seats 3, 4, and 8 all checked. Do you check as well, or do you bet $12, and why?

> Starting Hand (Pocket): **6♣ 3♣**
> This Pocket's Win Rate: **2.4%**
> Win Rate Rank: **106 of 169 possible**

Situation #49: Answer

Don't you just hate Texas Hold'em? One card earlier I felt like I was tearing out my opponents' lungs. Now I felt like the great poker god in the sky had just cut my head off and handed it to me.

The only hands I knew I was vulnerable to were a higher straight and a Diamond flush. Now both seemed like very real possibilities. Not only did I get a Diamond on the river, I got the 6 of Diamonds!

Suddenly every nightmarish scenario began to run through my mind. Did one of my opponents hold A♦ K/Q♦ and hit his flush draw? Could someone have actually stayed in on A♦ 8♦ and played for the flush/straight draw? Did someone hold A-3 for the low end of the straight, and with it half the pot? Was this $3-$6 game so loose that someone played the whole way with pocket 8s? Worse still, did someone actually play one of those hands, hit it, and then check when they caught their river card, hoping to check-raise a river bet?

I was now becoming physically ill at the thought of betting this hand. Somehow—I just didn't know how—I knew I was going to lose this hand, so I checked as well.

At the showdown, Seat 3 turned over pocket Aces, Seat 4 turned over pocket Kings, and Seat 8 turned over pocket Jacks (for three Jacks). After raking in the $338 pot, I tossed the dealer a $25 tip and decided that there really is no such thing as a great poker god in the sky. Is there?

★ = *Players still in the hand*   BB = *Big Blind*

● = *Dealer Button*   SB = *Small Blind*

GAME: $4–$8

* Pot amount does not include the house rake which might vary slightly from casino to casino, but usually is 10% up to a $3 maximum, plus $1 for some sort of house jackpot.

House Dealer

Seat 10

Seat 1

Seat 9

Seat 2

SB   BB

$ in the pot before you act:
$14*

Seat 8

Seat 3

YOU →

Seat 7

Seat 4

Seat 6

Seat 5

Flop

| Flop Cards Yet to Be Dealt | Flop Cards Yet to Be Dealt | Flop Cards Yet to Be Dealt |

Turn

Turn Card Yet to Be Dealt

River

River Card Yet to Be Dealt

Pocket

3♥   2♥

Situation #50

You have been dealt the suited connectors 3♥ 2♥ in your pocket. Seats 2 and 4 both called the $4 big blind bet. It is now your turn to act. With two callers already in the hand and four players to act after you, do you fold, call the $4, or raise to $8, and why?

Starting Hand (Pocket): **3♥ 2♥**

This Pocket's Win Rate: **0.7%**

Win Rate Rank: **120 of 169 possible**

Situation #50: Answer

Sometimes suited connectors such as this can be a bit enticing. It's easy to envision straights and flushes coming as often as not. Unfortunately, as shown by the above win rate of just 0.7 percent, those straights and flushes do not come very often.

Another aspect to consider when playing this hand is the pot odds. With only two players in the pot ahead of you and no assurances of how many others will jump in after you, you can't be certain that the pot odds will be enough to make calling this hand a correct move. Someone might even raise it, driving out potential callers, thereby lessening the pot and, by extension, the pot odds for you.

Again, this sort of pocket hand can be enticing. One time I had occasion to spend about four hours playing Hold'em in the San Francisco area. During that four-hour period, I received a 3-2 pocket (sometimes suited, sometimes not) six times and folded every time. Four times I would have made full houses, once I'd have made a set, and once I'd have made two pair. I would have won all six hands! Okay, I figured, maybe all those poker books I'd read were wrong somehow. Since I occasionally chart the progress of the poker hands I play, I decided to give 3-2 a try and chart my progress. Over the course of the next few weeks, I played 3-2 pockets twenty-four times...and *lost* all twenty-four times!

So what happened to the San Francisco experience? It helped to reinforce the principle that in gambling, anything can happen in the short run. Play the percentages you know are right. Fold this hand.

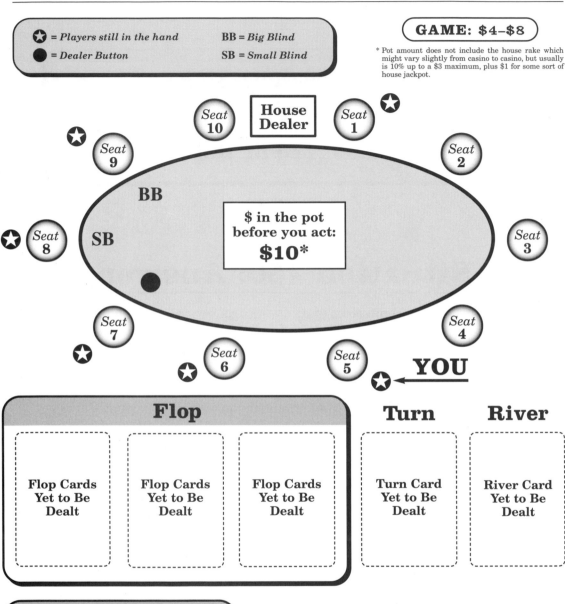

GAME: $4–$8

Seat 10   **House Dealer**   Seat 1

Seat 9

Seat 2

BB

$ in the pot before you act:
$10*

SB

Seat 8

Seat 3

Seat 7

Seat 4

Seat 6   Seat 5   **YOU**

Flop

| Flop Cards Yet to Be Dealt | Flop Cards Yet to Be Dealt | Flop Cards Yet to Be Dealt |

Turn

Turn Card Yet to Be Dealt

River

River Card Yet to Be Dealt

Pocket

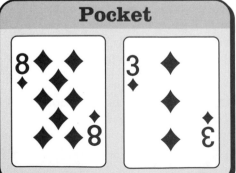

Situation #51

You have been dealt the 8 and 3 of Diamonds in your pocket. Seat 1 is the only caller in front of you with four players folding. With four players to act after you, including the blinds, do you fold, call the $4, or raise to $8, and why?

Starting Hand (Pocket): **8♦ 3♦**

This Pocket's Win Rate: **0.4%**

Win Rate Rank: **146 of 169 possible**

Situation #51: Answer

This situation is similar to the previous one in that your pocket contains two suited cards, but this time they're not connected, which actually makes this a worse hand than the 3-2 suited pocket. Again, suited pocket cards are tempting to play and many, many beginning and/or poor players will play almost any two suited pocket cards in any situation. You shouldn't be one of them. You have to pick your spots for playing a hand like this (which should be rare, such as the scenario I discussed in Situations 46–49).

With only one player in the pot ahead of you and no certainty of what is going to occur behind you because of your poor position (i.e., not many callers or a raise which will drive out the callers you need to make this hand playable), you should fold this hand.

About a year into my poker playing career, I learned a valuable principle about Texas Hold'em that I still use today to help me determine whether or not a hand is worth playing. I ask, "Would I be happy playing this pocket hand one thousand times in a row?" If I can't answer, "Yes," to that question, then I have my answer as to whether or not I should play it even one time.

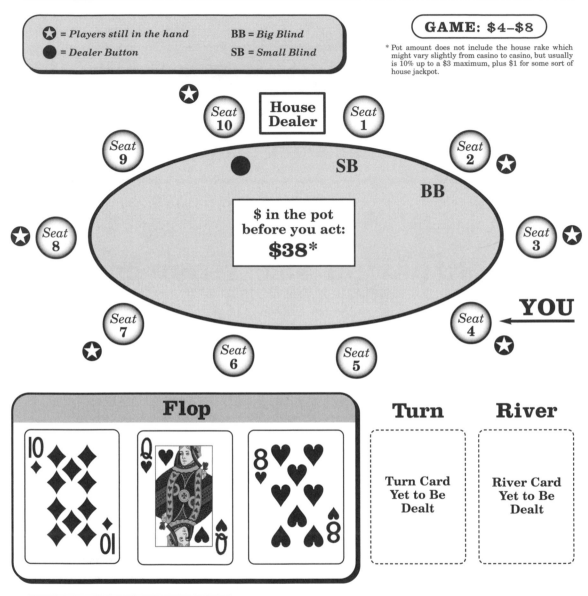

GAME: $4–$8

★ = *Players still in the hand*   BB = *Big Blind*

● = *Dealer Button*   SB = *Small Blind*

* Pot amount does not include the house rake which might vary slightly from casino to casino, but usually is 10% up to a $3 maximum, plus $1 for some sort of house jackpot.

House Dealer

Seat 10

Seat 1

Seat 9

Seat 2

SB

BB

$ in the pot before you act: **$38***

Seat 8

Seat 3

Seat 7

YOU

Seat 4

Seat 6

Seat 5

Flop

Turn

Turn Card Yet to Be Dealt

River

River Card Yet to Be Dealt

Pocket

Situation #52

Situations 52–54 all deal with the same hand at the last three betting stages.

You were dealt the Jack and 9 of Spades in your pocket. There were six callers in the pot for one bet before the flop. After the flop, Seat 2 (the first to act) bet $4. Seat 3 raised to $8. Do you fold, call the $8, or raise to $12, and why?

Starting Hand (Pocket): **J♠ 9♠**

This Pocket's Win Rate: **27.9%**

Win Rate Rank: **31 of 169 possible**

Situation #52: Answer

This is the kind of situation you like to be in. There are six callers in the pot, you flopped the absolute nuts, and there is a bet and a raise in front of you. There is no possible hand that any other player could presently hold that will beat you. The worst that could happen at this point is for another player to hold a Jack-9 just like you for a split pot.

This situation after the flop is not without its dangers, but right now you positively have the best hand. There are two schools of thought as to whether you should just call or raise at this point. To a certain degree, you will have to assess the players and the game you're in to know which is right for you on this particular hand.

You could call, hoping to keep as many players in the hand as possible since you already have the nuts, thereby creating a bigger pot. A raise might scare out some potential callers and their money, which is decidedly headed in your direction at the moment.

A raise, on the other hand, might just drive someone out of the hand who is sitting on three of a kind, two pair, a Heart flush draw, or a higher straight draw.

As for me, because there are so many possible ways for me to still lose this hand, and because of the two Hearts on the board, I'm going to raise it to $12 and hope it drives someone with a weak calling hand out of the pot.

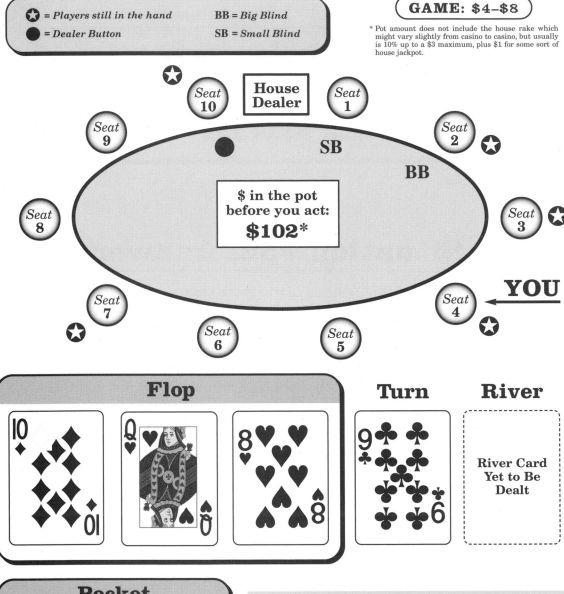

GAME: $4–$8

* Pot amount does not include the house rake which might vary slightly from casino to casino, but usually is 10% up to a $3 maximum, plus $1 for some sort of house jackpot.

Seat 10
House Dealer
Seat 1
Seat 9
Seat 2
SB
BB
$ in the pot before you act: **$102***
Seat 8
Seat 3
YOU
Seat 4
Seat 7
Seat 6
Seat 5

Flop

Turn   **River**

River Card Yet to Be Dealt

Pocket

Situation #53

Situations 52–54 all deal with the same hand at the last three betting stages.

After the 9♣ came on the turn, Seat 2 bet $8 and Seat 3 called. With two players still to act after you, do you fold, call the $8, or raise to $16, and why?

Starting Hand (Pocket): **J♠ 9♠**

This Pocket's Win Rate: **27.9%**

Win Rate Rank: **31 of 169 possible**

Situation #53: Answer

You received a chink in your armor when the 9 came on the turn. Now anyone holding King-Jack has you beat. The good news is that your raise after the flop drove out one player, and at least the turn card wasn't a Heart and the board didn't pair, so those on Heart draws and those hoping to catch a full house will have to wait (and pay) for the river card.

If you just call this hand (in effect deferring to the King-Jack possibility), you will not only project weakness but you might allow those on Heart draws and those hoping for a full house who are getting queasy stomachs about now to limp in for one bet.

If you raise the bet to $16 (which I would do), you will continue to project strength. You might also drive out the queasiest of the queasy bunch. If you get reraised, don't panic. It doesn't necessarily mean your opponent has the King-Jack pocket you dread. He could just have a Jack like you for the same straight and be trying to drive out the queasy people too. If you do happen to get reraised, play it safe and just call, don't cap the betting. The pot is already huge for a $4-$8 game. Besides, you still have to worry about players drawing out a flush or full house on the river.

Seat 10 | House Dealer | Seat 1

Seat 9

SB

Seat 2 ★

BB

$ in the pot before you act: **$190***

Seat 8

Seat 3

Seat 7

YOU

Seat 4

Seat 6 | Seat 5

★

Flop

Turn   River

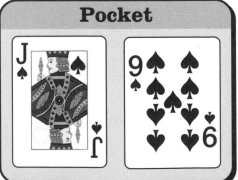

Pocket

Situation #54

Situations 52–54 all deal with the same hand at the last three betting stages.

After the 2♥ came on the river, Seats 2 and 3 checked, you bet $8, and Seat 10 then raised to $16. With reluctant body language, Seat 2 calls, making the comment, "The pot's too big to get out now." Seat 3 folds. Do you fold, call the additional $8, or raise to $24, and why?

Starting Hand (Pocket): **J♠ 9♠**

This Pocket's Win Rate: **27.9%**

Win Rate Rank: **31 of 169 possible**

Situation #54: Answer

Your raise after the turn drove out another opponent, leaving the hand with four players before the river. With the pot already so large and no more cards to come, now is not the time to get cutesy. If you've got it, bet it. When Seats 2 and 3 didn't bet it, that meant they didn't have enough to beat the flush possibility that came on the river.

When you bet after Seats 2 and 3 checked, you were taking the calculated gamble that no one was on a flush draw. When Seat 10 raised you, that calculation got shot down in flames. Unless, of course, he just had a straight, same as you, and was trying to project that he had a flush, hoping to get one or more players to fold and thereby decreasing the number of players in a split pot.

In any event, Seat 2 was correct when he said the pot was too big to get out now. Even though Seat 10's action leads you to believe he hit his flush draw, you have to call this bet. Another cardinal rule of Hold'em poker is that it's better to make a handful of $8 mistakes (calling when you have reason to believe you're already beaten) than to make one $190 mistake (folding a hand that would have won because the raiser was bluffing).

Expect the worst, hope for the best, and call the bet.

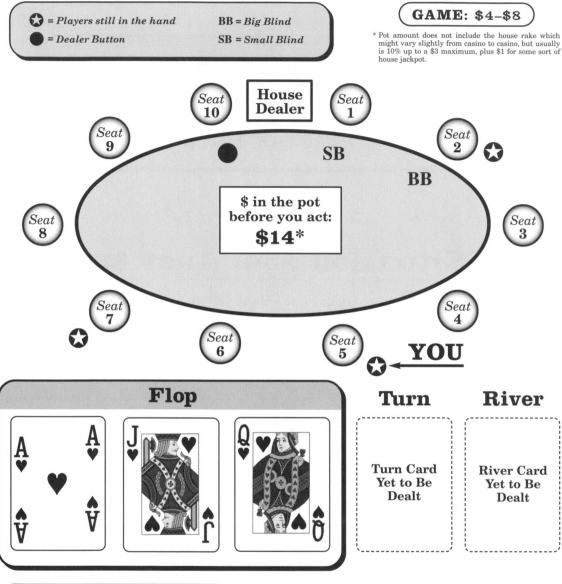

GAME: $4–$8

* Pot amount does not include the house rake which might vary slightly from casino to casino, but usually is 10% up to a $3 maximum, plus $1 for some sort of house jackpot.

$ in the pot before you act:

$14*

Flop

Turn

Turn Card Yet to Be Dealt

River

River Card Yet to Be Dealt

Pocket

Situation #55

You were dealt the King and 10 of Hearts in your pocket. Three players, including you, called one bet to see the flop. After the flop, Seat 2 checks. It is now your turn to act. Do you check or bet $4, and why?

Starting Hand (Pocket): **K♥ 10♥**

This Pocket's Win Rate: **40.9%**

Win Rate Rank: **19 of 169 possible**

Situation #55: Answer

To say that you've flopped the nuts is an understatement. You've flopped a royal flush and there is no possibility that either of the other two players can beat you or somehow tie you for a split pot scenario, no matter what cards they hold or what cards may come on the turn and river. The problem for you on this hand is making the most money you possibly can, and there is more to consider here than just the pot, but I'll get to that in a moment.

No one raised before the flop, so, in effect, no one projected any power. Then the flop came up ALL power. Seat 2 has already checked, so either that means he doesn't like the flop or he has a good hand and he doesn't want to scare anyone out of the pot until it grows. Which is how YOU should be looking at this hand right now. If you bet now, with the board being what it is, you're likely to scare out both opponents.

What you should do is check and hope that one or both players catch something on the turn and/or river that gives them cause to bet their hands so you can at least call and drag things out a bit longer and win a larger pot. Another reason to check at this point is that some establishments award jackpots for certain hands, including royal flushes, but they also usually require that the pots be of a certain amount, such as $20 or $30. If you bet now and scare out the other two players, you won't have enough in the pot to claim the jackpot. (You'll also take yourself out of a bad beat jackpot possibility. What if you're opponent holds A-K and two more Aces come on the turn and river?) If possible, wait until you reach at least that minimum pot requirement before you do any betting or raising. Check the bet, cross your fingers, and hope someone else bets first so you can call and build the pot to where you need it to be.

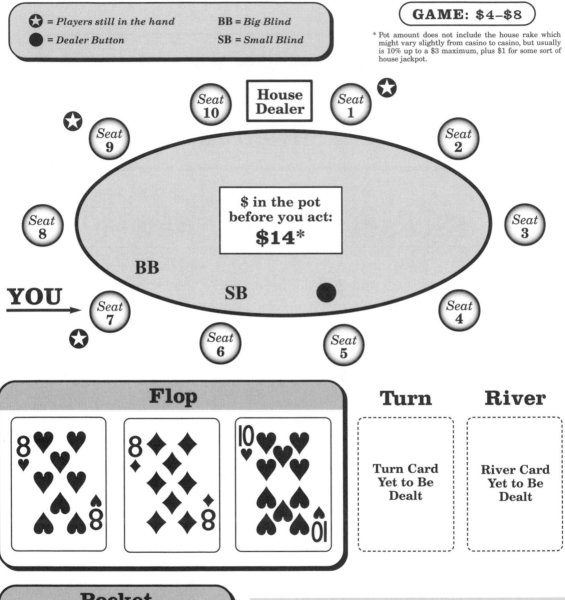

GAME: $4–$8

Players still in the hand = ⭐

Dealer Button = ⚫

BB = *Big Blind*

SB = *Small Blind*

* Pot amount does not include the house rake which might vary slightly from casino to casino, but usually is 10% up to a $3 maximum, plus $1 for some sort of house jackpot.

$ in the pot before you act: **$14***

Seat 10 · House Dealer · Seat 1 · Seat 2 · Seat 3 · Seat 4 · Seat 5 · Seat 6 · Seat 7 · Seat 8 · Seat 9

BB · SB · YOU →

Flop

Turn

Turn Card Yet to Be Dealt

River

River Card Yet to Be Dealt

Pocket

Situation #56

You were dealt pocket Kings in the big blind. Seats 9 and 1 called your big blind bet and everyone else folded. You checked instead of raising before the flop. After the flop, you are the first to act. Do you check or bet $4, and why?

Starting Hand (Pocket): **K♣ K♦**

This Pocket's Win Rate: **74.6%**

Win Rate Rank: **2 of 169 possible**

Situation #56: Answer

You should bet. While you do have a good hand, it is still vulnerable. It is also second best if someone holds an 8. There are two reasons why you should bet out of the gate in this situation.

First, by betting now you are gaining information. If you get reraised back, then it might be an indication your opponent is holding either an 8 or a 10. If your opponent(s) just call, then it might be a good indication that they don't have an 8 or a 10, or, if they do have a 10, they might have a weak kicker to go with it, such as a 10-5 suited hand.

Second, by betting now, if your opponents do not hold an 8 or 10 (or even an Ace-Something), they might be likely to fold to your bet, which keeps them from drawing out on you and making you do things like gnashing your teeth, tearing your hair out, and cussing Texas Hold'em.

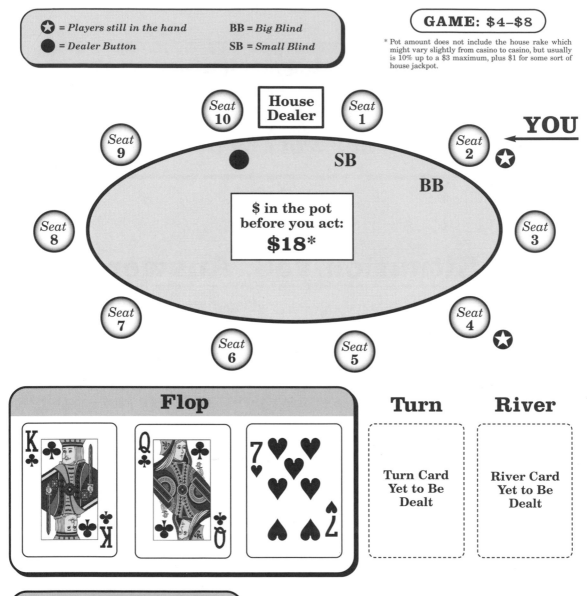

⭐ = *Players still in the hand*   BB = *Big Blind*

⬤ = *Dealer Button*   SB = *Small Blind*

GAME: $4–$8

* Pot amount does not include the house rake which might vary slightly from casino to casino, but usually is 10% up to a $3 maximum, plus $1 for some sort of house jackpot.

Seat 10   **House Dealer**   Seat 1

Seat 9

YOU

Seat 2 ⭐

SB

BB

Seat 8

$ in the pot before you act:
$18*

Seat 3

Seat 7

Seat 4 ⭐

Seat 6   Seat 5

Flop

K♣ Q♣ 7♥

Turn

Turn Card Yet to Be Dealt

River

River Card Yet to Be Dealt

Pocket

A♣ 9♣

Situation #57

You were dealt the Ace and 9 of Clubs in your pocket while in the big blind position. Seat 4 raised before the flop and everyone folded except you, and you called the raise. After the flop, you are the first to act. Do you check or bet $4, and why?

Starting Hand (Pocket): **A♣ 9♣**

This Pocket's Win Rate: **40.5%**

Win Rate Rank: **20 of 169 possible**

Situation #57: Answer

You've flopped four cards to a nut flush, but you're in a heads up situation. This means you'll only be getting even money on any action that takes place from here on out. The odds of you hitting your flush by the river are about one in three (35 percent). So, strictly speaking, getting a 1-to-1 return on your bets for a statistical probability that is 2-to-1 against you is a bad proposition.

However, you don't necessarily need to hit your flush to win the hand. The first thing you need to do is gain some information about what your opponent thinks of his hand. By betting first, you will give him pause to consider what you possibly hold in your hand. If he folds, you win. If he calls your bet, it would likely be an indication that the King, Queen, or some combination thereof makes him nervous.

If he raises you, then you have to reassess the situation. What kind of a player is he? Is he wild and loose, or tight? Once you take everything into consideration, you can decide whether or not to fold, call his raise, or reraise him, although the latter would not be advised since you don't even have a pair at this point.

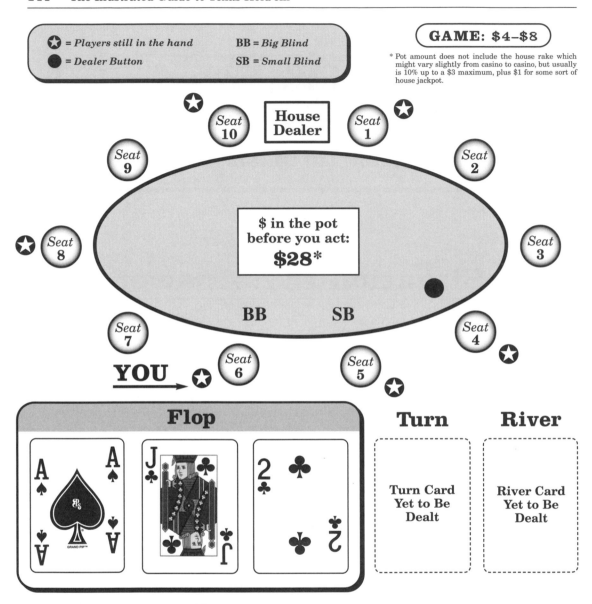

GAME: $4–$8

* Pot amount does not include the house rake which might vary slightly from casino to casino, but usually is 10% up to a $3 maximum, plus $1 for some sort of house jackpot.

$ in the pot before you act: **$28***

Situation #58

You were dealt a pair of 2s in your pocket while in the big blind position. Since none of the other five players still in the hand raised before it got back to you, you called, announcing, "Big enough." After the flop, Seat 5 bet $4. It is now your turn to act. With four players still to act after you, should you fold, call the $4, or raise to $8, and why?

Starting Hand (Pocket): **2♦ 2♥**

This Pocket's Win Rate: **4.0%**

Win Rate Rank: **72 of 169 possible**

Situation #58: Answer

The only two pocket hands that can beat you right now are a pair of Aces and a pair of Jacks, so you likely have the high hand at this point since no one raised before the flop.

However, since 2s are the lowest rank of all, and because many players in low limit Hold'em typically play Ace-Anything (which means you've got to assume that there's at least one Ace, maybe two, out there in someone's hand), you need to drive your opponents out of this hand if possible. Consequently, you should raise the bet to $8. A wise poker axiom says that you should never slow play the bottom set, or any set for that matter, against a flush or straight draw.

Now some things to beware of. Since Seat 5 bet when he was first to act after the flop, I'd assume that he's holding one of the Aces. Hopefully he's not holding Ace-Jack, because if another Ace or Jack comes on the turn or river, it will give him a higher full house than it will give you.

Also, anyone holding a pocket pair of any rank could still catch a third card of the same rank on the turn or river, and if an Ace or Jack comes as well, you're again beaten by a higher full house. That's the problem with 2s; there are so few outs that make them ultimately winnable.

So after you raise, pay particularly close attention to what everyone does. This is not a hand on which you can let your guard down.

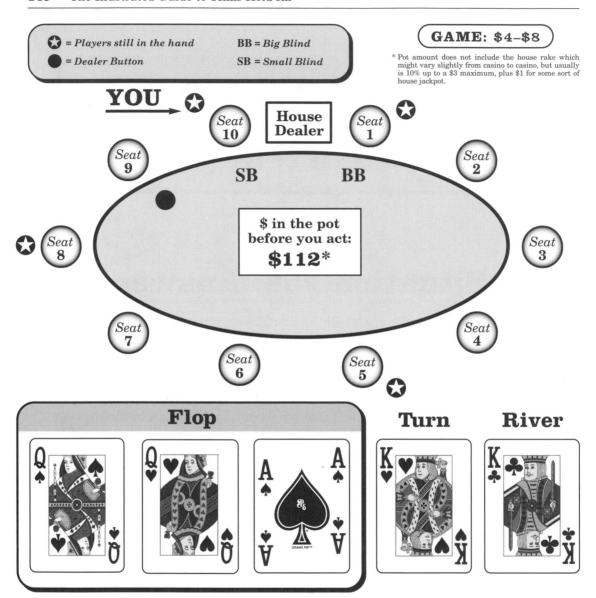

★ = *Players still in the hand*   BB = *Big Blind*

● = *Dealer Button*   SB = *Small Blind*

GAME: $4–$8

* Pot amount does not include the house rake which might vary slightly from casino to casino, but usually is 10% up to a $3 maximum, plus $1 for some sort of house jackpot.

YOU ★

Seat 10

House Dealer

Seat 1 ★

Seat 9

Seat 2

SB   **BB**

★ Seat 8

$ in the pot before you act: $112*

Seat 3

Seat 7

Seat 4

Seat 6

Seat 5

★

Flop

Q♠ Q♥ A♠

Turn

K♥

River

K♣

Pocket

A♦ 3♦

Situation #59

The same four players still in the hand at the end have been the only players in the hand from the beginning. No one raised before the flop. After the flop, you were first to act, and, seeking information, bet $4. The others all called. After the turn, you bet $8 and the others all called again. After the river you bet $8. Seat 1 raised to $16, Seat 5 reraised to $24, and Seat 8 folded. Do you fold, call the $24, or cap it at $32, and why?

Starting Hand (Pocket): **A♦ 3♦**

This Pocket's Win Rate: **21.3%**

Win Rate Rank: **33 of 169 possible**

Situation #59: Answer

This hand proceeded in a classic, orderly fashion. You had an okay hand to begin with, especially considering you were in the small blind and it only cost you $2 to play. Before the flop, an Ace-3 suited gave you a shot at a straight, a flush, and even a straight flush, so it was worth playing at the time.

After two Queens came on the flop, it was time to start getting nervous, but since you were the first to act, you could use your position to gain information. When you bet and the others only called, and didn't raise, that told you that probably no one was holding a Queen.

When the King came on the turn and you bet first, continuing to seek information, your opponents all called, and again no one raised. It should have been obvious by now that your three opponents were afraid of the Ace, which likely meant that none of them held one in their hand and that the worst you were facing was a pocket pair of some rank lower than Queens, a King-Something, or a Spade and/or Heart flush draw.

But when the river revealed a second King on the board and you not only got raised, but reraised, it should have become obvious that two players were likely holding Kings in their hands, giving them full houses on the river. Furthermore, when the King came on the river, you should have just checked instead of betting. In the face of likely full houses, you could have saved $8. Since it's highly unlikely that two players would be bluffing after the river, it's time to fold this hand as you are almost certainly beaten.

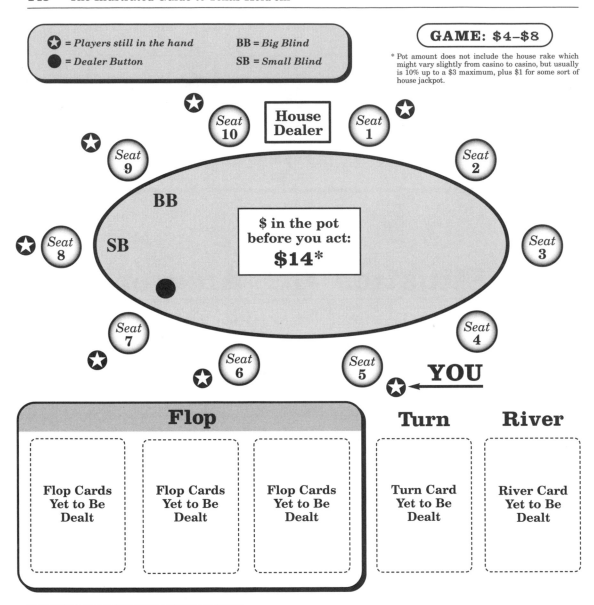

GAME: $4–$8

* Pot amount does not include the house rake which might vary slightly from casino to casino, but usually is 10% up to a $3 maximum, plus $1 for some sort of house jackpot.

★ = *Players still in the hand*   BB = *Big Blind*

● = *Dealer Button*   SB = *Small Blind*

$ in the pot before you act:
$14*

Flop

| Flop Cards Yet to Be Dealt | Flop Cards Yet to Be Dealt | Flop Cards Yet to Be Dealt |

Turn

Turn Card Yet to Be Dealt

River

River Card Yet to Be Dealt

Pocket

Situation #60

You have been dealt the 9 and 7 of Spades in your pocket. Seats 10 and 1, the first two players to act, bet and call, respectively. Seats 2, 3, and 4 all fold. It is now your turn to act. With four players yet to act after you, do you fold, call the $4 bet, or raise to $8, and why?

Starting Hand (Pocket): **9♠ 7♠**

This Pocket's Win Rate: **5.8%**

Win Rate Rank: **65 of 169 possible**

Situation #60: Answer

A hand of 9-7 suited can look attractive at first glance. You have a chance to make a flush or a straight (or both!), so oftentimes this hand gets played by many low limit Hold'em players. If you'll look at the chart above, you can see that 9-7 suited wins only 5.8 percent of the time.

While 9-7 suited can certainly be played in some situations, like in the blinds, or even late position with a lot of callers and no raisers in front of you, this isn't one of them. With two early position bettors you've been given the information that they are projecting power, which 9-7 suited is not.

You also don't know how the other four players behind you are going to act. What if they all fold? Then you're left in the hand against two players with strong hands. What if there's a raise and a reraise? Then it's going to cost you at least three bets, and maybe four, to play a hand that is mediocre at best.

A 9-7 suited hand is like the sirens of ancient mythology, who sang their hypnotic songs to the wayfaring sailors, causing them to wreck their ships upon the rocks.

Fold this hand in this position before you, too, sail onto the rocks of Texas Hold'em.

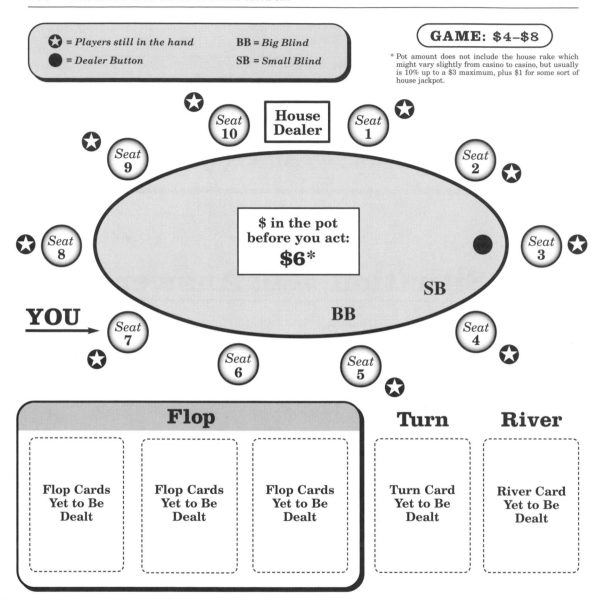

* Pot amount does not include the house rake which might vary slightly from casino to casino, but usually is 10% up to a $3 maximum, plus $1 for some sort of house jackpot.

GAME: $4–$8

⭐ = *Players still in the hand*   BB = *Big Blind*

⚫ = *Dealer Button*   SB = *Small Blind*

House Dealer

$ in the pot before you act: **$6***

YOU →

Seat 10, Seat 1, Seat 9, Seat 2, Seat 8, Seat 3, Seat 7, Seat 4, Seat 6, Seat 5

SB   BB

Flop

Flop Cards Yet to Be Dealt	Flop Cards Yet to Be Dealt	Flop Cards Yet to Be Dealt

Turn

Turn Card Yet to Be Dealt

River

River Card Yet to Be Dealt

Pocket

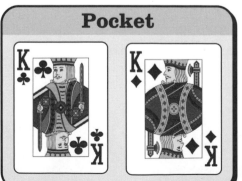

Situation #61

Situations 61–64 all deal with the same hand at the four betting stages of a hand the author was actually involved in.

You have been dealt pocket Kings. Seat 6, the first to act, folds. It is now your turn to act. Do you fold, call the $4 big blind bet, or raise to $8, and why?

Starting Hand (Pocket): **K♣ K♦**

This Pocket's Win Rate: **74.6%**

Win Rate Rank: **2 of 169 possible**

Situation #61: Answer

You should raise the bet to $8 in an effort to drive out anyone holding an Ace with a poor kicker, anyone holding a small pair, and anyone holding medium suited connectors, such as 10-9s, for example, who might decide to take a shot at the hand if it's only one bet. The last thing you want to see happen to you with a powerful starting hand like this is someone drawing out on you.

★ = *Players still in the hand*   BB = *Big Blind*

● = *Dealer Button*   SB = *Small Blind*

GAME: $4–$8

* Pot amount does not include the house rake which might vary slightly from casino to casino, but usually is 10% up to a $3 maximum, plus $1 for some sort of house jackpot.

Seat 10

House Dealer

Seat 1

Seat 9

Seat 2

$ in the pot before you act:
$62*

Seat 8

Seat 3

SB

YOU →

Seat 7 ★

BB

Seat 4

Seat 6

Seat 5 ★

Flop

6♥ K♥ 2♥

Turn

Turn Card Yet to Be Dealt

River

River Card Yet to Be Dealt

Pocket

K♣ K♦

Situation #62

Situations 61–64 all deal with the same hand at the four betting stages of a hand the author was actually involved in.

Your raise before the flop drove out five players. The other four players all called your raise. After the flop, Seat 5 bet $4, you raised to $8, Seats 10, 1, and 3 all folded, then Seat 5 reraised to $12. Do you fold, call the $12, or raise to $16, and why?

Starting Hand (Pocket): **K♣ K♦**

This Pocket's Win Rate: **74.6%**

Win Rate Rank: **2 of 169 possible**

Situation #62: Answer

Seat 5 was the first to act after the flop. When he bet first he was either projecting strength, betting for information, or maybe both. When you raised him back, you were not only seeking information as to whether the three Hearts really helped him or not, you were projecting strength as well. The other three players all understood what was going on here; there were two players who were going to go after each other and, since they didn't have hands that fit with the flop, they folded.

In what has now become a heads-up situation, Seat 5 reraised you. You should now seriously consider the possibility that he flopped a flush. He did, after all, come out of the gate betting after the three Hearts flopped and he raised your raise. He's either got the flush or he's on a nut flush draw, possibly with top pair as well (meaning he's holding the Ace of Hearts and the King of Spades).

Seat 5's reraise indicates it's time to exercise a bit of caution, so just call the $12 and see if you get some help on the turn in the way of a board pair which will give you a full house and you can blow his flush to kingdom come.

★ = *Players still in the hand*   BB = *Big Blind*

● = *Dealer Button*   SB = *Small Blind*

GAME: $4–$8

* Pot amount does not include the house rake which might vary slightly from casino to casino, but usually is 10% up to a $3 maximum, plus $1 for some sort of house jackpot.

Seat 10

House Dealer

Seat 1

Seat 9

Seat 2

$ in the pot before you act:

$106*

Seat 8

Seat 3

SB

YOU →

Seat 7

★

BB

Seat 4

Seat 6

Seat 5

★

Flop

6♥

K♥

2♥

Turn

K♠

River

River Card Yet to Be Dealt

Pocket

K♣   K♦

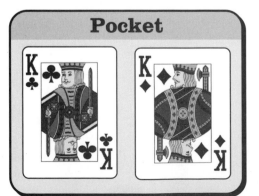

Situation #63

Situations 61–64 all deal with the same hand at the four betting stages of a hand the author was actually involved in.

After the turn, Seat 5 bet $8, you raised to $16, and he reraised to $24. Should you now fold, call the $24, or cap the betting at $32, and why?

> Starting Hand (Pocket): **K♣ K♦**
>
> This Pocket's Win Rate: **74.6%**
>
> Win Rate Rank: **2 of 169 possible**

Situation #63: Answer

By all means, cap the betting at $32 because you have the best hand. There are no two cards he can possibly hold that will beat you. Perhaps he doesn't believe the second King on the board gave you a full house (and it didn't, technically, since you hit four of a kind, or **quads**) or perhaps in his own exuberance of holding the nut flush he didn't notice the full house possibility.

In any event, at this point you have the best hand and he's not going to fold anyway, so make him pay another $8 for his own foolishness.

⭐ = *Players still in the hand*   BB = *Big Blind*

⬤ = *Dealer Button*   SB = *Small Blind*

GAME: $4–$8

* Pot amount does not include the house rake which might vary slightly from casino to casino, but usually is 10% up to a $3 maximum, plus $1 for some sort of house jackpot.

Seat 10   **House Dealer**   Seat 1

Seat 9   Seat 2

$ in the pot before you act:
$162*

Seat 8   ⬤   Seat 3

SB

YOU ➡   Seat 7   BB   Seat 4

⭐

Seat 6   Seat 5

⭐

Flop

6♥   K♥   2♥

Turn

K♠

River

4♥

Pocket

K♣   K♦

Situation #64

Situations 61–64 all deal with the same hand at the four betting stages of a hand the author was actually involved in.

After the river card was dealt, Seat 5 bet $8 and you raised to $16. With a slight smile, Seat 5, a known tight player, raises to $24 and comments, "Got a full house, huh?" Do you fold, call the $24, or cap the betting at $32, and why?

Starting Hand (Pocket): **K♣ K♦**

This Pocket's Win Rate: **74.6%**

Win Rate Rank: **2 of 169 possible**

Situation #64: Answer

When your opponent, a known tight player, made the comment, "Got a full house, huh?" *after he raised,* that should have sent up some red flags. Almost as many red flags as the 4♥ on the river. He obviously wasn't afraid of a full house, which meant he had at least four of a kind. But the only possible four of a kind hand was the Kings, which you hold. So what could he have that could beat four of a kind?

Ah, the straight flush. But would he have really called a raise before the flop with just a 3♥ 5♥ with only one other player in the hand? And would he really have played after the turn with two Kings on the board? I didn't think so, so I capped the betting at $32. When my opponent happily called my reraise and promptly turned over the 3♥ 5♥, he scooped in the $186 pot and I had my first truly **bad beat** story to tell.

The moral of this story is, *if you don't have the absolute nuts, you* don't *have the absolute nuts.*

= *Players still in the hand*   BB = *Big Blind*

= *Dealer Button*   SB = *Small Blind*

* Pot amount does not include the house rake which might vary slightly from casino to casino, but usually is 10% up to a $3 maximum, plus $1 for some sort of house jackpot.

Seat 10

House Dealer

Seat 1

Seat 9

Seat 2

YOU

Seat 8

$ in the pot before you act:
$30*

Seat 3

SB

BB

Seat 7

Seat 4

Seat 6

Seat 5

Flop

J♥   9♠   8♠

Turn

Turn Card Yet to Be Dealt

River

River Card Yet to Be Dealt

Pocket

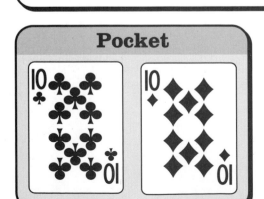

Situation #65

Situations 65–67 all deal with the same hand at the last three betting stages.

There were five players, including you, who stayed in for one bet before the flop. After the flop, Seat 5 bet $4 and Seat 7 called. It is now your turn to act with Seats 10 and 2 still to act after you. Do you fold, call the $4, or raise to $8, and why?

Starting Hand (Pocket): **10♣ 10♦**

This Pocket's Win Rate: **60.8%**

Win Rate Rank: **8 of 169 possible**

Situation #65: Answer

You should call the $4 bet. Right now you only have a pair of 10s, but you do have an open-ended straight draw with enough callers to make the pot odds for calling proper. (You have eight outs to make your straight, the four Queens and the four 7s, with two cards yet to come.) This translates into the mathematical equation:

$$(39 \div 8) \div 2 = 2.44\text{-to-}1$$

Put into percentages, this means you have a 31 percent chance of hitting this or any other open-ended straight draw with two cards to go.

With the amount of money already in the pot, and the prospect of several players remaining in the hand, you are getting better than pot odds to make this call. There is $30 already in the pot and the bet you're being asked to make is $4. Thus, $30 \div 4 = 7.5$-to-1.

There are several issues of concern, however, on this hand. Even if you do hit your straight, it doesn't mean it will be the highest straight. Someone could already be holding a Queen-10 and if a 7 comes up you will hold the idiot end of the straight. Also, someone might already hold King-Queen and if a 10 comes up on the turn or river they'll have a higher straight. Your only salvation then will be to have the board pair for a full house, which you're going to need anyway if someone hits their Spade draw, another point of concern.

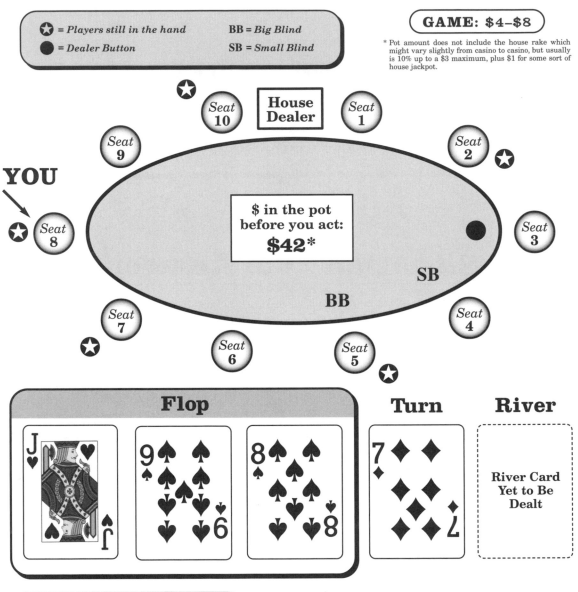

GAME: $4–$8

* Pot amount does not include the house rake which might vary slightly from casino to casino, but usually is 10% up to a $3 maximum, plus $1 for some sort of house jackpot.

⭐ = Players still in the hand   BB = Big Blind

⚫ = Dealer Button   SB = Small Blind

Seat 10
House Dealer
Seat 1
Seat 9
Seat 2
YOU
Seat 8

$ in the pot before you act:
$42*

Seat 3
SB
BB
Seat 7
Seat 4
Seat 6
Seat 5

Flop   **Turn**   **River**

J♥   9♠   8♠   7♦   River Card Yet to Be Dealt

Pocket

10♣   10♦

Situation #66

Situations 65–67 all deal with the same hand at the last three betting stages.

Seat 5's $4 bet after the flop was called by all four other players. After the turn card was revealed, Seats 5 and 7 both checked. Do you check as well or bet $8, and why?

Starting Hand (Pocket): **10♣ 10♦**

This Pocket's Win Rate: **60.8%**

Win Rate Rank: **8 of 169 possible**

Situation #66: Answer

You've hit your straight on the turn and Seats 5 and 7 both checked. This either means they're afraid of the potential straights, they missed their Spade draw, didn't improve their set, overpair, or two pair, or they've hit a straight and are contemplating a check-raise.

Despite all the possibilities (and eventual possibilities) out there, most of which are in your favor at this point, you should bet your hand, which is a made hand, and see what happens. This bet is both for value and for information. If an opponent had held a Queen-10 in his hand, he would have likely raised it after the flop in an effort to drive out those on flush draws.

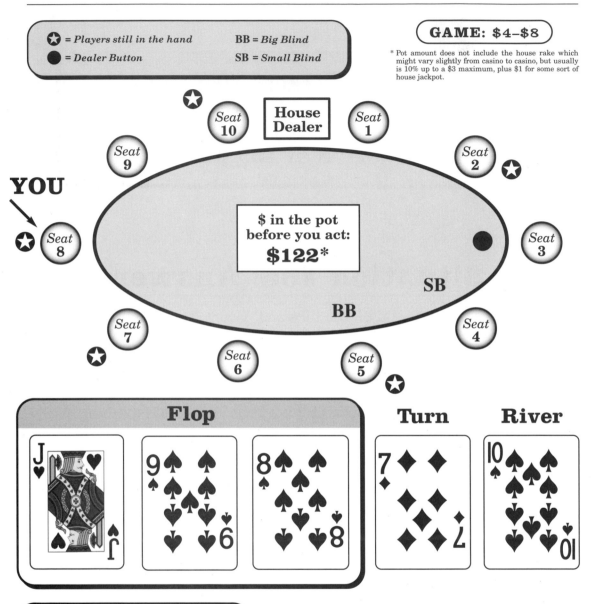

★ = *Players still in the hand*   BB = *Big Blind*

● = *Dealer Button*   SB = *Small Blind*

GAME: $4–$8

* Pot amount does not include the house rake which might vary slightly from casino to casino, but usually is 10% up to a $3 maximum, plus $1 for some sort of house jackpot.

House Dealer

Seat 10 Seat 1 Seat 9 Seat 2 Seat 8 **YOU** Seat 3 Seat 7 Seat 4 Seat 6 Seat 5

$ in the pot before you act: $122*

SB BB

Flop **Turn** **River**

Pocket

Situation #67

Situations 65–67 all deal with the same hand at the last three betting stages.

After the river card was dealt, Seats 5, 7, and you all checked. Seat 10 bet $8, Seats 2 and 5 called, and then Seat 7 (who checked earlier) raised to $16. Do you fold, call the $16, or raise to $24, and why?

Starting Hand (Pocket): **10♣ 10♦**

This Pocket's Win Rate: **60.8%**

Win Rate Rank: **8 of 169 possible**

Situation #67: Answer

What a disastrous card for you. Without knowing what the other players hold in their hands, if you could have picked one card *not* to come up, it would have been the 10 of Spades. Why? Because now anyone holding a Queen has a higher straight than you. And anyone holding two Spades now has a flush. This card literally opened the flood gates on you.

Seat 10 bet into the flush and Queen-high straight possibilities, so he probably has one or the other, both of which beat you. Seats 2 and 5 called, so they at the very least are willing to gamble on playing the board, which is as good as your hand now.

The real killer, however, is Seat 7 who check-raised. You've got to believe he has something good. It may not be the nuts, but it's almost certainly better than you.

The river card did you in on this hand. You should fold, even though the pot is quite large.

GAME: $4–$8

* Pot amount does not include the house rake which might vary slightly from casino to casino, but usually is 10% up to a $3 maximum, plus $1 for some sort of house jackpot.

Seat 10   **House Dealer**   Seat 1

Seat 9   Seat 2

BB

$ in the pot before you act:
$22*

Seat 8   **SB**   Seat 3

●

Seat 7   Seat 4

Seat 6   Seat 5   **YOU**

Flop

| Flop Cards Yet to Be Dealt | Flop Cards Yet to Be Dealt | Flop Cards Yet to Be Dealt |

Turn

Turn Card Yet to Be Dealt

River

River Card Yet to Be Dealt

Pocket

J♦ 9♦

Situation #68

Situations 68–71 all deal with the same hand at the four betting stages.

You are in middle position before the flop (sixth to act). You received Jack-9 suited in your pocket. Of the five players to act in front of you, four have called for $4. (Only Seat 1 has bowed out.) With four players to act behind you, including the two blinds, should you fold, call the $4, or raise to $8, and why?

Starting Hand (Pocket): **J♦ 9♦**

This Pocket's Win Rate: **27.9%**

Win Rate Rank: **31 of 169 possible**

Situation #68: Answer

Your pocket cards rank thirty-first on the win rate chart, about at the bottom end of playable hands, so long as you have the right circumstances. Before the flop you are in middle position (sixth), but after the flop you're going to be in late position (eighth), which strengthens your position in the hand. You've got four callers in front of you, one certain caller behind you (the big blind), and another probable caller behind you (the small blind). This means you will have a minimum of seven players in the hand including yourself. You have a shot at a straight *and* a flush, among other hands. These are all the right circumstances for playing a hand such as this.

At this point you should certainly call the $4 as well. A raise wouldn't be in order because it could scare out any or all of the four players behind you, and you want their money in the pot to help make the pot odds appropriate for later in the hand when, in all probability, you'll still have to hit some kind of drawing hand to win this pot. By all means, get in this pot, but get in as cheaply as possible.

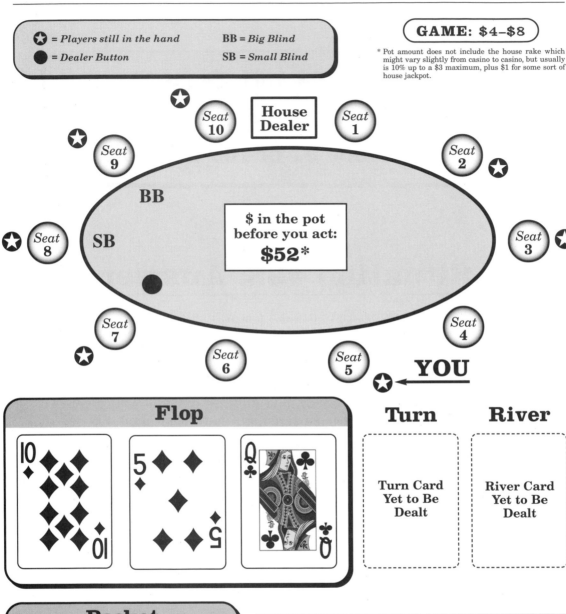

GAME: $4–$8

* Pot amount does not include the house rake which might vary slightly from casino to casino, but usually is 10% up to a $3 maximum, plus $1 for some sort of house jackpot.

⭐ = *Players still in the hand*   BB = *Big Blind*
● = *Dealer Button*   SB = *Small Blind*

$ in the pot before you act: **$52***

Flop

Turn
Turn Card Yet to Be Dealt

River
River Card Yet to Be Dealt

Pocket

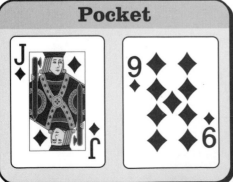

Situation #69

Situations 68–71 all deal with the same hand at the four betting stages.

Only two players dropped out before the flop. After the flop, Seat 8 bet $4. Seats 9, 10, 2, and 3 all called. Seat 4 folded. With only one player to act after you (Seat 7), should you fold, call the $4 bet, or raise to $8, and why?

Starting Hand (Pocket): **J♦ 9♦**

This Pocket's Win Rate: **27.9%**

Win Rate Rank: **31 of 169 possible**

Situation #69: Answer

You should raise. This is a good opportunity to make more money. By raising now, everyone who called for one bet will likely call for two bets. You have seventeen solid outs that will likely win you all the pot if you hit and nearly a 50-50 chance of getting there. Even if your raise makes Seat 7 fold, and you miss on the turn, everyone else will likely check to you on the turn and you could see the river for free.

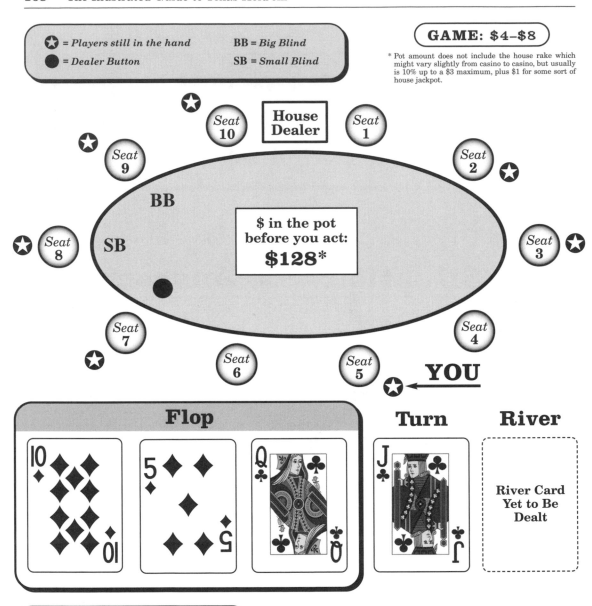

GAME: $4–$8

* Pot amount does not include the house rake which might vary slightly from casino to casino, but usually is 10% up to a $3 maximum, plus $1 for some sort of house jackpot.

= Players still in the hand   BB = Big Blind

= Dealer Button   SB = Small Blind

Seat 10   House Dealer   Seat 1

Seat 9   Seat 2

BB

SB   **$ in the pot before you act:** **$128***   Seat 3

Seat 8   Seat 4

Seat 7   Seat 6   Seat 5   **YOU**

Flop

Turn   ## River

River Card Yet to Be Dealt

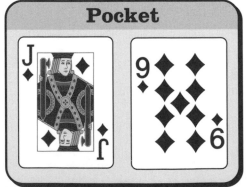

Pocket

Situation #70

Situations 68–71 all deal with the same hand at the four betting stages.

Seven players remained to see the turn. After the turn card was revealed, Seat 8 again bet out of the gate, for $8. Seats 9, 10, 2, and 3 all called. With one player still to act after you, do you fold, call the $8 as well, or raise to $16, and why?

Starting Hand (Pocket): **J♦ 9♦**

This Pocket's Win Rate: **27.9%**

Win Rate Rank: **31 of 169 possible**

Situation #70: Answer

You can't very well raise the bet since all you have is a pair of Jacks with straight and flush draws. You shouldn't fold because you still have too much potential to hit a winning hand. Besides the straight and flush draws, it's possible that three Jacks could win this hand since no one has raised Seat 8's bets yet and there are a lot of players still in the hand.

Just call the bet again and hope Seat 7 doesn't raise, thereby allowing you to stay in and see the river card for only one bet. But if they do raise, the pot odds will be big enough to call since you have approximately 4.5-to-1 odds of making a flush and winning the hand.

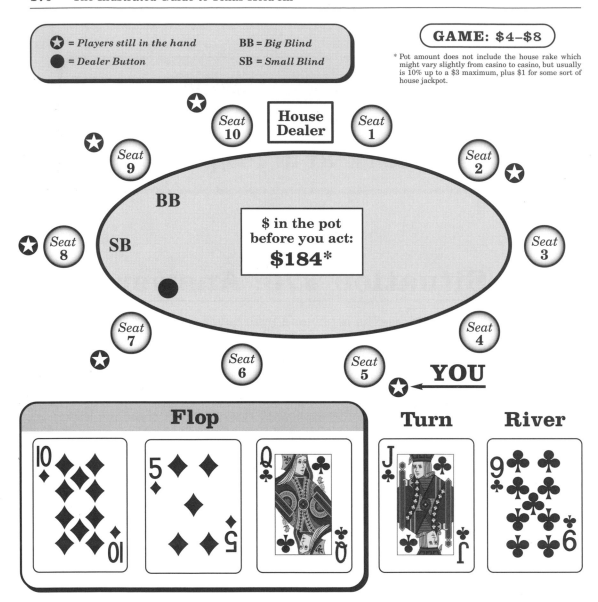

GAME: $4–$8

* Pot amount does not include the house rake which might vary slightly from casino to casino, but usually is 10% up to a $3 maximum, plus $1 for some sort of house jackpot.

Seat 10   House Dealer   Seat 1

Seat 9   Seat 2

BB

$ in the pot before you act: **$184***

SB

Seat 8   Seat 3

Seat 7   Seat 4

Seat 6   Seat 5   **YOU**

Flop

10♦   5♦   Q♣

Turn

J♣

River

9♣

Pocket

J♦   9♦

Situation #71

Situations 68–71 all deal with the same hand at the four betting stages.

All seven players remained in the hand for one bet to see the river. Once the river card was revealed, Seat 8 (who had been betting out of the gate) checked. Seat 9 bet $8, Seat 10 raised to $16, and Seat 2 called. Seat 3 folded. With one player still to act after you, do you fold, call the $16, or raise to $24, and why?

Starting Hand (Pocket): **J♦ 9♦**

This Pocket's Win Rate: **27.9%**

Win Rate Rank: **31 of 169 possible**

Situation #71: Answer

The river improved your hand from one pair to two pair. Unfortunately, it wasn't the improvement you were looking for. Seat 8, who had been betting first under the gun after the flop and turn, now checked. Either he's afraid of the Club flush possibility or he likes it and is planning on check-raising.

Seat 9, who had been calling, is now betting. Seat 10, who had also been calling, is now raising. So these two players obviously liked the river card. Seat 2 called, which means he wasn't impressed with the river, but he also isn't entirely afraid of it, and there are obvious straight and flush draws showing.

It would be safe to say that after the river, these first three players in front of you all have you beat. And you still don't even know about Seats 7 and 8 yet.

There are a number of ways a winning Texas Hold'em player becomes a winning player, and this is one of them:

CARDINAL RULE

Fold your hand when it's obvious you are beaten. Don't throw more money into a pot, "Just in case," or "Just to see."

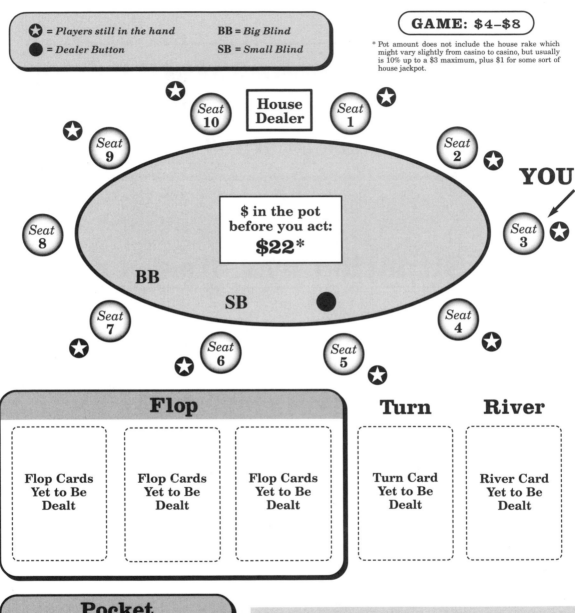

= Players still in the hand   BB = Big Blind

= Dealer Button   SB = Small Blind

GAME: $4–$8

* Pot amount does not include the house rake which might vary slightly from casino to casino, but usually is 10% up to a $3 maximum, plus $1 for some sort of house jackpot.

Seat 10   House Dealer   Seat 1

Seat 9   Seat 2

YOU

$ in the pot before you act: **$22***

Seat 8   Seat 3

BB

SB

Seat 7   Seat 4

Seat 6   Seat 5

Flop

Flop Cards Yet to Be Dealt

Flop Cards Yet to Be Dealt

Flop Cards Yet to Be Dealt

Turn

Turn Card Yet to Be Dealt

River

River Card Yet to Be Dealt

Pocket

8♠   8♥

Situation #72

You have received a pair of 8s in your pocket. You are in middle position before the flop (sixth). Four of the players in front of you call the $4 big blind bet. Do you fold, call the $4 as well, or raise to $8, and why?

Starting Hand (Pocket): **8♠ 8♥**

This Pocket's Win Rate: **51.8%**

Win Rate Rank: **13 of 169 possible**

Situation #72: Answer

You should call the bet. With a win rate of 51.8 percent, a pair of 8s in the pocket is a hand you want to play if the conditions are right. In this hand, the conditions are right to call. You have four callers in the hand already with the prospect of at least two more (the blinds), so the pot odds are good enough to call this bet and should be good enough to call on the turn, depending on the flop.

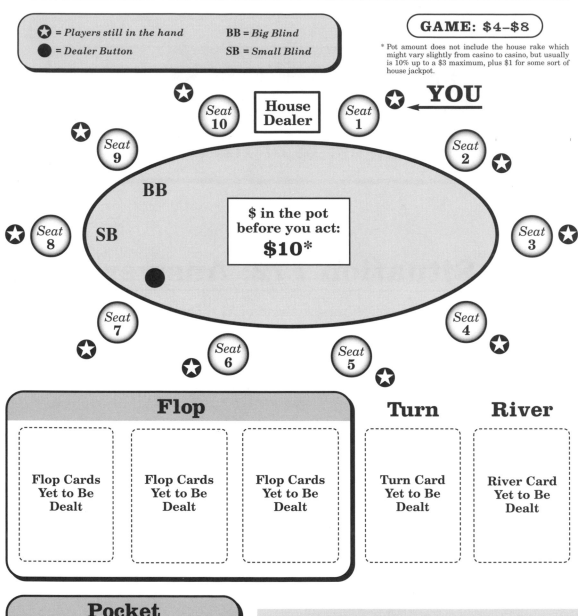

= *Players still in the hand*   BB = *Big Blind*

= *Dealer Button*   SB = *Small Blind*

GAME: $4–$8

* Pot amount does not include the house rake which might vary slightly from casino to casino, but usually is 10% up to a $3 maximum, plus $1 for some sort of house jackpot.

Seat 10
Seat 9
Seat 1
Seat 2
YOU

House Dealer

BB

SB

$ in the pot before you act: $10*

Seat 8
Seat 3

Seat 7
Seat 4

Seat 6
Seat 5

Flop

| Flop Cards Yet to Be Dealt | Flop Cards Yet to Be Dealt | Flop Cards Yet to Be Dealt |

Turn

Turn Card Yet to Be Dealt

River

River Card Yet to Be Dealt

Pocket

Situation #73

Situations 73–75 all deal with the same hand at the first three betting stages.

You received a pair of 9s in your pocket. Seat 10 acted first and bet $4. With eight players yet to act after you, do you fold, call the $4, or raise to $8, and why?

Starting Hand (Pocket): **9♠ 9♦**

This Pocket's Win Rate: **55.4%**

Win Rate Rank: **11 of 169 possible**

Situation #73: Answer

Pocket 9s is a good starting hand, overall, as can be seen in the chart above with its 55.4 percent win rate. It would be better if you had this hand in late position with a number of callers and no raisers in front of you, but it is still playable in this position.

A case could be made for raising this hand in order to drive out all those players holding hands with Aces and bad kickers, small pairs, mid-level suited connectors and the like, but in low limit Hold'em a lot of players will call a raise anyway with those hands. Also, Seat 10 did bet out of the gate so you have to assume he has some kind of strong hand. If you raise, you might get reraised by Seat 10 or even another player before it ever gets back to Seat 10.

So for now, with this hand in this position, the best thing to do would be to call the $4 and see what the flop brings.

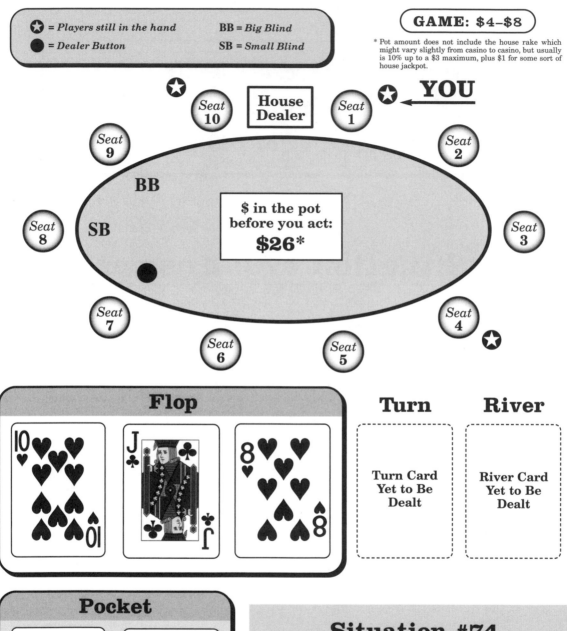

⭐ = *Players still in the hand*   BB = *Big Blind*

⬤ = *Dealer Button*   SB = *Small Blind*

GAME: $4–$8

* Pot amount does not include the house rake which might vary slightly from casino to casino, but usually is 10% up to a $3 maximum, plus $1 for some sort of house jackpot.

Seat 10 — House Dealer — Seat 1 — **YOU**

Seat 9   Seat 2

BB

Seat 8   **$ in the pot before you act:** **$26***   Seat 3

SB

Seat 7   Seat 4

Seat 6   Seat 5

Flop

Turn
Turn Card Yet to Be Dealt

River
River Card Yet to Be Dealt

Pocket

Situation #74

Situations 73–75 all deal with the same hand at the first three betting stages.

Four players, including you, stayed in to see the flop for one bet. After the flop, Seats 9, 10, and you all checked. Seat 4 bet $4. Seat 9 folded and Seat 10 calls the bet. Do you fold, call $4 as well, or raise to $8, and why?

Starting Hand (Pocket): **9♠ 9♦**

This Pocket's Win Rate: **55.4%**

Win Rate Rank: **11 of 169 possible**

Situation #74: Answer

First, the good news: you flopped an open-ended straight draw. Now, the bad news: you don't have a straight yet, there are two overcards on the board, and you're facing a Heart flush draw as well.

Simple analysis of what you've got going for you and against you with this hand should at least make it obvious that you're not going to raise this hand. Now the issue becomes whether to fold or call. Well, let's calculate our odds and then decide.

There are eight cards which will give you the straight; the four 7s and the four Queens. There are forty-seven cards that remain unseen, so any of the eight cards you need could be in that group of forty-seven unseen cards. So, 47 - 8 = 39. This means there are thirty-nine cards that won't make your straight and eight that will. You calculate your odds of getting a straight this way: 39 ÷ 8 = 4.875, or a shade under 5-to-1 odds against you. However, you still have two chances to catch the card you need (the turn and the river), so you have to divide 4.875 by 2 to get the correct odds, which is: 4.875 ÷ 2 = 2.438, or about 2.5-to-1.

There is $26 in the pot right now, and you are being asked to make a $4 bet, which translates into: $26 ÷ $4 = $6.50-to-1 money odds. So, since the odds against you of hitting the straight on the turn are about 5-to-1, and the money return is 6.5-to-1, then the correct play is to call this bet. Remember, however, that if you do hit your straight, it doesn't necessarily mean you'll win. If a Queen comes up, someone could be holding an Ace-King for a higher straight. Or the Heart flush could hit.

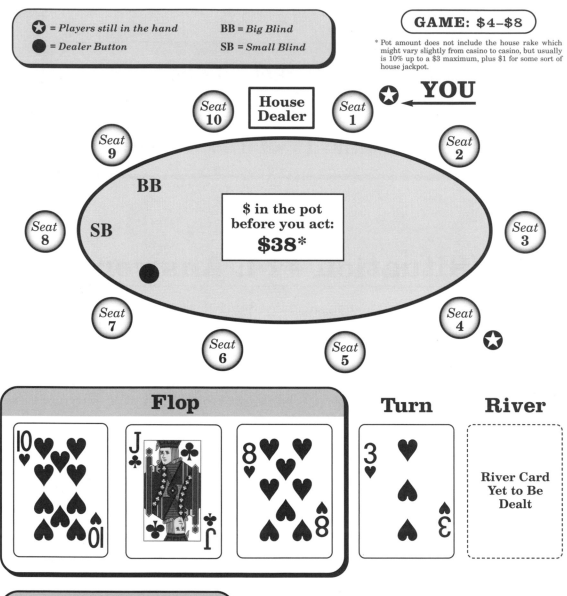

GAME: $4–$8

* Pot amount does not include the house rake which might vary slightly from casino to casino, but usually is 10% up to a $3 maximum, plus $1 for some sort of house jackpot.

⭐ **YOU** ←

Seat 10   **House Dealer**   Seat 1

Seat 9   Seat 2

BB

$ in the pot before you act:
$38*

SB   Seat 8   Seat 3

Seat 7   Seat 4 ⭐

Seat 6   Seat 5

Flop

10♥   J♣   8♥

Turn

3♥

River

River Card Yet to Be Dealt

Pocket

9♠   9♦

Situation #75

Situations 73–75 all deal with the same hand at the first three betting stages.

After the turn card was dealt, Seat 10 and you both checked. Seat 4 bet $8 and Seat 10 folded, leaving you in a heads up situation with Seat 4. Do you fold, call the $8, or raise to $16, and why?

Starting Hand (Pocket): **9♠ 9♦**

This Pocket's Win Rate: **55.4%**

Win Rate Rank: **11 of 169 possible**

Situation #75: Answer

The turn card didn't help you at all. In fact, it killed you if your opponent was on a Heart draw. And if he's holding something else, such as Ace-Jack and one of the cards is a Heart, he now has a legitimate Heart draw to go with whatever else he was working on.

So we know we're not going to raise this hand, but let's calculate the odds to see if it makes sense to call this bet or not.

There are now forty-six unseen cards, eight of which will still give us a straight. 38 ÷ 8 = 4.75-to-1 odds, and since there is only one card yet to be dealt, those are our odds.

Now for the pot odds. The pot contains $38 minus the $3 rake and the $1 jackpot deductions for a correct total of $34. You are being asked to make a bet of $8 in order to win $34. $34 ÷ $8 = $4.25-to-1 pot odds. This means that you are being asked to make a bet where the odds against you are 4.75-to-1 for a return of only 4.25-to-1. While it wouldn't be the end of the world if you made this call with its slight odds disadvantage, you should still fold this hand because of that and the three Hearts on the board.

There will be a lot of hands that will come your way in Texas Hold'em that you can get excited about. This ain't one of 'em.

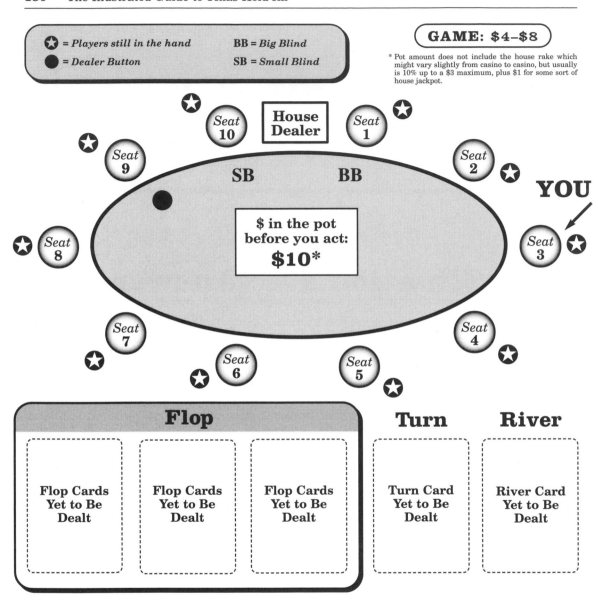

* Pot amount does not include the house rake which might vary slightly from casino to casino, but usually is 10% up to a $3 maximum, plus $1 for some sort of house jackpot.

★ = *Players still in the hand*   BB = *Big Blind*

● = *Dealer Button*   SB = *Small Blind*

House Dealer

Seat 10

Seat 1

Seat 9

Seat 2

SB   BB

YOU

$ in the pot before you act: **$10***

Seat 8

Seat 3

Seat 7

Seat 4

Seat 6

Seat 5

Flop

| Flop Cards Yet to Be Dealt | Flop Cards Yet to Be Dealt | Flop Cards Yet to Be Dealt |

Turn

Turn Card Yet to Be Dealt

River

River Card Yet to Be Dealt

Pocket

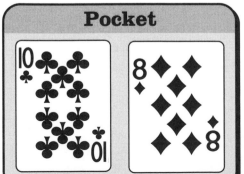

Situation #76

You received 10-8 offsuit in your pocket. Seat 2 was first to act and he bet $4. It is now your turn to act. Do you fold, call the $4, or raise to $8, and why?

Starting Hand (Pocket): **10♣ 8♦**

This Pocket's Win Rate: **3.9%**

Win Rate Rank: **76 of 169 possible**

Situation #76: Answer

As you can see from the chart above, this is a very weak hand, having a win rate of less than 4 percent. When you mix into the equation the fact that you are in early position it turns this hand from weak to terrible.

Seat 1's bet under the gun is a projection of power and you don't know what the eight other players behind you are going to do. And even if you did know what they were going to do, this isn't a hand worth playing. For example, let's say you and everyone else called this hand for a total of ten players. Since this hand only wins one time in twenty-five, is it worth calling when the maximum return you're going to get is 9-to-1?

In the world of low limit Texas Hold'em, you will see many players play such hands time and again. You should be grateful when your opponents play this kind of hand because if they do so against you on a regular basis, you are going to take all their chips. It will only be a matter of time. This hand is an open-and-shut case for folding.

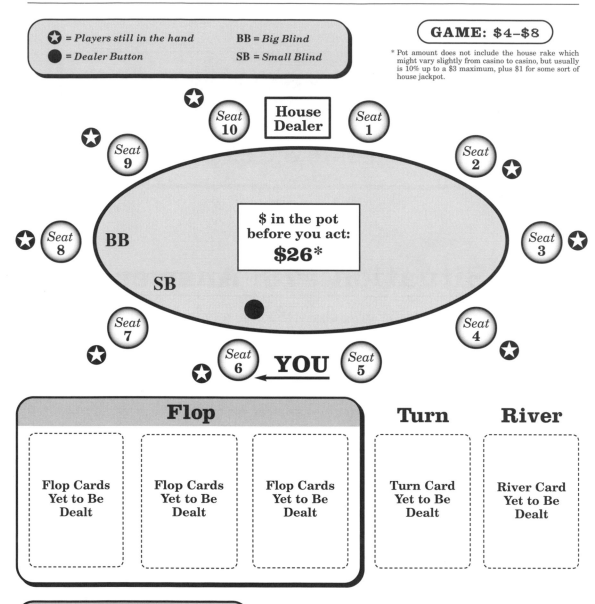

* Pot amount does not include the house rake which might vary slightly from casino to casino, but usually is 10% up to a $3 maximum, plus $1 for some sort of house jackpot.

GAME: $4–$8

★ = Players still in the hand   BB = Big Blind

● = Dealer Button   SB = Small Blind

House Dealer

Seat 10   Seat 1   Seat 9   Seat 2   Seat 8   Seat 3   Seat 7   Seat 4   Seat 6   Seat 5

BB

SB

$ in the pot before you act: $26*

YOU

Flop

Flop Cards Yet to Be Dealt

Flop Cards Yet to Be Dealt

Flop Cards Yet to Be Dealt

Turn

Turn Card Yet to Be Dealt

River

River Card Yet to Be Dealt

Pocket

Situation #77

You received a pair of Aces in your pocket. Seat 9 was the first to act and he bet $4. Seats 10, 2, 3, and 4 all called the bet. It is now your turn to act. Do you fold, call the $4 as well, or raise to $8, and why?

Starting Hand (Pocket): **A♥ A♠**

This Pocket's Win Rate: **86.1%**

Win Rate Rank: **1 of 169 possible**

Situation #77: Answer

Seat 9 bet under the gun, so he is projecting power, but right now it doesn't matter because you, too, have power. In fact, you have the number one power pocket hand in Texas Hold'em—a pair of Aces. The best hand any other player at the table can hold right now is a pair of pocket Aces, just like you, for a tie.

You are in the dream position for a Hold'em hand, holding pocket Aces on the button, meaning you get to act last on the final three betting rounds.

CARDINAL RULE

When you have the best hand, make your opponents pay.

Right now you have the best hand, so raise and make them pay.

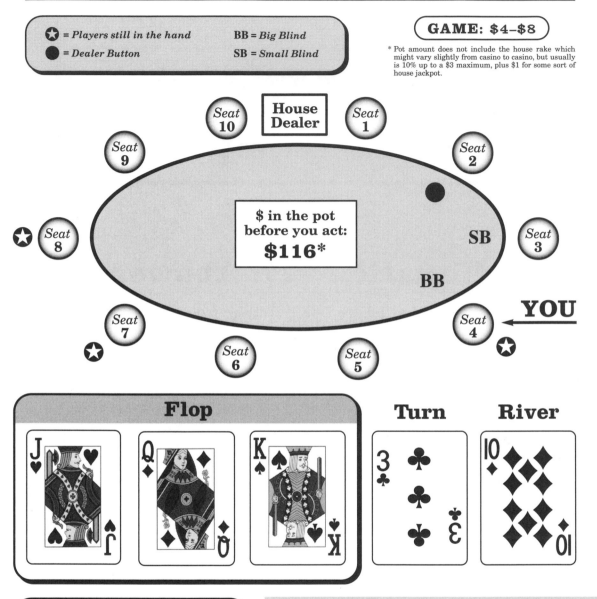

⭐ = *Players still in the hand*   **BB** = *Big Blind*

⚫ = *Dealer Button*   **SB** = *Small Blind*

GAME: $4–$8

* Pot amount does not include the house rake which might vary slightly from casino to casino, but usually is 10% up to a $3 maximum, plus $1 for some sort of house jackpot.

House Dealer

Seat 10
Seat 1
Seat 9
Seat 2
Seat 8 ⭐
Seat 3
Seat 7 ⭐
Seat 6
Seat 5
Seat 4

SB
BB
YOU ←

$ in the pot before you act:
$116*

Flop

Turn

River

Pocket

Situation #78

You received 10-9 suited in your pocket while in the big blind. There were five callers, including you, for one bet to see the flop. After the flop, you hit a straight and were first to act. You bet $4 and had three callers. After the turn, you bet first and again had three callers. After the river, you bet first and Seat 7 raised to $16. Seat 8 reraised to $24 and Seat 2 folded. Do you fold, call the $24, or raise to $32, and why?

Starting Hand (Pocket): **10♣ 9♣**

This Pocket's Win Rate: **38.3%**

Win Rate Rank: **24 of 169 possible**

Situation #78: Answer

When the 10♦ came on the river, it gave straights to anyone holding an Ace or a 9. With the obvious open-ended straight draw on the board, and considering that Ace-Anything is held and played routinely in low limit Hold'em, you have to figure that at least one, if not both, of your opponents still in this hand hold Ace-high straights, especially Seat 8.

As mentioned previously in this book, another key element to playing winning Hold'em is to know when you are beaten and to fold your hand as soon as you recognize it. Routinely staying in hands one bet too many is an effective way of being a losing player. Despite the size of the pot, you should fold this hand because you are most assuredly beaten.

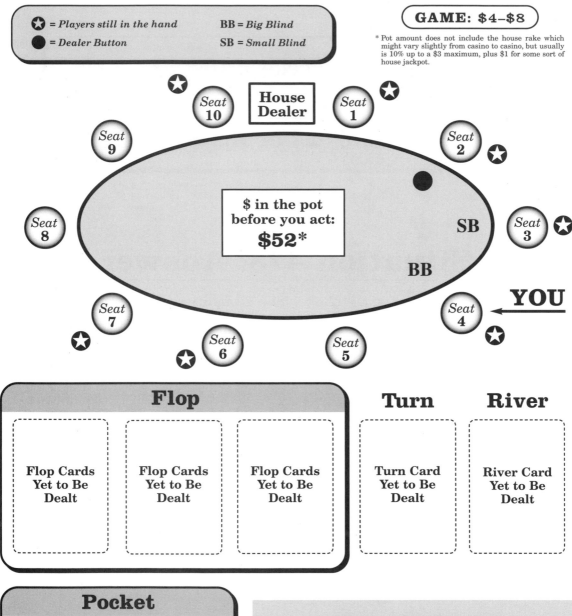

GAME: $4–$8

* Pot amount does not include the house rake which might vary slightly from casino to casino, but usually is 10% up to a $3 maximum, plus $1 for some sort of house jackpot.

⭐ = Players still in the hand   **BB = Big Blind**

⚫ = Dealer Button   **SB = Small Blind**

Seat 10 • House Dealer • Seat 1 • Seat 2 • Seat 3 • Seat 4 (YOU) • Seat 5 • Seat 6 • Seat 7 • Seat 8 • Seat 9

$ in the pot before you act:
$52*

SB

BB

YOU ←

Flop

| Flop Cards Yet to Be Dealt | Flop Cards Yet to Be Dealt | Flop Cards Yet to Be Dealt |

Turn

Turn Card Yet to Be Dealt

River

River Card Yet to Be Dealt

Pocket

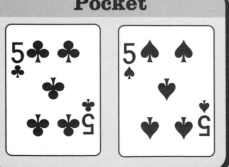

Situation #79

Situations 79–82 all deal with the same hand at the four betting stages of a hand the author was actually involved in.

You were dealt a pair of 5s in your pocket while in the big blind position. Seat 6 raised to $8. Seats 7, 10, 1, 2, and 3 all called the raise. As the last to act, do you fold, call the $8, or raise to $12, and why?

Starting Hand (Pocket): **5♣ 5♠**

This Pocket's Win Rate: **20.7%**

Win Rate Rank: **34 of 169 possible**

Situation #79: Answer

With a raise and five calls in front of you, you are certainly an underdog with your pocket 5s. However, that doesn't necessarily mean you should fold the hand. Let's calculate the odds and see.

Clearly, at least at this point in the hand, you are going to need another 5 to have any hope of winning this pot. There are fifty unseen cards, with two of them being the 5s you need, and you have five shots of catching a third 5 by the river. So, the formula would be calculated thusly:

(48 ÷ 2) ÷ 5 = 4.8, or 4.8-to-1 odds *by the river*

Now, let's calculate the odds of hitting a third 5 on just the flop:

(48 ÷ 2) ÷ 3 = 8, or 8-to-1 odds *on the flop*

Going with the flop odds of 8-to-1 then, we'd have to get at least 8-to-1 on our money to make this a correct call. There is $52 in the pot, *including our $4 big blind bet we were forced to put in at the beginning of the hand,* which doesn't count as part of what we are now required to bet. That means we are only being asked to bet $4 to win $52, and that is 13-to-1 on our money ($52 ÷ $4 = 13). Strictly from the standpoint of pot odds, this is a great bet. Now, it may be another story whether or not the three 5s will hold up if we hit them, but it's a correct bet at this point. Do what I did when I had this hand and call the bet for $8.

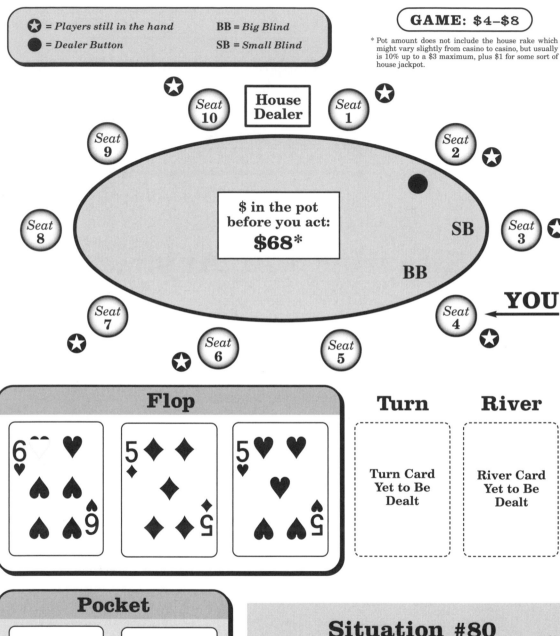

GAME: $4–$8

* Pot amount does not include the house rake which might vary slightly from casino to casino, but usually is 10% up to a $3 maximum, plus $1 for some sort of house jackpot.

Seat 10   **House Dealer**   Seat 1

Seat 9

Seat 2

$ in the pot before you act: **$68***

SB

Seat 8

Seat 3

BB

YOU

Seat 7   Seat 4

Seat 6   Seat 5

Flop

Turn

Turn Card Yet to Be Dealt

River

River Card Yet to Be Dealt

Pocket

Situation #80

Situations 79–82 all deal with the same hand at the four betting stages of a hand the author was actually involved in.

After the flop, Seat 3 checked, as did you. Seats 6, 7, 10, and 1 also checked. Seat 2, possibly seeking information, bet $4. Seat 3 then called. It is now your turn to act. Do you call the $4 or check-raise to $8, and why?

Starting Hand (Pocket): **5♣ 5♠**

This Pocket's Win Rate: **20.7%**

Win Rate Rank: **34 of 169 possible**

Situation #80: Answer

Every once in a while you'll flop a monster, as I did with this hand. The problem now was keeping everyone in the pot so I could maximize the potential of this hand.

If you check-raise this hand now, you're practically telling your opponents you have at least one 5 in your hand, and some or all of the five players who initially checked after the flop will undoubtedly fold their hands. Your main focus now should be to keep as many players in the hand as long as possible because you have a hand that is almost unbeatable. Since so many players stayed in the hand to begin with after Seat 6's pre-flop raise, and then all but one checked after the flop, it tells me that they obviously have big cards or pocket pairs that the flop just plain missed. I was hoping for an Ace, King, or Queen to come on the turn since any of these three big cards would likely help one or two of their hands.

At this point I would (and did) just call Seat 2's bet.

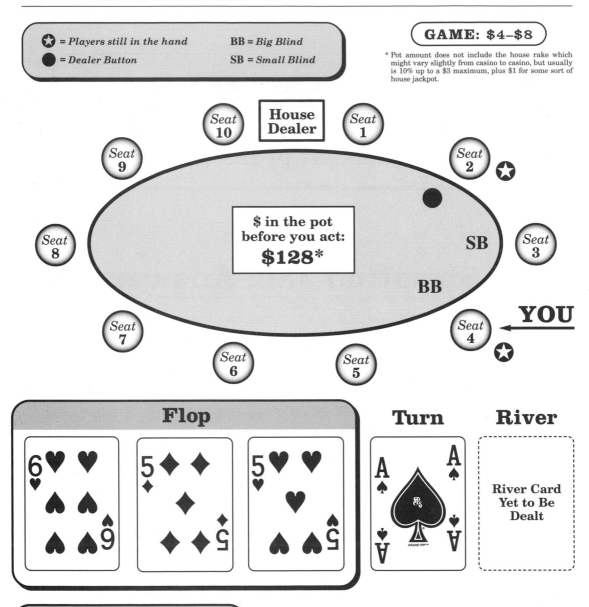

★ = *Players still in the hand*   BB = *Big Blind*

● = *Dealer Button*   SB = *Small Blind*

GAME: $4–$8

* Pot amount does not include the house rake which might vary slightly from casino to casino, but usually is 10% up to a $3 maximum, plus $1 for some sort of house jackpot.

Seat 10   **House Dealer**   Seat 1

Seat 9

Seat 2 ★

Seat 8

$ in the pot before you act:
$128*

SB

Seat 3

BB

Seat 7

YOU ←

Seat 4 ★

Seat 6   Seat 5

Flop

6♥   5♦   5♥

Turn   **River**

A♠

River Card Yet to Be Dealt

Pocket

5♣   5♠

Situation #81

Situations 79–82 all deal with the same hand at the four betting stages of a hand the author was actually involved in.

After the turn, Seat 3 bet $8, you raised to $16, Seat 7 folded, Seat 2 raised to $24, and Seat 3 folded. Now in a heads up situation with Seat 2, do you fold, call the additional $8 for a total of $24, or cap the betting at $32, and why?

Starting Hand (Pocket): **5♣ 5♠**

This Pocket's Win Rate: **20.7%**

Win Rate Rank: **34 of 169 possible**

Situation #81: Answer

Unfortunately, in spite of just calling Seat 2's bet after the flop, three of the other players folded, leaving just four of us in the hand for the turn. The good news, however, was that an Ace came up on the turn and I knew it had to help someone's hand. It would have been nice if it had been the Ace of Hearts instead of Spades to give someone a flush or flush draw, but hey, beggars can't be choosers.

As for the situation at hand, Seat 2's raise of your raise was a delight to see, since there's nothing he can hold at this point that can beat you. He's obviously not going anywhere if you reraise him, so by all means, cap the betting at $32.

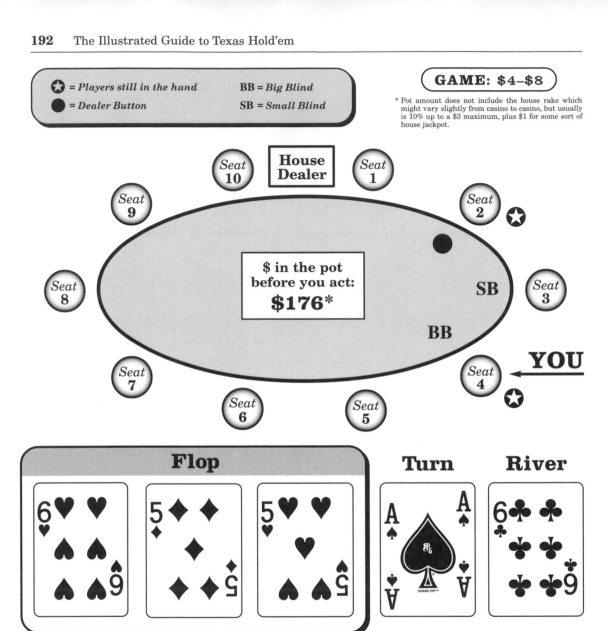

= *Players still in the hand*   BB = *Big Blind*

= *Dealer Button*   SB = *Small Blind*

GAME: $4–$8

* Pot amount does not include the house rake which might vary slightly from casino to casino, but usually is 10% up to a $3 maximum, plus $1 for some sort of house jackpot.

House Dealer

Seat 10 · Seat 1 · Seat 9 · Seat 2 · Seat 8 · Seat 3 · Seat 7 · Seat 4 · Seat 6 · Seat 5

$ in the pot before you act: $176*

SB

BB

YOU

Flop

6♥ · 5♦ · 5♥

Turn

A♠

River

6♣

Pocket

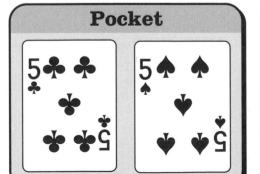

5♣ · 5♠

Situation #82

Situations 79–82 all deal with the same hand at the four betting stages of a hand the author was actually involved in.

After the flop, you bet $8. Seat 2 raised to $16. Do you fold, call the $16, or reraise to $24, and why?

Starting Hand (Pocket): **5♣ 5♠**

This Pocket's Win Rate: **20.7%**

Win Rate Rank: **34 of 169 possible**

Situation #82: Answer

Seat 2's raise after my bet on the river again brought a smile to my face. I quickly reraised him, pushing another $16 in front of me. He then reraised me, capping the betting at $32, which I gladly called. This $220 pot was going to be mine.

Until he turned over his pocket 6s. Once again, I learned the hard way:

CARDINAL RULE

Until you have the nuts, you don't have the nuts.

Admittedly, this was a bad beat. But I also have to admit that in my excitement to get my money into the pot, I never even saw four 6s as a real possibility. Even if I had, I still would have done the same thing.

As I watched my opponent scoop in the huge pot, I began to reflect on the hand and wondered if I'd done anything wrong, but decided I hadn't, with the possible exception of reraising him on the river. I could have just called the $16, allowing for the possibility of quad 6s. But since he flopped a full house, he wasn't going anywhere, no matter how hard I would have raised in the early going. If anything, I saved myself some money by restraining my betting until later in the hand. Sometimes a bad beat is just that—a bad luck beat.

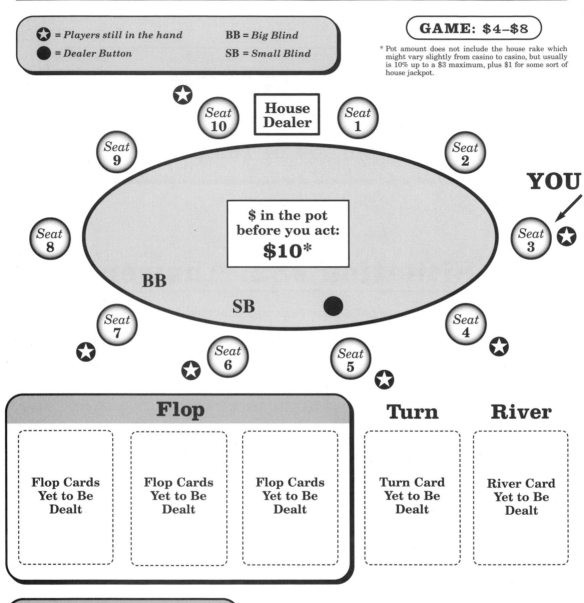

⭐ = *Players still in the hand*   BB = *Big Blind*

⚫ = *Dealer Button*   SB = *Small Blind*

GAME: $4–$8

* Pot amount does not include the house rake which might vary slightly from casino to casino, but usually is 10% up to a $3 maximum, plus $1 for some sort of house jackpot.

Seat 10   **House Dealer**   Seat 1

Seat 9   Seat 2

YOU

$ in the pot before you act: **$10***

Seat 8   Seat 3 ⭐

BB

SB

Seat 7   Seat 4 ⭐

Seat 6   Seat 5 ⭐

Flop

| Flop Cards Yet to Be Dealt | Flop Cards Yet to Be Dealt | Flop Cards Yet to Be Dealt |

Turn

Turn Card Yet to Be Dealt

River

River Card Yet to Be Dealt

Pocket

8♥ 5♥

Situation #83

You were dealt 8-5 suited in your pocket. On the previous two hands, there were many 8s and 5s brought on the board, suggesting a poor mix by the dealer. Of the five players who acted in front of you, only Seat 10 called, the others all folded. It is now your turn to act. With four players yet to act behind you, including the blinds, do you fold, call the $4 bet, or raise to $8, and why?

Starting Hand (Pocket): **8♥ 5♥**

This Pocket's Win Rate: **3.9%**

Win Rate Rank: **77 of 169 possible**

Situation #83: Answer

Regardless of what turned up on the board during the two previous hands, this is still a poor hand, as its 3.9 percent winning rate attests. There is nothing scientific or statistically reliable to prove that more 8s and 5s will come on the board a third consecutive time. I have played against players who go with "hunches" such as this, and they go with them about as often as they go to the ATM to get more cash.

Each hand should be played on its own merits, not on some hunch. The merit of this hand is that you didn't have to put any money into the pot before folding, which is what you should do.

Again, don't fall into the trap that so many low limit Hold'em players do when they play any two suited cards from any position. An early bettor indicates power of some kind. Four folds in front of you keeps you from getting a large pot, which is what you need when you play a statistically poor drawing hand like this because you need the pot odds.

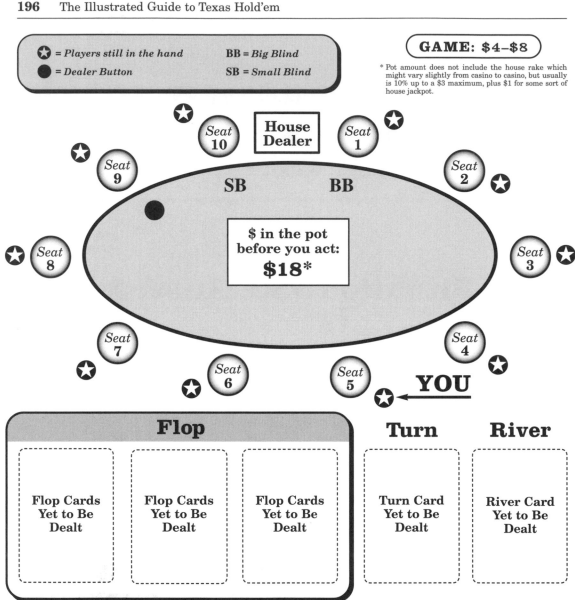

= Players still in the hand   BB = Big Blind

= Dealer Button   SB = Small Blind

GAME: $4–$8

* Pot amount does not include the house rake which might vary slightly from casino to casino, but usually is 10% up to a $3 maximum, plus $1 for some sort of house jackpot.

Seat 10   House Dealer   Seat 1

Seat 9   Seat 2

SB   BB

$ in the pot before you act: $18*

Seat 8   Seat 3

Seat 7   Seat 4

Seat 6   Seat 5   **YOU**

Flop

| Flop Cards Yet to Be Dealt | Flop Cards Yet to Be Dealt | Flop Cards Yet to Be Dealt |

Turn

Turn Card Yet to Be Dealt

River

River Card Yet to Be Dealt

Pocket

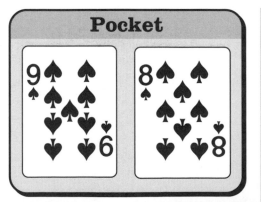

Situation #84

Situations 84–87 all deal with the same hand at the four betting stages.

You were dealt 9-8 suited in your pocket. You are fourth to act in a game that has been, for the most part, loose and passive. The first three players in front of you all called the $4 big blind bet. With six players yet to act after you, including the blinds, do you fold, call the $4 as well, or raise to $8, and why?

Starting Hand (Pocket): **9♠ 8♠**

This Pocket's Win Rate: **9.8%**

Win Rate Rank: **44 of 169 possible**

Situation #84: Answer

There are several key aspects to determining whether or not to play this hand since it falls a bit below the level of starting hands you'd ideally like to play. First, the fact that you're involved in a passive game means it is possible that no one will raise behind you, thereby allowing you to see the flop for one bet. Second, your hand is suited, not unsuited, and that increases your odds significantly. An unsuited 9-8 pocket has a winning rate of 3.8 percent while a suited 9-8 stands at 9.8 percent.

With a hand like this you need at least four callers, and more would be better. Since three players have already called, and you know the big blind will stay in and the small blind will probably stay in, you've likely got five callers right now with four others to decide. This should give you enough in the way of pot odds to at least see the flop, then you can go from there. If you happen to catch two pair, a set, or four cards to a flush or an open-ended straight draw, you've got a shot at this pot.

There are several things to be aware of on this hand. If you flop a 10-Jack-Queen, you've got the bottom end of the straight, and any Kings and Aces lurking out there could eventually give someone a higher straight. Also, if three or four Spades come on the board, your hand is only a 9-high flush, which could easily be beaten.

These warnings notwithstanding, go ahead and call the bet and see if your hand fits the flop.

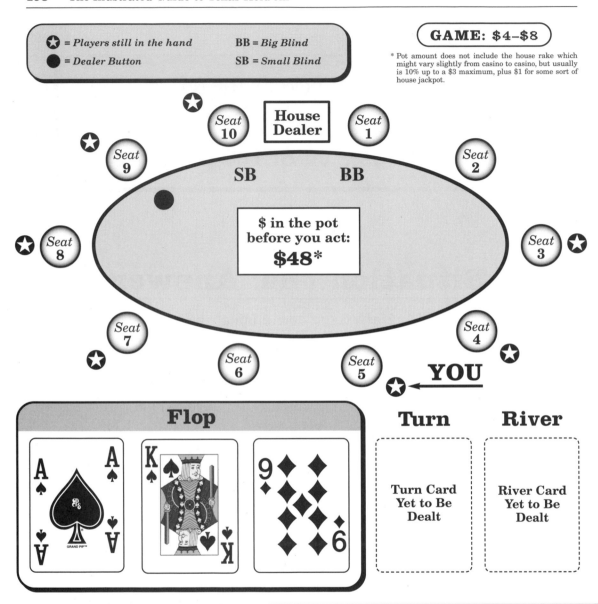

GAME: $4–$8

* Pot amount does not include the house rake which might vary slightly from casino to casino, but usually is 10% up to a $3 maximum, plus $1 for some sort of house jackpot.

★ = *Players still in the hand*   BB = *Big Blind*

● = *Dealer Button*   SB = *Small Blind*

Seat 10   House Dealer   Seat 1

Seat 9   Seat 2

SB   BB

Seat 8   **$ in the pot before you act: $48***   Seat 3

Seat 7   Seat 4

Seat 6   Seat 5   **YOU**

Flop

Turn

Turn Card Yet to Be Dealt

River

River Card Yet to Be Dealt

Pocket

Situation #85

Situations 84–87 all deal with the same hand at the four betting stages.

Before the flop, only one player folded and none of the nine players remaining in the hand raised. After the flop, Seat 10, the first to act, bet $4. Seats 1 and 2 folded. Seats 3 and 4 called. It is now your turn to act. With three players yet to act after you, do you fold, call the $4, or raise to $8, and why?

Starting Hand (Pocket): **9♠ 8♠**

This Pocket's Win Rate: **9.8%**

Win Rate Rank: **44 of 169 possible**

Situation #85: Answer

The flop certainly fit your hand, but not good enough to raise. Right now you only have bottom pair and a flush draw. You also no longer have a chance for a straight

What you do have is a fair number of outs. If any of the other nine Spades come on the board you'll have a flush. It won't necessarily be the highest, but it will be a flush all the same. If either of the other two nines appear on the turn, you'll have a set, and that could be good enough to win this hand, since right now no one can possibly hold a straight or a flush. Even another 8 improves your hand to two pair.

At this point, you're not strong enough to raise and you're not so weak that you have to fold, especially for just one bet. Call the bet and see what the turn brings. And if someone behind you should raise, the pot odds are good enough right now for you to call the raise as well.

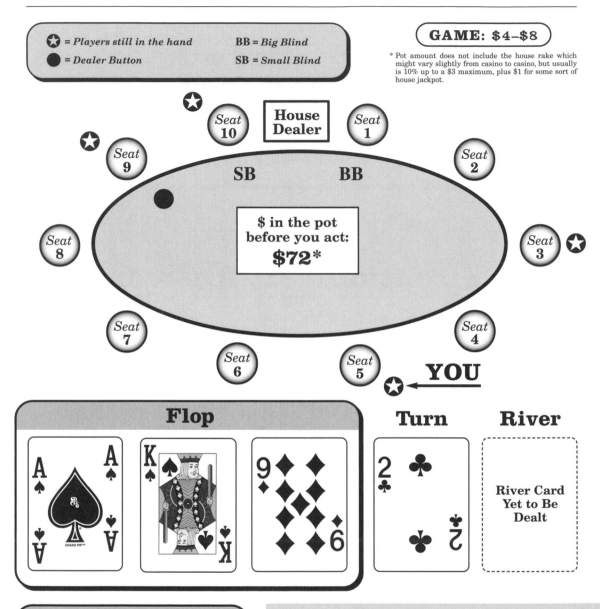

GAME: $4–$8

*Pot amount does not include the house rake which might vary slightly from casino to casino, but usually is 10% up to a $3 maximum, plus $1 for some sort of house jackpot.

Seat 10   House Dealer   Seat 1

Seat 9   Seat 2

SB   BB

$ in the pot before you act: **$72***

Seat 8   Seat 3

Seat 7   Seat 4

Seat 6   Seat 5   **YOU**

Flop

A♠   K♠   9♦

Turn

2♣

River

River Card Yet to Be Dealt

Pocket

9♠   8♠

Situation #86

Situations 84–87 all deal with the same hand at the four betting stages.

When you called after the flop, two more players folded and one more called, leaving five players to see the turn. After the turn, Seat 10, the first to act, again bet out of the gate, this time for $8. Seat 3 called and Seat 4 folded. With Seat 9 yet to act behind you, do you fold, call the $8, or raise to $16, and why?

Starting Hand (Pocket): **9♠ 8♠**

This Pocket's Win Rate: **9.8%**

Win Rate Rank: **44 of 169 possible**

Situation #86: Answer

On the surface it would appear that very little changed after the turn card, except that now you have one less chance to hit what you need to improve your hand to the point where you could play it to the showdown. It's unlikely that the 2♣ on the turn helped anybody, unless someone happened to be playing Ace-2 suited, for example.

Seat 10 continued to bet out of the gate, so he's the one you've got to be the most concerned with. He very likely has an Ace in his pocket. If he held only a King-high hand, it's not likely he'd be betting into the Ace possibility. The other callers, just like you, are needing some help.

You still have fourteen cards that can improve your hand to the point where you could win this pot, but you're not there yet. Just call the bet and see what the river brings.

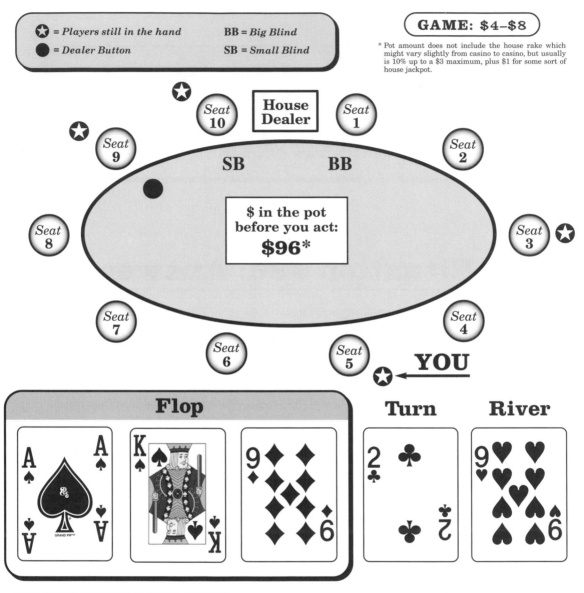

★ = *Players still in the hand*   BB = *Big Blind*

● = *Dealer Button*   SB = *Small Blind*

GAME: $4–$8

* Pot amount does not include the house rake which might vary slightly from casino to casino, but usually is 10% up to a $3 maximum, plus $1 for some sort of house jackpot.

House Dealer

Seat 10   Seat 1   Seat 2   Seat 3   Seat 4   Seat 5   Seat 6   Seat 7   Seat 8   Seat 9

SB   BB

$ in the pot before you act: $96*

YOU

Flop

A♠   K♠   9♦

Turn

2♣

River

9♥

Pocket

9♠   8♠

Situation #87

Situations 84–87 all deal with the same hand at the four betting stages.

No one folded after the turn. After the river, Seats 10 and 3 both checked. It is now your turn to act. With Seat 9 still yet to act after you, do you check (concerned about the full house possibilities), check (with the intent of raising if Seat 9 bets), or do you bet $8, and why?

Starting Hand (Pocket): **9♠ 8♠**

This Pocket's Win Rate: **9.8%**

Win Rate Rank: **44 of 169 possible**

Situation #87: Answer

In all likelihood, this was a very good card for you. Seat 10, who had been betting under the gun, now checked after the river. That means one of two things. Either he's afraid of the three 9s or full house possibilities, or he has the full house and his check was actually intended to be a check-raise.

Seat 3 continued to check, so it's unlikely that the 9 on the river helped him, unless he was holding two pair and hit a full house and is intending on check-raising as well. One thing is certain: the river card definitely helped you, and unless someone is holding the 9♣ with a better kicker than you or is holding pocket Aces, Kings, or 2s, you have the best hand.

It's hard to imagine that Seats 3 or 9 would have just checked during the first three betting stages with pocket Aces or Kings, and it's just as unlikely they would have continued to play after the flop with pocket 2s. Therefore, my conclusion would be that the worst you have against you is two pair, with the outside possibility of three 9s with a higher kicker (Queen, Jack, or 10).

Feeling fairly confident that you hold the best hand, you should bet it now and not hold out for the check-raise. If you bet now, it's likely you'll get one, two, or even three callers just because they "want to see it," thereby making another $8-$24. If you just check in hopes of getting a check-raise situation, you might not get any more money. In the unlikely event you get check-raised, you should just call the raise.

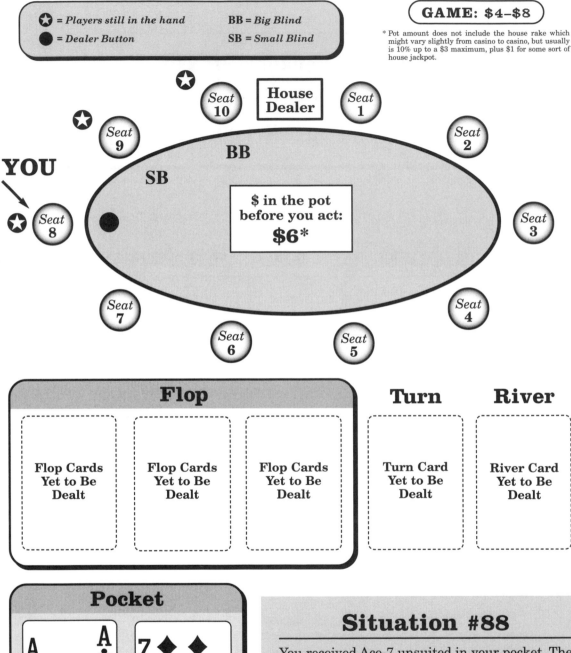

★ = *Players still in the hand*   BB = *Big Blind*

● = *Dealer Button*   SB = *Small Blind*

GAME: $4–$8

* Pot amount does not include the house rake which might vary slightly from casino to casino, but usually is 10% up to a $3 maximum, plus $1 for some sort of house jackpot.

Seat 10   House Dealer   Seat 1

Seat 9   Seat 2

BB

YOU

SB

Seat 8   **$ in the pot before you act: $6***   Seat 3

Seat 7   Seat 4

Seat 6   Seat 5

Flop

| Flop Cards Yet to Be Dealt | Flop Cards Yet to Be Dealt | Flop Cards Yet to Be Dealt |

Turn

Turn Card Yet to Be Dealt

River

River Card Yet to Be Dealt

Pocket

A♣ 7♦

Situation #88

You received Ace-7 unsuited in your pocket. The first seven players in front of you all folded. It is now your turn to act. With only the two blinds to act after you, do you fold as well, call the $4 big blind bet, or raise to $8, and why?

Starting Hand (Pocket): **A♣ 7♦**

This Pocket's Win Rate: **10.2%**

Win Rate Rank: **41 of 169 possible**

Situation #88: Answer

There are several reasons you would not normally play a pocket hand of Ace-7 unsuited. First, your chances for making an Ace-high flush are slim, at best. Second, there is little chance to make a straight. Third, even if you do catch an Ace on the board, your 7 is not a very good kicker. So you've got a lot of things working against you when you play a hand like this. *Normally*.

But this situation is not normal. When everyone folded in front of you, it left you alone in the hand with the two blinds. Statistically speaking, the blinds probably don't have very good hands. Most small blinds are played for just the additional two dollars and most big blinds are played "big enough."

While you could certainly call this hand in this situation, it would be better to raise to $8 in order to **steal the blinds**. This means to raise in late position when only the blinds are left in an attempt to get the blinds to fold, thereby giving you the $6 pot. Most of the time the blinds will fold in the face of such a raise because most of the time they won't have any kind of a hand worth playing. (Again, statistically speaking.)

On those occasions where one or both blinds do call your raise, indicating that they have some sort of playable hand, you still have two things working for you. One is your Ace. If they're playing a small or medium pair, you can still beat them if an Ace comes up. Second, you still have position on them with the knowledge of their hands. After the flop and their action, you can decide whether or not to continue on with the hand.

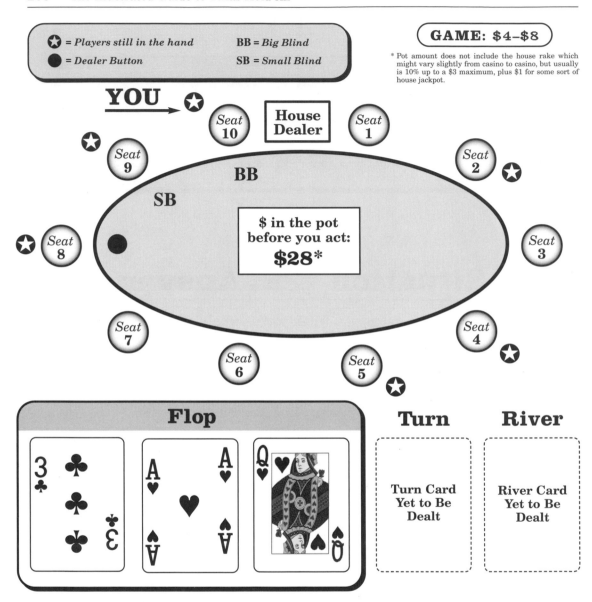

★ = *Players still in the hand*   BB = *Big Blind*

● = *Dealer Button*   SB = *Small Blind*

GAME: $4–$8

* Pot amount does not include the house rake which might vary slightly from casino to casino, but usually is 10% up to a $3 maximum, plus $1 for some sort of house jackpot.

YOU ★

Seat 10

House Dealer

Seat 1

Seat 9

Seat 2

BB

SB

$ in the pot before you act:

$28*

Seat 8

Seat 3

Seat 7

Seat 4

Seat 6

Seat 5

Flop

3♣   A♥ A♥   Q♥

Turn

Turn Card Yet to Be Dealt

River

River Card Yet to Be Dealt

Pocket

4♦   3♦

Situation #89

You received 4-3 suited in your pocket while in the big blind position. Since there were five callers and no raisers before the flop, when it was your turn to act you said, "Big enough," indicating a call. After the flop, Seat 9 bet $4. It is now your turn to act. Do you fold, call the $4, or raise to $8, and why?

Starting Hand (Pocket): **4♦ 3♦**

This Pocket's Win Rate: **1.6%**

Win Rate Rank: **110 of 169 possible**

Situation #89: Answer

The only reason you're still in this hand is because it didn't cost you anything more than the required big blind bet. You flopped bottom pair and no more.

To stay in this hand with five other players and an Ace and a Queen already on the board would border on suicide, because your only realistic chance of winning this hand is to catch another 3. To catch another 3 would require you to be, in effect, **chasing** a 3, and there are only two 3s left in the deck out of forty-seven possible cards. Not very good odds, is it? Chasing is a poor way to play Texas Hold'em.

Even if you catch another 4 for two pair, you can almost rest assured several players already have at least a pair of Aces, Queens, or a pocket pair bigger than your pair of 3s, and if they pair up their other hole card or a board card, their two pair or three of a kind will beat your two pair.

Fold the hand now before you get in any deeper.

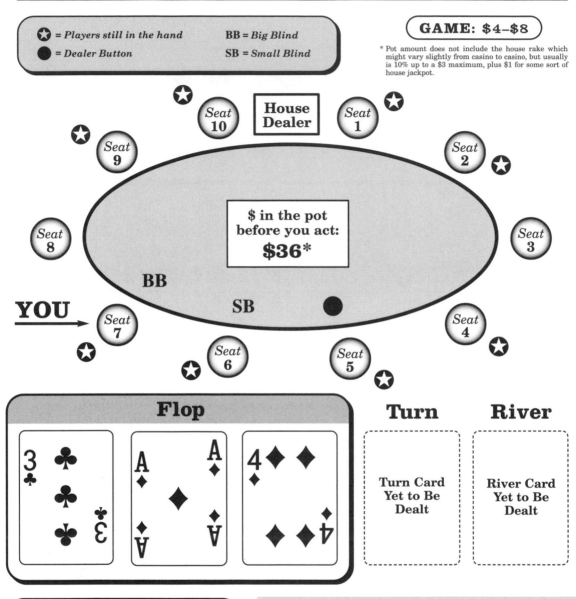

* = *Players still in the hand*   BB = *Big Blind*

● = *Dealer Button*   SB = *Small Blind*

GAME: $4–$8

* Pot amount does not include the house rake which might vary slightly from casino to casino, but usually is 10% up to a $3 maximum, plus $1 for some sort of house jackpot.

Seat 10 | House Dealer | Seat 1

Seat 9

Seat 2

$ in the pot before you act:
$36*

Seat 8

Seat 3

BB

YOU → Seat 7

SB

Seat 4

Seat 6

Seat 5

Flop

3♣ A♦ A♦ 4♦♦

Turn

Turn Card Yet to Be Dealt

River

River Card Yet to Be Dealt

Pocket

5♥ 2♠

Situation #90

Situations 90–92 all deal with the same hand at the last three betting stages.

You received 5-2 unsuited in your pocket while in the big blind position. Since there were seven callers and no raisers before the flop, you declined to raise, announcing, "Big enough." After the flop, Seat 6 bet $4. It is now your turn to act. Do you fold, call the $4, or raise to $8, and why?

Starting Hand (Pocket): **5♥ 2♠**

This Pocket's Win Rate: **0.3%**

Win Rate Rank: **160 of 169 possible**

Situation #90: Answer

Even though you have one of the worst possible starting hands, you were allowed to stay in the pot because no one raised. And now you've flopped the nuts. Oftentimes after flopping the nuts it is wise to just check or call in order to keep as many players in the pot as long as possible so as to make a bigger pot that you ultimately expect to win.

That is not the case in this instance. Yes, you flopped the nuts, but there are seven other players in the hand and there is no telling what some of them might have stayed in on. (For example, maybe the small blind stayed in on 5-6 suited for $2. Now look what he has, especially if they're Diamonds.) Maybe the first bettor in has pocket Aces but got no one to raise him. Now all he has to do is pair the board and his full house will bury your straight. And don't forget the obvious, the Diamond draw.

Since there are so many possible ways for you to eventually lose on this nuts hand, you should raise right now and try to drive some of your opponents out of the hand.

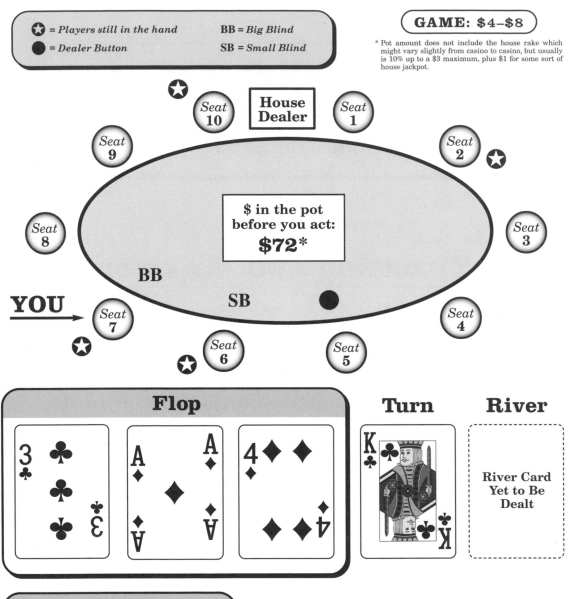

★ = *Players still in the hand*   BB = *Big Blind*

● = *Dealer Button*   SB = *Small Blind*

GAME: $4–$8

* Pot amount does not include the house rake which might vary slightly from casino to casino, but usually is 10% up to a $3 maximum, plus $1 for some sort of house jackpot.

House Dealer

Seat 10
Seat 1
Seat 9
Seat 2
Seat 8
Seat 3

$ in the pot before you act:

$72*

BB
SB

YOU →

Seat 7
Seat 6
Seat 5
Seat 4

Flop

3♣   A♦ A♦   4♦

Turn

K♣

River

River Card Yet to Be Dealt

Pocket

5♥   2♠

Situation #91

Situations 90–92 all deal with the same hand at the last three betting stages.

Your raise after the flop succeeded in getting four players to fold. The other three all called your raise. After the turn, Seat 6 again bet under the gun, this time $8. With two players still to act after you, do you fold, call the $8, or raise to $16, and why?

Starting Hand (Pocket): **5♥ 2♠**

This Pocket's Win Rate: **0.3%**

Win Rate Rank: **160 of 169 possible**

Situation #91: Answer

The worst you can do at this point is split the pot with another player, but he'd have to be holding 5-2 like you, and it's highly unlikely another player would hold such a hand. Since there is no hand that any of your opponents could possibly hold that will beat you at this time, you should raise.

The only things that developed on the turn was a possible Club flush draw and possible two pair for anyone holding Ace-King, or three of a kind for anyone holding pocket Kings.

Red flags for you to be aware of going into the river are: another Club, another Diamond, another Ace, or another King.

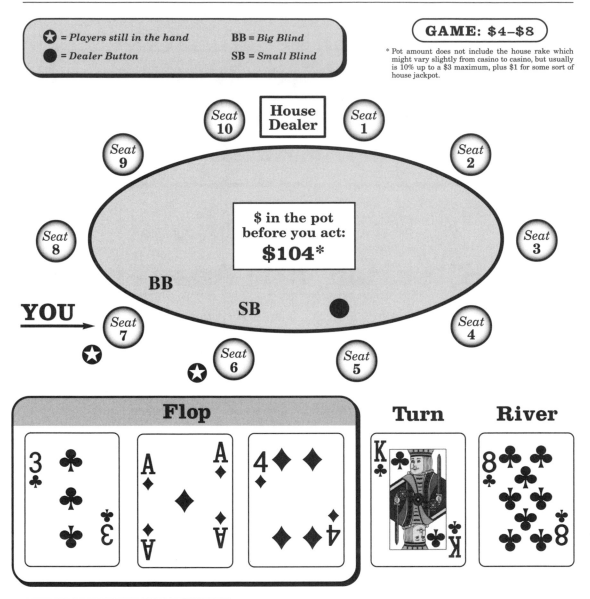

* Pot amount does not include the house rake which might vary slightly from casino to casino, but usually is 10% up to a $3 maximum, plus $1 for some sort of house jackpot.

GAME: $4–$8

★ = Players still in the hand   BB = Big Blind

● = Dealer Button   SB = Small Blind

Seat 10 · House Dealer · Seat 1

Seat 9 · Seat 2

Seat 8 · $ in the pot before you act: $104* · Seat 3

BB

YOU → Seat 7 · SB · Seat 4

Seat 6 · Seat 5

Flop

3♣ A♦A♦ 4♦

Turn

K♣

River

8♣

Pocket

5♥ 2♠

Situation #92

Situations 90–92 all deal with the same hand at the last three betting stages.

Your raise after the turn succeeded in getting two more players to fold, with Seat 6 again calling your raise. After the river card was revealed, Seat 6 once again bet under the gun. Given the possible Club flush on the board, do you fold, call the $8, or raise to $16, and why?

Starting Hand (Pocket): **5♥ 2♠**

This Pocket's Win Rate: **0.3%**

Win Rate Rank: **160 of 169 possible**

Situation #92: Answer

Raise. But why, you ask, would you raise your straight with a possible Club flush out there? Simple. Because Seat 6 doesn't have a Club flush. How do we know?

Well, let's back track on the hand. After the flop, Seat 6 came out betting. Either he had an Ace (probable) or he was seeking information (probable, too). He probably didn't have pocket Aces or he'd have checked them, afraid of running people out of a pot he could have reasonably expected to win at that point. He may or may not have been betting two Diamonds, depending on the type of player he is. In any event, once you raised his bet, he only called after that, he didn't reraise. The same thing happened after the turn card. He bet first, you raised, he called.

Now, after the river, he again bets under the gun. But the only thing that could have happened to hurt you is if he made his Club flush. If he had made a Club flush, knowing that you were already raising after the flop (when there was only one Club on the board, so he figures you don't have Clubs), and knowing there is no possible hand you could hold that could beat his flush, he'd have checked after the river, figuring you'd bet again, and then he could check-raise you.

Since he bet in the face of the flush, he's trying to project to you that he has a flush, but he almost assuredly doesn't. Raise him.

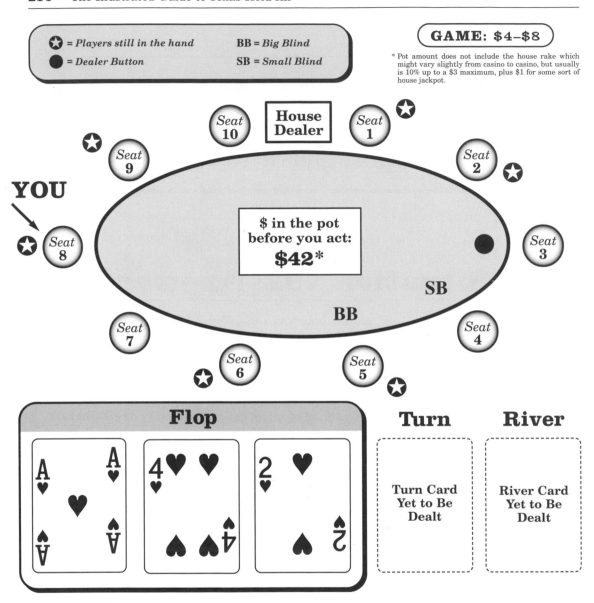

= Players still in the hand   BB = Big Blind

= Dealer Button   SB = Small Blind

GAME: $4–$8

* Pot amount does not include the house rake which might vary slightly from casino to casino, but usually is 10% up to a $3 maximum, plus $1 for some sort of house jackpot.

Seat 10   House Dealer   Seat 1

Seat 9   Seat 2

YOU

Seat 8

$ in the pot before you act:
$42*

Seat 3

SB

BB

Seat 7   Seat 4

Seat 6   Seat 5

Flop

A♥ 4♥ 2♥

Turn

Turn Card Yet to Be Dealt

River

River Card Yet to Be Dealt

Pocket

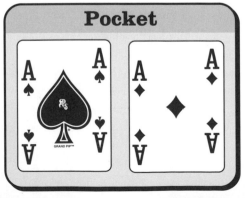

A♠ A♦

Situation #93

Situations 93–95 all deal with the same hand at the last three betting stages.

You received a pair of Aces in your pocket. You raised before the flop and received five callers. After the flop, Seats 5 and 6 both check. It is now your turn to act. With three other players to act after you, do you also check or do you bet $4, and why?

Starting Hand (Pocket): **A♠ A♦**

This Pocket's Win Rate: **86.1%**

Win Rate Rank: **1 of 169 possible**

Situation #93: Answer

Three Aces after the flop is a very nice hand indeed. But there are problems on the horizon. Not only is there a Heart flush possibility on the board, there's also a straight possibility. And a possible straight flush. Of course, you have a shot for a full house yourself, so you're not exactly without bullets in this war.

So, what to do? You could check as well, but that doesn't gain you any information. It only projects that you might be afraid of the flop, especially if you get raised and then only call the raise. If you bet now, while it's only $4, you not only could drive out some players who are holding weak draws, but you'll also gain the knowledge of who's projecting power if you get raised. And you'll be projecting power yourself.

Go ahead and make the $4 bet and see what happens.

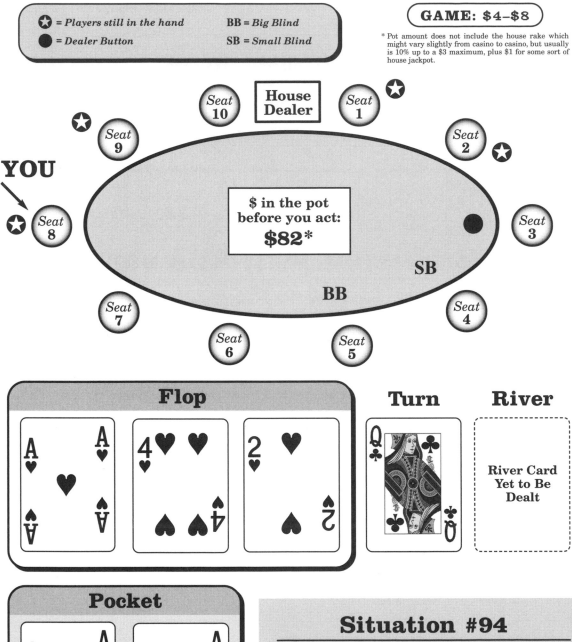

★ = *Players still in the hand*   BB = *Big Blind*

● = *Dealer Button*   SB = *Small Blind*

GAME: $4–$8

* Pot amount does not include the house rake which might vary slightly from casino to casino, but usually is 10% up to a $3 maximum, plus $1 for some sort of house jackpot.

Seat 10   **House Dealer**   Seat 1   ★

★   Seat 9   Seat 2   ★

YOU   ★ Seat 8

$ in the pot before you act:
$82*

●   Seat 3

SB

BB

Seat 7   Seat 4

Seat 6   Seat 5

Flop
A♥ 4♥ 2♥

Turn
Q♣

River
River Card Yet to Be Dealt

Pocket
A♠ A♦

Situation #94

Situations 93–95 all deal with the same hand at the last three betting stages.

Your bet after the flop succeeded in getting two players to fold (Seats 5 and 6). The other three called your bet. After the turn card, you are first to act and you check. Seat 9 bets $8 and Seats 1 and 2 both call. Do you fold, call as well, or raise to $16, and why?

Starting Hand (Pocket): **A♠ A♦**

This Pocket's Win Rate: **86.1%**

Win Rate Rank: **1 of 169 possible**

Situation #94: Answer

The Q♣ on the turn did nothing to hurt you, at least not at this point. It did, however, induce Seat 9 to bet after you checked. If you'll remember, Seat 9 only called your bet after the flop, so he was cautious of the flop. After the turn, Seat 9 bet. So what you have to ascertain is whether he was slow-playing his Heart flush or was genuinely helped by the Queen on the turn.

Since both Seats 1 and 2 called after Seat 9's bet on the turn, this would lead me to think that one or both are on Heart draws, or maybe one of them holds the fourth Ace. Either way, at this point Seat 9 is your main problem.

The only way to see how much he likes the three Hearts on the board is to bet into him. Raise to $16 and see what Seat 9 does in the face of your check-raise. If he reraises, you should just call and hope the board pairs on the river. If it does, it will give you the nut full house, which can only be beaten if another player happens to hold the 3 and 5 of Hearts (not very likely) or a pocket pair of whatever river card comes that pairs the board (four of a kind).

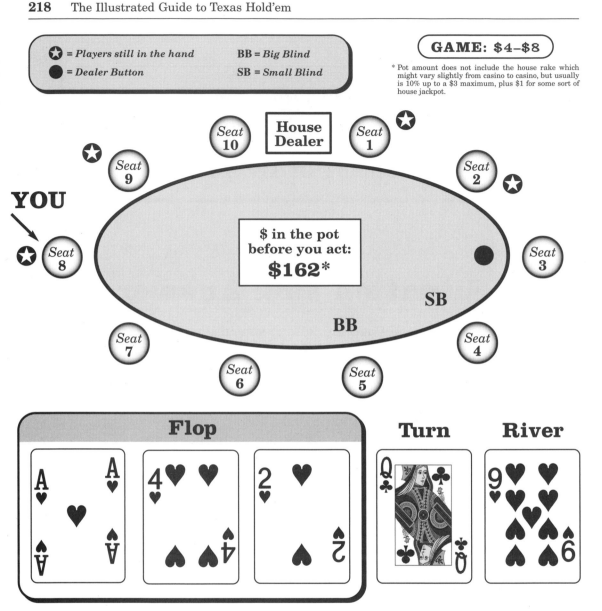

YOU

Seat 10   House Dealer   Seat 1

Seat 9   Seat 2

Seat 8 $ in the pot before you act: $162*   Seat 3

SB

BB

Seat 7   Seat 4

Seat 6   Seat 5

Flop   **Turn**   **River**

Pocket

Situation #95

Situations 93–95 all deal with the same hand at the last three betting stages.

Your check-raise after Seat 9's bet on the turn failed to drive anyone out of the pot. They all called your raise. After the river card was dealt, you checked and Seat 9 bet $8. Seat 1 raised to $16 and Seat 2 called. Do you fold, call the $16, or raise to $24, and why?

Starting Hand (Pocket): **A♠ A♦**

This Pocket's Win Rate: **86.1%**

Win Rate Rank: **1 of 169 possible**

Situation #95: Answer

This hand could be called the monster that couldn't scare. You raised before the flop. You bet after the flop. You (essentially) check-raised after the turn, yet still you have three opponents in the hand with you to the end. After the fourth Heart came on the river, leaving you with only a set of Aces, you were effectively done for, and that was evidenced by the bet, raise, and call by your three opponents.

It's hard to do with hands like this, especially when the pot is so large, but you have to fold it because one or more of your opponents has made a flush. They all three can't be bluffing.

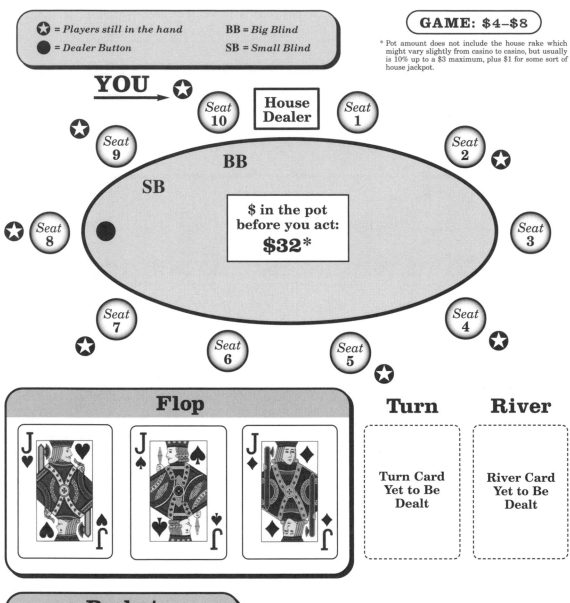

GAME: $4–$8

* Pot amount does not include the house rake which might vary slightly from casino to casino, but usually is 10% up to a $3 maximum, plus $1 for some sort of house jackpot.

YOU ➜

Seat 10   House Dealer   Seat 1

Seat 9   Seat 2

BB

SB

Seat 8

$ in the pot before you act:

$32*

Seat 3

Seat 7   Seat 4

Seat 6   Seat 5

Flop

Turn

Turn Card Yet to Be Dealt

River

River Card Yet to Be Dealt

Pocket

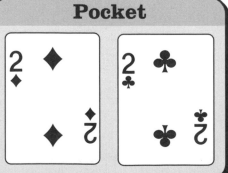

Situation #96

While in the big blind position, you were dealt pocket 2s. Including you, seven players stayed in to see the flop for one bet. When Seat 1 folded pre-flop, because of the careless way in which he held his cards, you—and only you—noticed that one of the cards he mucked was a Jack. After the flop, Seat 9, who was the first to act, bet $4. Do you fold, call the $4, or raise to $8, and why?

Starting Hand (Pocket): **2♦ 2♣**

This Pocket's Win Rate: **4.0%**

Win Rate Rank: **72 of 169 possible**

Situation #96: Answer

With six opponents still in the hand, your pocket 2s are almost worthless. The fact that you saw a Jack thrown into the muck is of practically no relevance. All it did was possibly change who the eventual winner of the pot was going to be and it likely wasn't going to be you in any event.

If any of the other six players still in the hand either has a pocket pair or pairs one of the cards in their pocket, so long as it's anything but a two, you're **drawing dead**. You have no chance.

You have only two chances to win this hand, neither of which is very enticing, and neither of which I could recommend. The first is for two more 2s to come on the turn and river, giving you four deuces. The odds of that are far higher than any possible pot odds you will be getting by staying in the hand.

The second is to bluff and bet like you have the fourth Jack. If anyone bets, raise them. To pull this off you have to commit to going all the way with it, no matter the cost. But if you run into pocket Aces, or if an Ace comes on the turn or river, you're not likely going to force an opponent out of the hand.

Fold the hand now rather continue on in the illusion that you actually have something.

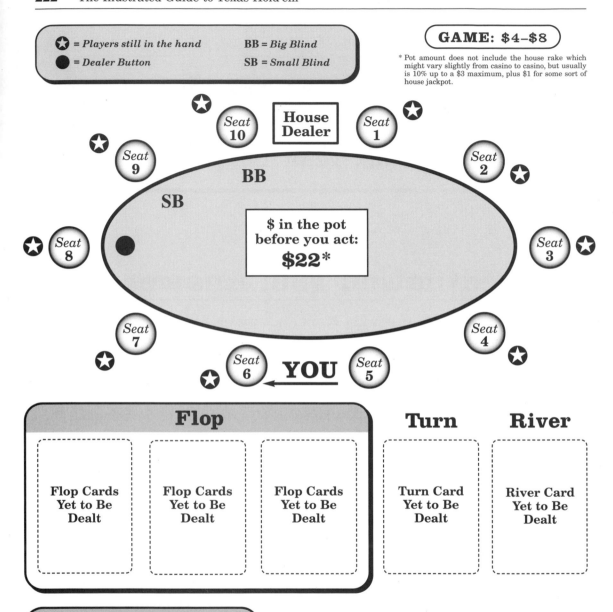

★ = *Players still in the hand*   BB = *Big Blind*

● = *Dealer Button*   SB = *Small Blind*

GAME: $4–$8

* Pot amount does not include the house rake which might vary slightly from casino to casino, but usually is 10% up to a $3 maximum, plus $1 for some sort of house jackpot.

Seat 10

House Dealer

Seat 1

Seat 9

Seat 2

BB

SB

$ in the pot before you act:

$22*

Seat 8

Seat 3

Seat 7

Seat 4

Seat 6

YOU

Seat 5

Flop

| Flop Cards Yet to Be Dealt | Flop Cards Yet to Be Dealt | Flop Cards Yet to Be Dealt |

Turn

Turn Card Yet to Be Dealt

River

River Card Yet to Be Dealt

Pocket

A♥ 5♥

Situation #97

Situations 97–100 all deal with the same hand at the four betting stages.

You were dealt Ace-5 suited in your pocket. Four of the first five players called for $4. It is now your turn to act. With four players yet to act after you (including the two blinds), do you fold, call the $4, or raise to $8, and why?

Starting Hand (Pocket): **A♥ 5♥**

This Pocket's Win Rate: **29.7%**

Win Rate Rank: **28 of 169 possible**

Situation #97: Answer

Ace-5 suited is a fairly decent starting hand, depending on your position, the number of players in the hand, etc. As of now, there are four callers in the pot with the likelihood of two more (the blinds). Having at least five other players in a hand gives you the necessary pot odds when you're trying to make straights and flushes, which this hand is trying to do at this point.

After the flop, you will be in late position, so this should be included in your decision as to whether or not to play the hand.

Certainly you won't fold the hand. The decision you face is one of calling or raising. If you call, you'll likely keep the blinds in the hand and possibly Seats 7 and 8. You'll also keep your hand disguised. If you raise, you might drive out all four of them and you'll project strength, although I doubt most of your opponents would put you on the hand you've got.

At this point, I would just call and keep the money in the pot. This hand is a perfect candidate for seeing the flop as cheaply as possible, because if you don't catch something very helpful on the flop, you'll probably have to fold.

★ = *Players still in the hand*   BB = *Big Blind*

● = *Dealer Button*   SB = *Small Blind*

Seat 10   **House Dealer**   Seat 1

Seat 9   Seat 2

BB

SB

$ in the pot before you act:

$40*

Seat 8   Seat 3

Seat 7   Seat 4

Seat 6   Seat 5

YOU →

Flop

| K♥ | K♣ | 3♥ |

Turn

Turn Card Yet to Be Dealt

River

River Card Yet to Be Dealt

Pocket

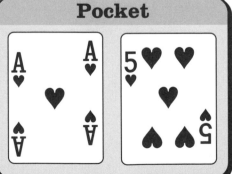

A♥   5♥

Situation #98

Situations 97–100 all deal with the same hand at the four betting stages.

Seven players stayed in to see the flop for one bet. After the flop, Seats 9 and 10 checked, Seat 1 bet $4, Seat 2 folded, and Seats 3 and 4 called. It is now your turn to act. Do you fold, call the $4, or raise to $8, and why?

Starting Hand (Pocket): **A♥ 5♥**

This Pocket's Win Rate: **29.7%**

Win Rate Rank: **28 of 169 possible**

Situation #98: Answer

You shouldn't raise because you don't even have a hand yet. You have four cards to the nut flush, and you have a long shot straight draw. What you have to be concerned about here are the two Kings. Anyone holding a King now has a set and is one card away from a full house, which will beat your flush if you hit it.

Seats 9 and 10 both checked, so unless they're planning on check-raising, they're not projecting any strength. Seats 3 and 4 only called Seat 1's bet, so they're not projecting strength either. They all seem to be cautious of the two Kings.

At this point, since only Seat 1 seems to be projecting strength, and since it's also statistically in your favor that he doesn't have pocket Kings or a pocket of King-3, call at least one more time and see what the turn brings. If you hit your flush you'll have an excellent chance of winning this hand.

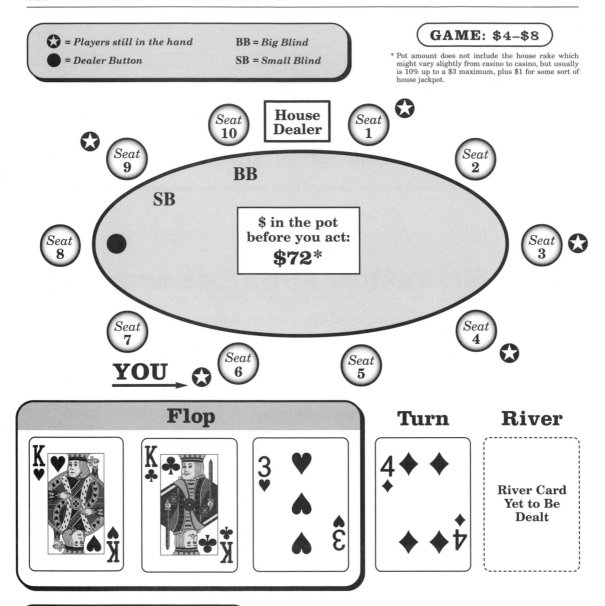

= Players still in the hand   BB = Big Blind

= Dealer Button   SB = Small Blind

GAME: $4–$8

* Pot amount does not include the house rake which might vary slightly from casino to casino, but usually is 10% up to a $3 maximum, plus $1 for some sort of house jackpot.

Seat 10   House Dealer   Seat 1

Seat 9   Seat 2

BB

SB

Seat 8   Seat 3

$ in the pot before you act:
$72*

Seat 7   Seat 4

YOU →   Seat 6   Seat 5

Flop

K♥ K♣ 3♥

Turn

4♦

River

River Card Yet to Be Dealt

Pocket

A♥ 5♥

Situation #99

Situations 97–100 all deal with the same hand at the four betting stages.

Five players stayed in the hand for one bet to see the turn. After the turn, Seat 9 checked, Seat 1 bet $8, and Seats 3 and 4 again both called. It is now your turn to act. Do you fold, call the $8, or raise to $16, and why?

Starting Hand (Pocket): **A♥ 5♥**

This Pocket's Win Rate: **29.7%**

Win Rate Rank: **28 of 169 possible**

Situation #99: Answer

Things are becoming more and more clear with this hand. Seat 1 has something worth betting and Seats 3, 4, and 9 are, like you, hanging around waiting for the card they need.

Seat 1 is betting like he has a King in his hand. Whether or not he already has a full house is open to conjecture, but it's hard to imagine he played either King-3, King-4, or pocket 3s.

Seats 3, 4, and 9 are playing like they have a pocket pair that hasn't hit a match on the board, or like they're on Heart draws.

From your perspective, you have to look at the pot odds. You're being asked to make an $8 call to win a $72 pot, or 9-to-1 money odds. You have thirteen outs (any Heart or a 2) to hit a flush or straight, either of which could likely win this pot. That means the odds against you making a flush or straight are 33-to-13, or about 2.5-to-1. With 9-to-1 pot odds, calling this hand is a great play.

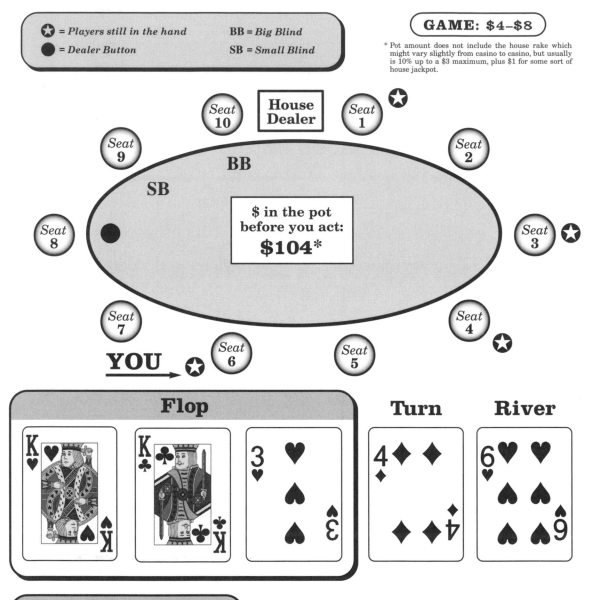

⭐ = *Players still in the hand*   BB = *Big Blind*

⬤ = *Dealer Button*   SB = *Small Blind*

GAME: $4–$8

* Pot amount does not include the house rake which might vary slightly from casino to casino, but usually is 10% up to a $3 maximum, plus $1 for some sort of house jackpot.

Seat 10

House Dealer

Seat 1 ⭐

Seat 9

Seat 2

BB

Seat 3 ⭐

SB

$ in the pot before you act:

$104*

Seat 8

Seat 7

Seat 4 ⭐

Seat 6

Seat 5

YOU ➡ ⭐

Flop

K♥ K♣ 3♥

Turn

4♦

River

6♥

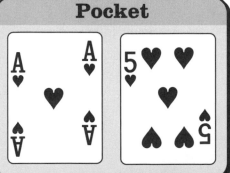

Pocket

A♥ 5♥

Situation #100

Situations 97–100 all deal with the same hand at the four betting stages.

Seat 9 folded after your call, leaving four players in the hand to see the river card. After the river card was dealt, Seat 1 checked. Seat 3 bet $8 and Seat 4 promptly raised to $16. Do you fold, call the $16, or raise to $24, and why?

Starting Hand (Pocket): **A♥ 5♥**

This Pocket's Win Rate: **29.7%**

Win Rate Rank: **28 of 169 possible**

Situation #100: Answer

Seat 1's check is an indication of one of two things. Either the third Heart on the river with its possible flush possibilities worries him, or he is holding King-6 in the pocket and is intending on raising any bet from a player who hopefully (for him) hit their flush.

Seat 3's bet would seem to indicate that he hit a flush, since it would be hard to imagine he held 5-2 or 5-7 and hit a straight. Seat 4's raise after the river would seem to indicate he also hit a flush, but is confident that his is better than Seat 3's. There is also a slight possibility that either Seat 3 or Seat 4 was holding a pocket of King-6 or 6-6 and was only checking the whole way because they weren't feeling too confident about their kicker (the 6), which now has turned into a full house.

The King-6 or pocket 6s scenarios, while possible, seem the least likely given the betting patterns during this hand. While it appears that Seats 3 and 4 both hit flushes, and that Seat 1 is worried about the flush, you should still only call the raise. The two Kings on the board still allow for the possibility of a full house, which beats your nut flush.

⭐ = *Players still in the hand*   BB = *Big Blind*

⚫ = *Dealer Button*   SB = *Small Blind*

GAME: $4–$8

* Pot amount does not include the house rake which might vary slightly from casino to casino, but usually is 10% up to a $3 maximum, plus $1 for some sort of house jackpot.

⭐ YOU ←

Seat 10   House Dealer   Seat 1   ⭐

⭐   Seat 9   Seat 2   ⭐

$ in the pot before you act:
$18*

⭐ Seat 8   BB   Seat 3 ⭐

SB   ⚫

Seat 7   Seat 4

⭐   Seat 6 ⭐   Seat 5   ⭐

Flop

| Flop Cards Yet to Be Dealt | Flop Cards Yet to Be Dealt | Flop Cards Yet to Be Dealt |

Turn

Turn Card Yet to Be Dealt

River

River Card Yet to Be Dealt

Pocket

Situation #101

Situations 101–103 all deal with the same hand at the first three betting stages.

You have been dealt King-Queen suited in your pocket. You are fourth to act. The first three players in front of you all called the $4 big blind bet. With six players yet to act behind you, do you fold, call the $4, or raise to $8, and why?

Starting Hand (Pocket): **K♠ Q♠**

This Pocket's Win Rate: **54.6%**

Win Rate Rank: **12 of 169 possible**

Situation #101: Answer

A pocket hand of King-Queen suited is a very good starting hand and has a solid degree of success as evidenced by the 54.6 percent win rate noted in the chart above.

While it is a playable hand, at this point it's still only a King-high hand. You certainly shouldn't fold, but neither should you raise. Call the $4 and do your part to build a larger pot which will give you better pot odds for the flush and straight draws you will potentially be drawing for after the flop.

Since the first three bettors didn't raise, they haven't projected powerful hands yet. If someone raises after you, there will already be enough in the pot to justify calling that raise and seeing what the flop brings.

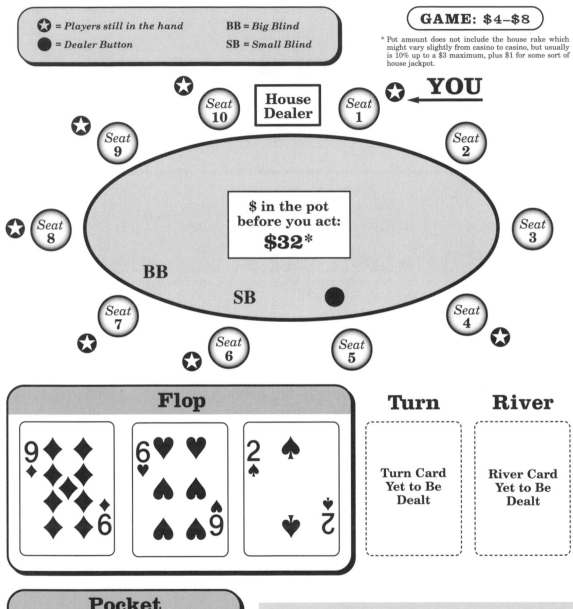

GAME: $4–$8

* Pot amount does not include the house rake which might vary slightly from casino to casino, but usually is 10% up to a $3 maximum, plus $1 for some sort of house jackpot.

Seat 10   House Dealer   Seat 1   **YOU**

Seat 9

Seat 2

$ in the pot before you act:
$32*

Seat 8

Seat 3

BB

Seat 7

SB

Seat 4

Seat 6   Seat 5

Flop   **Turn**   **River**

9♦   6♥   2♠

Turn Card Yet to Be Dealt   River Card Yet to Be Dealt

Pocket

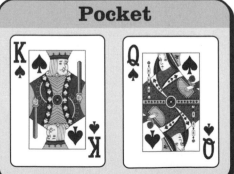

Situation #102

Situations 101–103 all deal with the same hand at the first three betting stages.

Seven players ended up staying in the hand for one bet to see the flop. After the flop, the first four players to act all checked before Seat 10 bet $4. With only one player yet to act after you, do you fold, call the $4, or raise to $8, and why?

Starting Hand (Pocket): **K♠ Q♠**

This Pocket's Win Rate: **54.6%**

Win Rate Rank: **12 of 169 possible**

Situation #102: Answer

On this particular situation, strangely enough, a case could just about be made for doing any of the three, and it would be correct. Let's take a look at it.

By folding you are negating your chance to win a pot that pot odds says is worth calling, although the actual odds of hitting a flush or straight are against you since you need to hit runner-runner for either of them. On the other hand, it may not take a flush or straight to win this hand. One big pair might do it. But to do that requires a King or Queen to come on the turn or river. The odds are against that.

By calling you will be receiving proper pot odds for the flush and straight draws, although, again, the actual odds are against you.

By raising you might possibly get four or five of your opponents to fold (since four of them already checked after the flop in front of you), leaving you with only one or two opponents, meaning it could take a lesser hand to win the pot. But if you do that, you could find yourself in a heads up situation with only a King-Queen. Any Ace or any pair will beat you.

At this point we'll go with calling this hand and seeing what the turn brings.

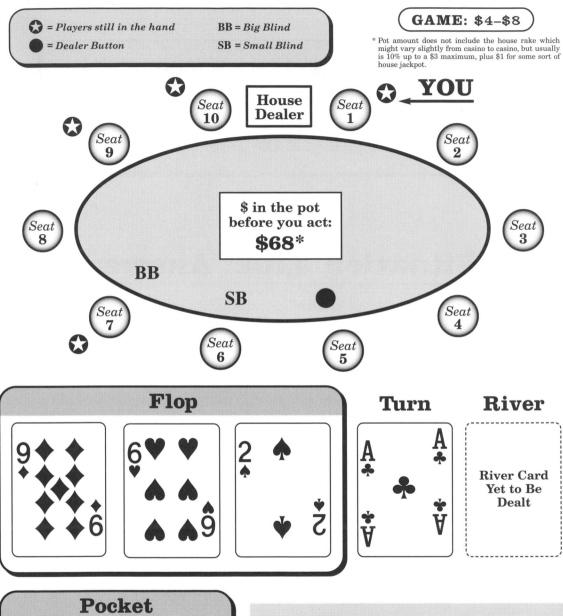

★ = *Players still in the hand*   BB = *Big Blind*

● = *Dealer Button*   SB = *Small Blind*

GAME: $4–$8

* Pot amount does not include the house rake which might vary slightly from casino to casino, but usually is 10% up to a $3 maximum, plus $1 for some sort of house jackpot.

Seat 10 — House Dealer — Seat 1 — **YOU**

Seat 9 | Seat 2

$ in the pot before you act:
$68*

Seat 8 | Seat 3

BB

SB

Seat 7 | Seat 4

Seat 6 | Seat 5

Flop

9♦ | 6♥ | 2♠

Turn

A♣ A♣

River

River Card Yet to Be Dealt

Pocket

K♠ Q♠

Situation #103

Situations 101–103 all deal with the same hand at the first three betting stages.

After you called Seat 10's bet on the flop, two other players called as well. Three folded, leaving four of you in the hand. After the turn, Seat 7 bet $8 and was called by both Seats 9 and 10. You are last to act and it is now your turn. Do you fold, call the $8, or raise to $16, and why?

Starting Hand (Pocket): **K♠ Q♠**

This Pocket's Win Rate: **54.6%**

Win Rate Rank: **12 of 169 possible**

Situation #103: Answer

The turn card was a very bad one for you. You lost any chance for a flush or straight. You didn't pair up. And now you have an overcard on the board. Seat 7 has now become the new first bettor after the Ace was dealt. This is a strong indication he has an Ace.

Also, Seats 9 and 10 called, so the Ace didn't impact them so much that they decided to fold. They've obviously got something playable and, looking at this board, it would be safe to say that all three of your opponents have at least a pair, if not two pair. Or at least still a straight draw. You have none of those.

You should always be on the scout for two things: 1) What could potentially be out there to beat you? 2) What is the best hand I can still make? The best you can hope for now is a pair of Kings or Queens. And, since neither will beat the pair of Aces that now seems to be out there, it's time to fold this hand.

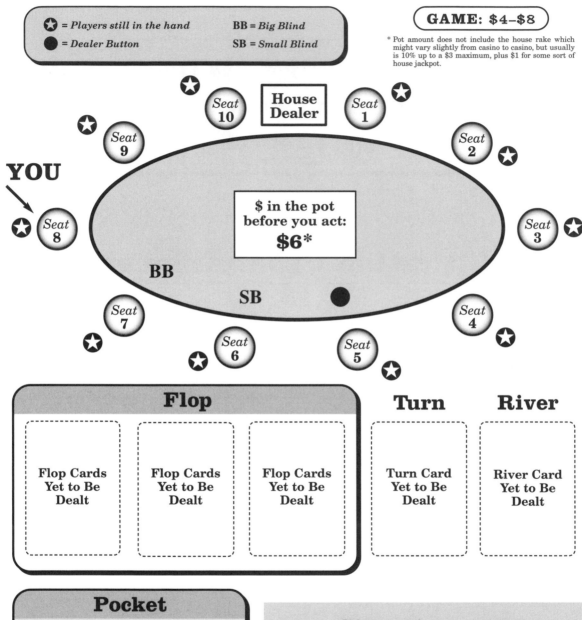

GAME: $4–$8

⭐ = *Players still in the hand*   BB = *Big Blind*

⚫ = *Dealer Button*   SB = *Small Blind*

YOU

$ in the pot before you act: **$6***

Flop

| Flop Cards Yet to Be Dealt | Flop Cards Yet to Be Dealt | Flop Cards Yet to Be Dealt |

Turn

Turn Card Yet to Be Dealt

River

River Card Yet to Be Dealt

Pocket

7♦   7♣

Situation #104

You have been dealt a pair of 7s in your pocket. You are the first to act. With nine players yet to act after you, do you fold, call the $4 big blind bet, or raise to $8, and why?

Starting Hand (Pocket): **7♦ 7♣**

This Pocket's Win Rate: **28.6%**

Win Rate Rank: **30 of 169 possible**

Situation #104: Answer

At issue here is whether or not a pair of 7s is worth playing in first position. A pair of 7s is about at the bottom end of playable hands *under the best of circumstances*. Calling or raising this hand in first position is not one of those. Having to act first without any knowledge of what the other nine players are going to do behind you is not an advantage.

At this point, your only reasonable outs are the two other 7s, and even if you catch one of them on the board it may not be enough to win. It makes no sense to put money into a pot right now when you have no knowledge or information about your opponents' hands, and when the statistical odds are so greatly against you. The smart move is to fold this hand in this position.

As a further note, when under the gun, it is *generally* recommended that you only play about a dozen starting hands. These would be:

A-A, K-K, Q-Q, J-J, 10-10, 9-9, A-K suited and unsuited, A-Q suited and unsuited, A-J suited, and K-Q suited.

The following hands could be played in first position, but you should think about folding them if you are raised:

10-10, 9-9, 8-8, A-J unsuited, A-10 suited, A-9 suited, A-8 suited, K-Q suited, K-J suited, and Q-J suited.

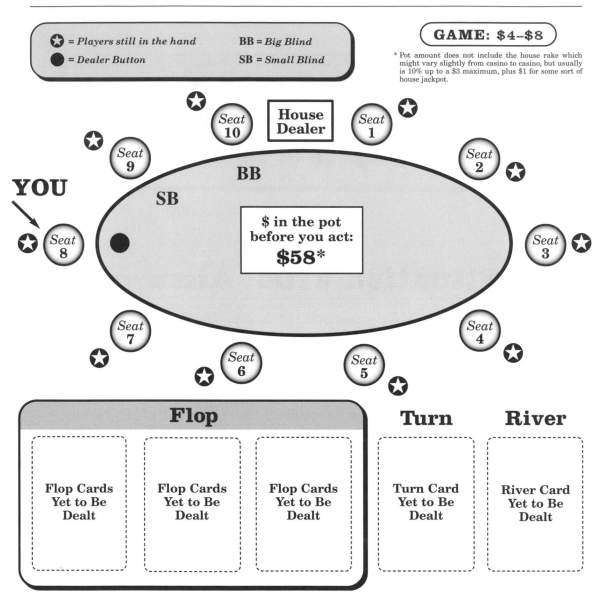

= Players still in the hand   BB = Big Blind

= Dealer Button   SB = Small Blind

GAME: $4–$8

* Pot amount does not include the house rake which might vary slightly from casino to casino, but usually is 10% up to a $3 maximum, plus $1 for some sort of house jackpot.

Seat 10   **House Dealer**   Seat 1

Seat 9   Seat 2

YOU   **BB**

SB

Seat 8   **$ in the pot before you act: $58***   Seat 3

Seat 7   Seat 4

Seat 6   Seat 5

Flop

Flop Cards Yet to Be Dealt   Flop Cards Yet to Be Dealt   Flop Cards Yet to Be Dealt

Turn

Turn Card Yet to Be Dealt

River

River Card Yet to Be Dealt

Pocket

Situation #105

You have been dealt a pair of 7s in your pocket. You are **on the button**, meaning the eighth to act before the flop and the last to act for the final three rounds of betting should you still be in the hand. Seat 1 bet $4. Seat 2 raised to $8. Seats 3 through 7 all called the $8. It is now your turn to act. With two players yet to act behind you, do you fold, call the $8, or raise to $12, and why?

Starting Hand (Pocket): **7♥ 7♠**

This Pocket's Win Rate: **28.6%**

Win Rate Rank: **30 of 169 possible**

Situation #105: Answer

You received the same starting hand as in the previous situation, but the circumstances are totally different. Instead of being first to act, you're last to act (after the flop). You now also have information on how almost all of your opponents are going to act. You also have a huge pot building which will give you appropriate pot odds for making this call.

Right now you have about 7-to-1 pot odds if you call this bet. But, as is typical for low limit Hold'em, when the first eight players all jump into the pot, the last two will almost as surely join in no matter what they hold in their hands because "the pot is too big to get out now." You are likely going to be getting 8- or 9-to-1 pot odds to see the flop. The odds of catching another 7 for three of a kind (which could be enough to win the hand without further improvement, although you could still improve) are, then:

$$(50 \div 2) \div 5 = 5\text{-to-}1$$

Your mathematical chances of catching another 7 are 5-to-1 while the pot odds (money return) is a likely 8- or 9-to-1.

Something else to consider is raising. If you raised to $12 and at least five players called you, you'd still be getting correct pot odds, and if six or more called your raise, you'd be getting better than pot odds. While most of your opponents wouldn't back out now if you raised since they are already in the pot for $8, you don't know that for sure. The best play here is to call the $8. This lets you see the flop for the least amount of money. Remember, however, that while the odds of making a set by the river are about 5-to-1, you will only make it on the flop once out of 8 times, so be prepared to fold after the flop depending on the cards brought.

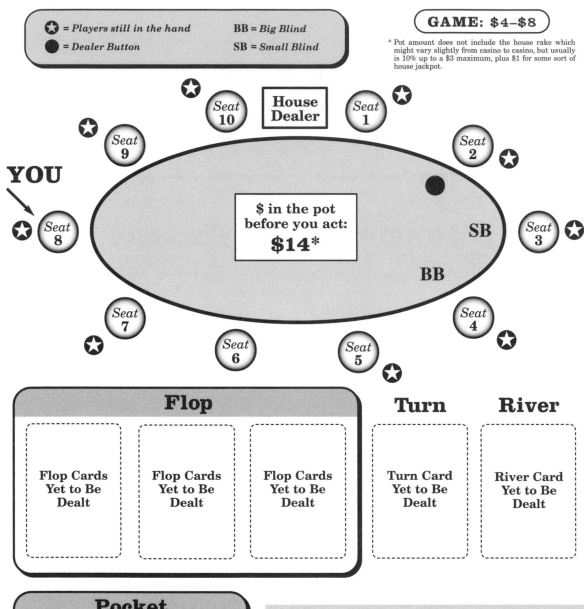

GAME: $4–$8

* Pot amount does not include the house rake which might vary slightly from casino to casino, but usually is 10% up to a $3 maximum, plus $1 for some sort of house jackpot.

Seat 10   House Dealer   Seat 1

Seat 9

YOU

Seat 8

$ in the pot before you act: **$14***

SB

BB

Seat 3

Seat 2

Seat 7   Seat 6   Seat 5   Seat 4

Flop

| Flop Cards Yet to Be Dealt | Flop Cards Yet to Be Dealt | Flop Cards Yet to Be Dealt |

Turn

Turn Card Yet to Be Dealt

River

River Card Yet to Be Dealt

Pocket

Situation #106

Situations 106–109 all deal with the same hand at the four betting stages.

You have been dealt Queen-Jack suited in your pocket. Two of the first three players to act have called the big blind bet of $4. It is now your turn to act. With six players yet to act behind you, do you fold, call the $4 as well, or raise to $8, and why?

Starting Hand (Pocket): **Q♦ J♦**

This Pocket's Win Rate: **44.2%**

Win Rate Rank: **17 of 169 possible**

Situation #106: Answer

Ranked seventeenth in win rate rank (with a healthy 44.2 percent win rate) of the 169 possible pocket hands one could hold, Queen-Jack suited is definitely a playable hand, even in middle position like this. It is not, however, a strong enough hand to raise with at this point.

You have three players in the pot already (the two callers plus the big blind) besides yourself, so you are close to getting proper pot odds on a decent drawing hand.

This hand is one that works well in multiway pots, i.e., straights and flushes. Keep in mind that you want as many callers as possible on drawing hands like this. Call this bet now, and if someone raises behind you, call that bet as well and see what the flop brings.

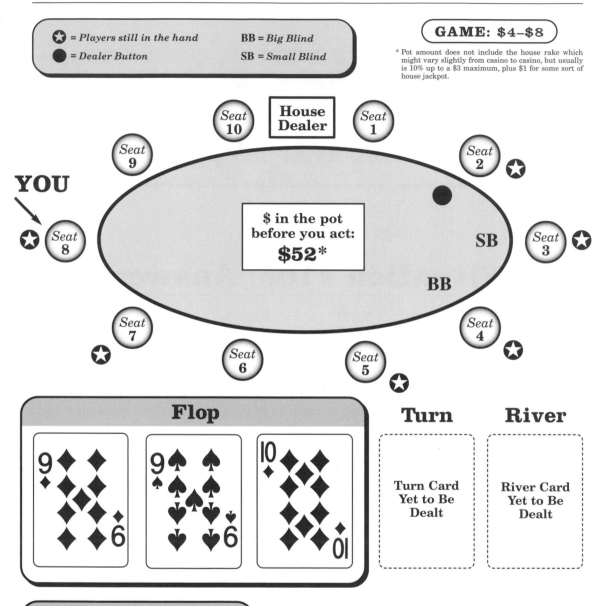

= Players still in the hand   BB = Big Blind

= Dealer Button   SB = Small Blind

GAME: $4–$8

* Pot amount does not include the house rake which might vary slightly from casino to casino, but usually is 10% up to a $3 maximum, plus $1 for some sort of house jackpot.

Seat 10   House Dealer   Seat 1

Seat 9   Seat 2

YOU

Seat 8

$ in the pot before you act: **$52***

SB

Seat 3

BB

Seat 7   Seat 4

Seat 6   Seat 5

Flop

9♦   9♠   10♦

Turn

Turn Card Yet to Be Dealt

River

River Card Yet to Be Dealt

Pocket

Q♦   J♦

Situation #107

Situations 106–109 all deal with the same hand at the four betting stages.

Six players stayed in the hand for one bet to see the flop. After the flop, Seat 3 bet $4 under the gun. Seat 4 raised to $8, and Seats 5 and 7 called. It is now your turn to act. With just one player to act behind you, do you fold, call the $8, or raise to $12, and why?

Starting Hand (Pocket): **Q♦ J♦**

This Pocket's Win Rate: **44.2%**

Win Rate Rank: **17 of 169 possible**

Situation #107: Answer

No doubt about it, the flop hit your hand really strongly, but you still don't have anything yet except the pair of 9s on the board, which everyone else has, too. And, the way Seats 3 and 4 came out betting and raising, you have to believe one or both of them are holding some combination of 9s and or 10s in their hands, probably with decent kickers.

You certainly won't fold this hand, but you can't raise it, either. You have a lot of outs for straights and flushes (seventeen to be exact). You also have six more outs for two pair (the other three Queens and Jacks). And if you do hit either a Jack or Queen on the turn or river, your two pair will include the top pair.

With twenty-three decent outs, call this hand, but keep an eye on the eventual possibilities for your opponents of the two 9s on the board (i.e., three of a kind and full house).

★ = *Players still in the hand*   BB = *Big Blind*

● = *Dealer Button*   SB = *Small Blind*

GAME: $4–$8

* Pot amount does not include the house rake which
might vary slightly from casino to casino, but usually
is 10% up to a $3 maximum, plus $1 for some sort of
house jackpot.

Seat 10

House Dealer

Seat 1

Seat 9

Seat 2

YOU

★ Seat 8

$ in the pot
before you act:
$88*

SB

Seat 3 ★

BB

Seat 7

Seat 4

★

Seat 6

Seat 5

★

★

Flop

9♦   9♠   10♦

Turn

K♠

River

River Card
Yet to Be
Dealt

Pocket

Q♦   J♦

Situation #108

Situations 106–109 all deal with the same hand at the four betting stages.

Five players remained in the hand after Seat 4's raise on the flop. Seat 2's fold put you in last position for the remainder of the way. After the turn, Seats 3 and 4 both checked. Seat 5 bet $8 and Seat 7 raised to $16. Now last to act, do you fold, call the $16, or raise to $24, and why?

Starting Hand (Pocket): **Q♦ J♦**

This Pocket's Win Rate: **44.2%**

Win Rate Rank: **17 of 169 possible**

Situation #108: Answer

The turn card brought one of your twenty-three outs and gave you a King-high straight, so now you have a made hand. But there is still plenty of danger lurking out there. With two Spades on the board there is still the possibility of a Spade flush coming on the river. The two 9s still give someone a full house possibility. Someone might even hold two Diamonds, one (or both) of which could be higher than your Queen, giving them a higher flush than you if another Diamond hits on the river.

When Seats 3 and 4 bet and raised after the flop, but checked after the turn, this made for a curious turn of events. Were they truly afraid of what the King could mean? Or, were they wanting to check-raise? And when Seats 5 and 7 now bet and raised, you have to wonder how the King suddenly seemed to help them.

Certainly you have to stay in the hand, but raising is totally out of the question at this point. There's too much going on here to get take a chance on getting burned any more than you have to. Call the $16 and see what the river brings.

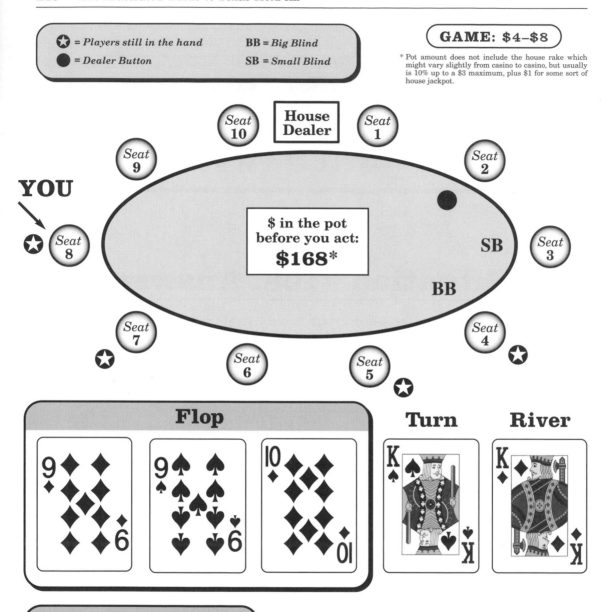

= Players still in the hand   BB = *Big Blind*

= Dealer Button   SB = *Small Blind*

GAME: $4–$8

* Pot amount does not include the house rake which might vary slightly from casino to casino, but usually is 10% up to a $3 maximum, plus $1 for some sort of house jackpot.

Seat 10

House Dealer

Seat 1

Seat 9

Seat 2

YOU

Seat 8

$ in the pot before you act:

$168*

SB

Seat 3

BB

Seat 7

Seat 4

Seat 6

Seat 5

Flop

Turn   **River**

Pocket

Situation #109

Situations 106–109 all deal with the same hand at the four betting stages.

Four players stayed in to see the river for two bets, with only Seat 3 folding. After the river card was dealt, Seat 4 bet $8, Seat 5 raised to $16, and Seat 7 called. You are last to act and it is your turn. Do you fold, call the $16, or raise to $24, and why?

Starting Hand (Pocket): **Q♦ J♦**

This Pocket's Win Rate: **44.2%**

Win Rate Rank: **17 of 169 possible**

Situation #109: Answer

What a card, huh? The board now holds possibilities of an Ace-high Diamond flush, King-high straights, quad 9s, quad Kings, and a gaggle of full house possibilities. None of which will beat your straight flush. This is what Hold'em players dream of, catching the best possible hand and having their opponents catch lots of good second-best hands.

You hit the absolute nuts on the river, so by all means, raise and hope someone reraises you, because whatever gets tossed into the pot at this point will end up in your stack a few moments after showdown.

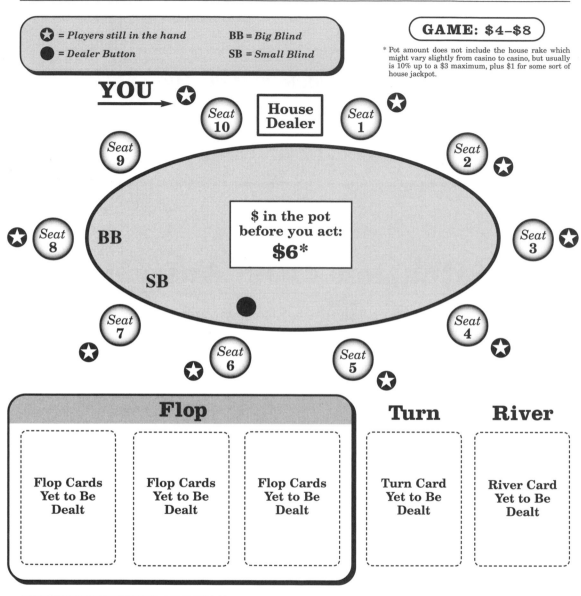

★ = *Players still in the hand*   BB = *Big Blind*

● = *Dealer Button*   SB = *Small Blind*

GAME: $4–$8

* Pot amount does not include the house rake which
might vary slightly from casino to casino, but usually
is 10% up to a $3 maximum, plus $1 for some sort of
house jackpot.

YOU →

Seat 10   House Dealer   Seat 1

Seat 9   Seat 2

$ in the pot before you act:
$6*

BB

Seat 8   Seat 3

SB

Seat 7   Seat 4

Seat 6   Seat 5

Flop

| Flop Cards Yet to Be Dealt | Flop Cards Yet to Be Dealt | Flop Cards Yet to Be Dealt |

Turn

Turn Card Yet to Be Dealt

River

River Card Yet to Be Dealt

Pocket

Situation #110

Situations 110–111 both deal with the same hand at the first two betting stages.

You have been dealt a pair of Queens in your pocket. The first player to act, Seat 9, folded. It is now your turn to act. With eight players yet to act behind you, do you fold, call the $4 big blind bet, or raise to $8, and why?

Starting Hand (Pocket): **Q♣ Q♠**

This Pocket's Win Rate: **68.5%**

Win Rate Rank: **4 of 169 possible**

Situation #110: Answer

You were dealt one of the best pocket hands you can have in the game of Hold'em, as the fourth highest win rate rank would attest. However, pocket Queens are very vulnerable because so many low limit Hold'em players will play Ace-Anything or King-Anything, and if they pair up their Ace or King on the board, you're dead.

But what your opponents might not do is play Ace-Lousy Kicker or King-Lousy Kicker for two bets. You should raise this hand now and try and drive out all the Ace/King-Lousy Kicker hands by making it too expensive to want to try and hit their big card.

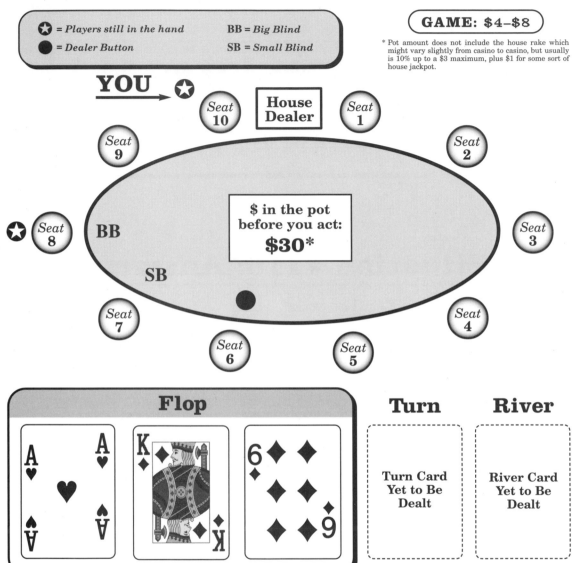

★ = *Players still in the hand*   BB = *Big Blind*

● = *Dealer Button*   SB = *Small Blind*

GAME: $4–$8

* Pot amount does not include the house rake which might vary slightly from casino to casino, but usually is 10% up to a $3 maximum, plus $1 for some sort of house jackpot.

YOU ★

Seat 10   House Dealer   Seat 1

Seat 9   Seat 2

Seat 8   BB   **$ in the pot before you act: $30***   Seat 3

SB

Seat 7   Seat 4

Seat 6   Seat 5

Flop

A♥ K♦ 6♦9

Turn

Turn Card Yet to Be Dealt

River

River Card Yet to Be Dealt

Pocket

Q♣ Q♠

Situation #111

Situations 110–111 both deal with the same hand at the first two betting stages.

Your pre-flop raise succeeded in getting everyone to fold except Seat 8 (the big blind), who called your $8 raise. After the flop, Seat 8 was first to act and he checked. Seeking information, you bet $4. Seat 8 raised to $8. Do you now fold, call the $8, or reraise to $12, and why?

Starting Hand (Pocket): **Q♣ Q♠**

This Pocket's Win Rate: **68.5%**

Win Rate Rank: **4 of 169 possible**

Situation #111: Answer

When you bet after the flop (and after Seat 8's check), you were seeking information, primarily because of the two overcards, secondarily because of the two Diamonds that flopped.

Seat 8's check-raise should provide you with all the information you need to make a decision about this hand. He's either totally bluffing or the flop helped him. Since he did call your raise pre-flop, it would be wise to assume he's not bluffing but does have some sort of a hand. In such a pre-flop situation that you presented to him with your raise, he likely called with at least a pair, Ace-Something, or two fairly high suited connectors.

You're not going to get better than even pot odds the rest of the way since it's a heads-up situation. Trying to win this hand with only long shot possibilities would be foolish. Given the two overcards, the two Diamonds, and your opponent's check-raise, you should fold this hand.

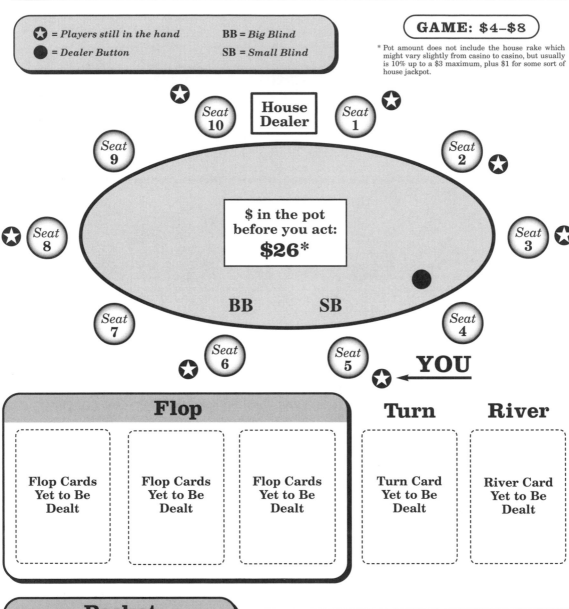

GAME: $4–$8

* Pot amount does not include the house rake which might vary slightly from casino to casino, but usually is 10% up to a $3 maximum, plus $1 for some sort of house jackpot.

Seat 10 | House Dealer | Seat 1

Seat 9

Seat 2

$ in the pot before you act:
$26*

Seat 8

Seat 3

BB   SB

Seat 7

Seat 4

Seat 6 | Seat 5 | **YOU**

Flop

| Flop Cards Yet to Be Dealt | Flop Cards Yet to Be Dealt | Flop Cards Yet to Be Dealt |

Turn

Turn Card Yet to Be Dealt

River

River Card Yet to Be Dealt

Pocket

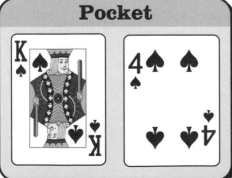

Situation #112

Situations 112–115 all deal with the same hand at the four betting stages.

You have been dealt King-4 suited in your pocket while in the small blind. Of the eight players in front of you, five called for $4. With only the big blind to act after you, do you fold, call the $4, or raise to $8, and why?

Starting Hand (Pocket): **K♠ 4♠**

This Pocket's Win Rate: **3.9%**

Win Rate Rank: **75 of 169 possible**

Situation #112: Answer

Under most circumstances it would not be correct to play King-4 suited. But let's take a closer look.

At this point, your best chance of winning this hand would be to catch a flush, since your kicker is so low in the event you make a pair of Kings. To make a flush you need to have three more Spades come on the board. Ideally, you would like to catch at least two Spades on the flop, and that will keep you in play for the turn and river, if need be, so long as the pot odds are correct. What are your chances?

Any time you hold two cards of the same suit, you have about an 11 percent chance of flopping two more of the same suit. This translates into odds of about 8-to-1. Since there is already $26 in the pot, and you are being asked to bet $2 (remember, you already had to put $2 in for the small blind anyway), this translates into 13-to-1 pot odds. So, based on pot odds, it would be correct to make this call in hopes of hitting two more Spades.

Keep in mind that holding just any two Spades wouldn't necessarily make this a correct call. If, for example, the two spades you held were 6-2, you could easily be beaten by a higher flush. By holding the King, the only flush that will beat you is one in which an opponent holds the Ace of Spades. And, if you miss the flush, you still might hit a King and have top pair, something that might allow you to keep playing the hand, depending on the rest of the flop and the betting that takes place.

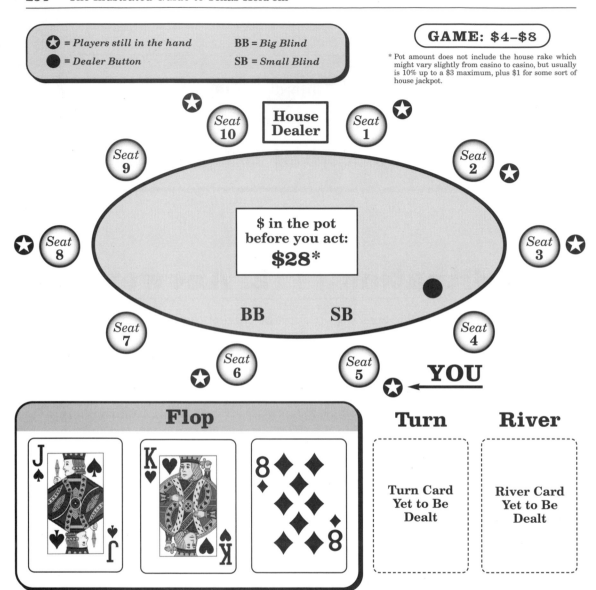

GAME: $4–$8

* Pot amount does not include the house rake which might vary slightly from casino to casino, but usually is 10% up to a $3 maximum, plus $1 for some sort of house jackpot.

= Players still in the hand   BB = Big Blind

= Dealer Button   SB = Small Blind

$ in the pot before you act:

$28*

Seat 10

House Dealer

Seat 1

Seat 9

Seat 2

Seat 8

Seat 3

BB   SB

Seat 7

Seat 4

Seat 6

Seat 5

YOU

Flop

Turn   **River**

Turn Card Yet to Be Dealt

River Card Yet to Be Dealt

Pocket

Situation #113

Situations 112–115 all deal with the same hand at the four betting stages.

Seven players stayed in to see the flop for one bet. After the flop, you are first to act. Do you check or bet $4, and why?

Starting Hand (Pocket): **K♠ 4♠**

This Pocket's Win Rate: **3.9%**

Win Rate Rank: **75 of 169 possible**

Situation #113: Answer

The flop improved your hand, giving you top pair and a third Spade. Almost as importantly, the flop didn't appear to hurt you. There's no Ace on the board, there's no possibility yet of a made straight, and the flop was a rainbow (meaning three different suits), so everyone else is at least two cards away from a flush as well.

You have something to work with here, but since it's not an overpowering hand that you hold, it's not a betting situation because of your position. A bet now could easily be raised and end up costing you more to see the turn card. Check for now and call a bet if it happens, which is likely with six other players still in the hand.

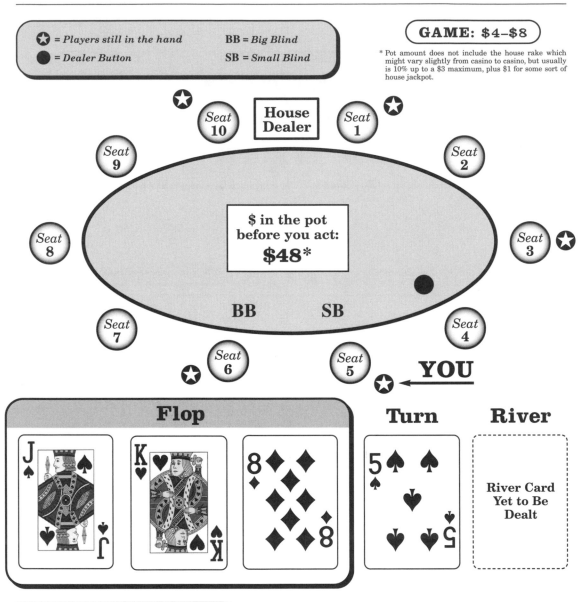

⭐ = *Players still in the hand*   **BB** = *Big Blind*

● = *Dealer Button*   **SB** = *Small Blind*

GAME: $4–$8

* Pot amount does not include the house rake which might vary slightly from casino to casino, but usually is 10% up to a $3 maximum, plus $1 for some sort of house jackpot.

Seat 10   House Dealer   Seat 1

Seat 9   Seat 2

Seat 8

$ in the pot before you act:
$48*

Seat 3

BB   SB

Seat 7   Seat 4

Seat 6   Seat 5   **YOU**

Flop

J♠   K♥   8♦

Turn

5♠

River

River Card Yet to Be Dealt

Pocket

K♠   4♠

Situation #114

Situations 112–115 all deal with the same hand at the four betting stages.

Five players stayed in for one bet to see the turn. Seat 10 bet, the other four still in, including you, called. After the turn, you are first to act. Do you check or bet $8, and why?

Starting Hand (Pocket): **K♠ 4♠**

This Pocket's Win Rate: **3.9%**

Win Rate Rank: **75 of 169 possible**

Situation #114: Answer

The situation after the turn is almost the same as after the flop except that you caught a fourth Spade, improving your chances. On the surface it would appear that the turn card was essentially a **blank**, meaning it didn't help anyone. There are still no straights possible with the four board cards shown, and the only flush possibility is Spades, which you have dominant (but not total) control of.

Unless someone has pocket Aces, two pair, or a set—and no one has yet bet like they have any of these—you are okay to go to the river. Again, just check for now and call a bet if one's made.

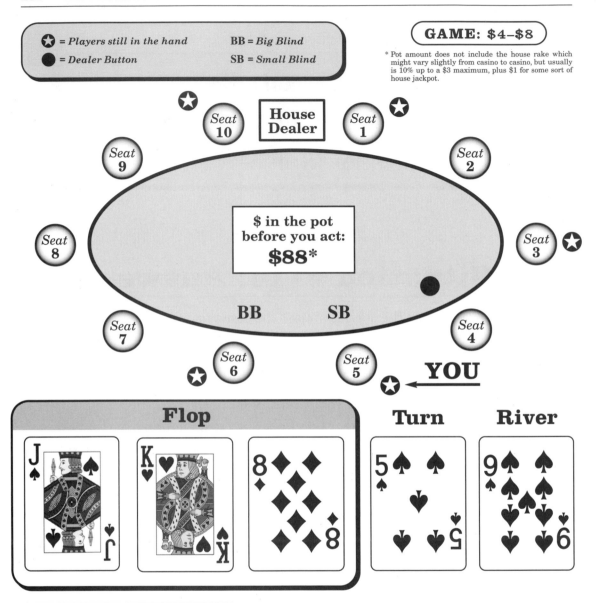

* Pot amount does not include the house rake which might vary slightly from casino to casino, but usually is 10% up to a $3 maximum, plus $1 for some sort of house jackpot.

Situation #115

Situations 112–115 all deal with the same hand at the four betting stages.

After the turn, the same five players stayed in for one bet to see the river. Seat 10 again bet and was called by the other four players. After the river, you are first to bet. Do you check or bet $8, and why?

Starting Hand (Pocket): **K♠ 4♠**

This Pocket's Win Rate: **3.9%**

Win Rate Rank: **75 of 169 possible**

Situation #115: Answer

The river card gave you a King-high flush. The only possibility of losing this hand is if one of your opponents holds two Spades, one of which is the Ace. Otherwise, you've got the nuts, and you should play it like you do until someone makes you think otherwise.

As to checking or betting, if you'll remember the betting has been very soft this hand, Seat 10 was the first to bet each of the last two hands. If you don't think the third Spade will scare him off, then check and raise him. If you think he's nervous about the third Spade coming on the board and will only check if it gets to him, go ahead and bet for value now.

If you bet and get raised, someone might be holding two Spades as well, which is fine so long as one of them isn't the Ace. You can play a raise cautiously and call, or you can reraise, depending on your assessment of the player. Personally, because the statistics are heavily on my side of anyone holding two Spades, Ace-high, I'd reraise.

⭐ = *Players still in the hand*   BB = *Big Blind*

⬤ = *Dealer Button*   SB = *Small Blind*

GAME: $4–$8

* Pot amount does not include the house rake which might vary slightly from casino to casino, but usually is 10% up to a $3 maximum, plus $1 for some sort of house jackpot.

⭐ **YOU** ←

Seat 10

House Dealer

Seat 1

Seat 9

Seat 2

SB   BB

⭐ Seat 8

$ in the pot before you act: **$26***

Seat 3 ⭐

Seat 7

Seat 4

Seat 6 ⭐

Seat 5

Flop

| Flop Cards Yet to Be Dealt | Flop Cards Yet to Be Dealt | Flop Cards Yet to Be Dealt |

Turn

Turn Card Yet to Be Dealt

River

River Card Yet to Be Dealt

Pocket

Situation #116

You have been dealt Jack-3 unsuited in your pocket while in the big blind position. Seat 3 bet $4. Seat 6 raised to $8 and Seat 8 called the raise. Everyone else folded. It is now your turn to act. Do you fold, call the additional $4 since you're already in for the $4 big blind bet, or raise to $12, and why?

Starting Hand (Pocket): **J♥ 3♠**

This Pocket's Win Rate: **0.4%**

Win Rate Rank: **141 of 169 possible**

Situation #116: Answer

The three players in the hand with you have all projected power: the early bettor, the raiser, and the player who called the raise. Your hand is atrociously weak. I have known a number of players who will call any bet into their blind for a variety of reasons, e.g., "Protecting my blind," "I'm already in for half the bet," etc.

There is no sense in throwing good money after a forced blind. By doing so, over the long term, you'd be surprised at how much money you fritter away. Fold this hand now and cut your losses.

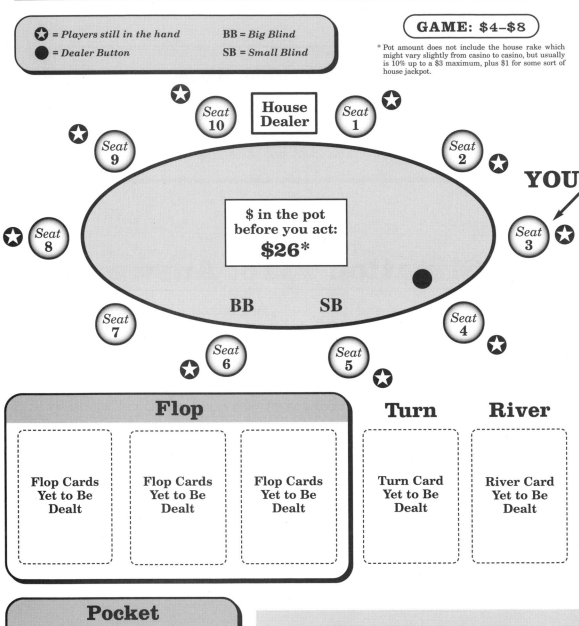

☆ = Players still in the hand BB = Big Blind

● = Dealer Button SB = Small Blind

GAME: $4–$8

* Pot amount does not include the house rake which might vary slightly from casino to casino, but usually is 10% up to a $3 maximum, plus $1 for some sort of house jackpot.

Seat 10

House Dealer

Seat 1

Seat 9

Seat 2

YOU

$ in the pot before you act:
$26*

Seat 3

Seat 8

BB SB

Seat 7

Seat 4

Seat 6

Seat 5

Flop

| Flop Cards Yet to Be Dealt | Flop Cards Yet to Be Dealt | Flop Cards Yet to Be Dealt |

Turn

Turn Card Yet to Be Dealt

River

River Card Yet to Be Dealt

Pocket

3♣ 3♥

Situation #117

Situations 117–120 all deal with the same hand at the four betting stages.

You have been dealt a pair of 3s in your pocket while in late position (seventh before the flop, ninth after the flop). Five of the six players in front of you have called the $4 big blind bet. Do you fold, call the $4 as well, or raise to $8, and why?

Starting Hand (Pocket): **3♣ 3♥**

This Pocket's Win Rate: **4.5%**

Win Rate Rank: **66 of 169 possible**

Situation #117: Answer

With a hand like pocket 3s, your only realistic expectation of winning this hand will be to hit a third 3 on the board, and even that might not be enough. But if it is, since the odds of hitting a set on the board with a pocket pair is 5-to-1 and the pot odds are already above that (6-,7-, or 8-to-1 depending on what the small blind and button do), then it would be a correct call at this point.

Keep in mind, however, that if a pair of anything higher than 3s comes on the board with this many players in the hand, at least one of your opponents will likely have hit his set, and his will beat yours, so you'll have to fold at that point.

Call this bet and be extremely mindful of the flop's potentialities.

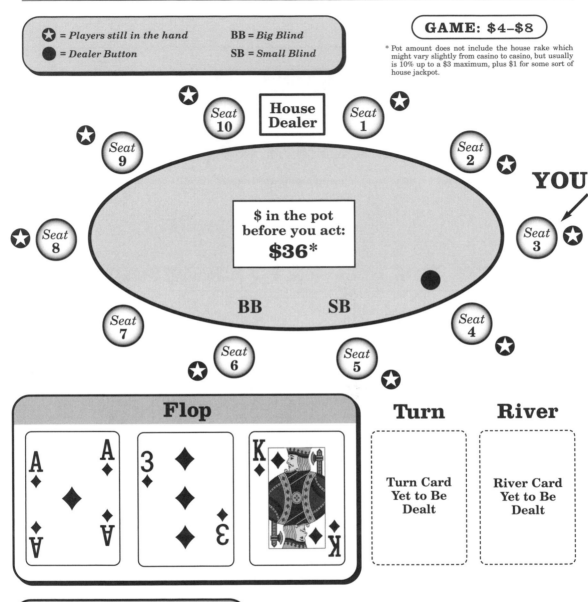

GAME: $4–$8

* Pot amount does not include the house rake which might vary slightly from casino to casino, but usually is 10% up to a $3 maximum, plus $1 for some sort of house jackpot.

★ = *Players still in the hand*   BB = *Big Blind*

● = *Dealer Button*   SB = *Small Blind*

$ in the pot before you act: **$36***

Situation #118

Situations 117–120 all deal with the same hand at the four betting stages.

It was almost a **family pot** as nine players remained in the hand to see the flop. Only Seat 7 folded. After the flop, all five players in front of you checked. Do you check, too, or do you bet $4, and why?

Starting Hand (Pocket): **3♣ 3♥**

This Pocket's Win Rate: **4.5%**

Win Rate Rank: **66 of 169 possible**

Situation #118: Answer

Boy, has this hand ever developed into a touchy situation! Especially for you. Certainly, you improved your hand. You got what you wanted to get. But…

Those three Diamonds. And the Ace. And the King. And five consecutive checks by your opponents. What are you to make of all this? For starters, don't panic. No one else knows what to make of it, either. That's why they've all checked to you.

Obviously you have to be concerned about the possibility of the Diamond flush. And pocket Aces and pocket Kings. However, no one raised before the flop. If anyone had been holding pocket Aces or Kings, they would have likely raised at that time just to avoid the mess they now find themselves in. With three Diamonds on the flop, everyone has been given reason to pause.

If you check now, your hand will stay disguised along with everyone else's (at least those in front of you). If you bet now, you will positively mislead everyone as to what you're holding. (Who'd believe with this flop that you're holding pocket 3s?) Also, if you bet now you'll likely get a number of players to fold, such as those who played a pair of 9s, or Ace-7 unsuited, and hands like that, especially those which contain no Diamonds.

Bet now and drive out some of the pesky problem hands being held by nervous players made very uneasy by this troublesome flop.

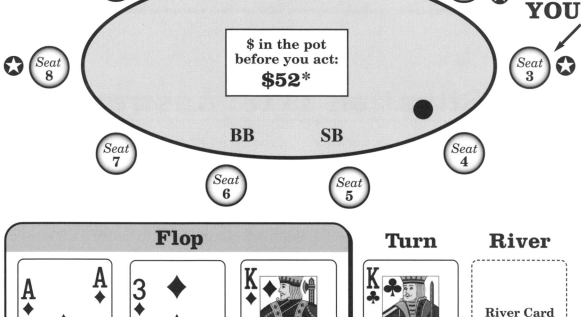

★ = *Players still in the hand*   BB = *Big Blind*

● = *Dealer Button*   SB = *Small Blind*

GAME: $4–$8

* Pot amount does not include the house rake which might vary slightly from casino to casino, but usually is 10% up to a $3 maximum, plus $1 for some sort of house jackpot.

Seat 10 — House Dealer — Seat 1

Seat 9

Seat 2

YOU

$ in the pot before you act: **$52***

Seat 3

Seat 8

Seat 7

BB   SB

Seat 4

Seat 6   Seat 5

Flop

A♦ 3♦ K♦

Turn

K♣

River

River Card Yet to Be Dealt

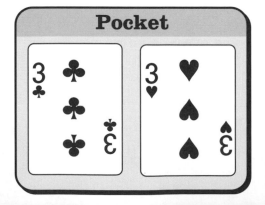

Pocket

3♣ 3♥

Situation #119

Situations 117–120 all deal with the same hand at the four betting stages.

Your bet after the flop succeeded in getting five players to fold, including the button, which now makes you last to act. Immediately after the turn card was revealed, the player in Seat 4 uttered a profanity and rolled his eyes skyward. Everyone checked to you. Do you check or bet $8, and why?

Starting Hand (Pocket): **3♣ 3♥**

This Pocket's Win Rate: **4.5%**

Win Rate Rank: **66 of 169 possible**

Situation #119: Answer

You not only bet the $8, but you smile like the cat that got the tweety bird as you're pushing your money out. When Seat 4 uttered his profanity and rolled his eyes skyward after the turn card was revealed, he practically told you he mucked a King. Not only that, he practically told everyone else at the table that he mucked a King, too. Which, by sublimation, tells all the other players you're not holding that King either. This may help convince them to call you now and/or after the river, confident that your hand isn't as powerful as you are projecting.

Since he mucked a King, that means that no one holds pocket Kings. Now your concern is if someone holds pocket Aces, but that is highly doubtful. If someone was holding pocket Aces they would have been betting them by now.

The likely worst case scenario you've got going against you is an Ace-Something or King-Something. You don't want the board to pair or a card to come up that pairs the other hole card of a player holding a King.

⭐ = *Players still in the hand*   BB = *Big Blind*

⚫ = *Dealer Button*   SB = *Small Blind*

* Pot amount does not include the house rake which might vary slightly from casino to casino, but usually is 10% up to a $3 maximum, plus $1 for some sort of house jackpot.

GAME: $4–$8

⭐

Seat 10   **House Dealer**   Seat 1

Seat 9

Seat 2 ⭐

YOU

Seat 8

$ in the pot before you act:

$100*

Seat 3 ⭐

BB   SB

Seat 7   Seat 4

Seat 6   Seat 5

Flop

A ♦ A   3 ♦   K ♦

Turn

K ♣

River

6 ♦ 9

Pocket

3 ♣   3 ♥

Situation #120

Situations 117–120 all deal with the same hand at the four betting stages.

Your bet after the turn caused Seat 8 to fold. Seats 10 and 2 both called your bet. After the river card was revealed, Seat 10 bet $8 and Seat 2 raised to $16. Do you fold, call the $16, or raise to $24, and why?

Starting Hand (Pocket): **3♣ 3♥**

This Pocket's Win Rate: **4.5%**

Win Rate Rank: **66 of 169 possible**

Situation #120: Answer

So, what are these two opponents betting and raising on? Did one of them go all the way to the river with King-6 unsuited, neither card being a Diamond? Not likely, especially in the face of the Ace and three Diamonds on the flop. Did someone go all the way to the river with pocket 6s? Again, very unlikely given the same reasons.

No, what's almost surely happened here is that both of your opponents were staying in with Diamond draws and hit them (one maybe with Queen high, the other with Jack high), exactly what you were hoping for. Neither of them has placed you on pocket Aces, pocket Kings, or Ace-King (which is correct), and both are likely feeling confident that you are holding three Kings or two pair.

Raise to $24. You don't have the nuts, but you do have the probable best hand, and that warrants a raise.

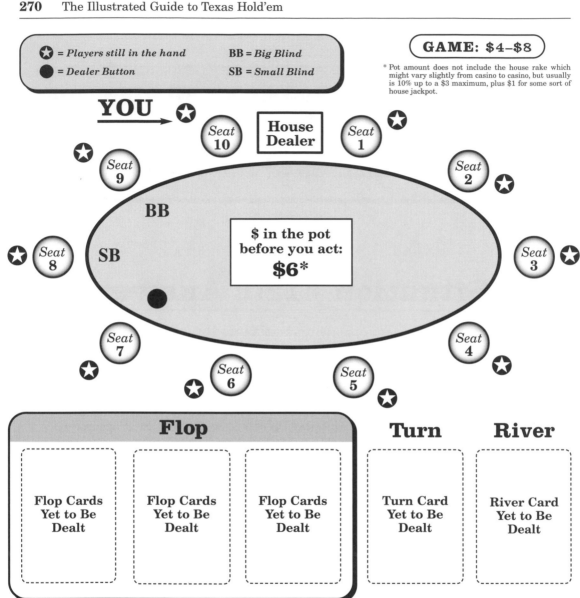

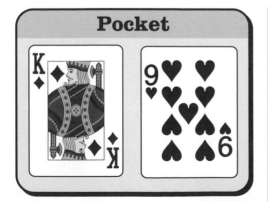

Situation #121

You have been dealt King-9 unsuited ("canine") in your pocket. You are first to act. Because you trained dogs in the military and are now a K9 police officer, the King-9 hand has become your favorite hand to play and you always play it regardless of your position. Being in first position, with the other nine players to act after you, should you just call the big blind bet of $4 or should you raise it to $8, and why?

Starting Hand (Pocket): **K♦ 9♥**

This Pocket's Win Rate: **8.2%**

Win Rate Rank: **62 of 169 possible**

Situation #121: Answer

You need to do two things. First, fold the hand. Second, get the idea of favorite hand out of your mindset; your new favorite hand becomes pocket Aces.

Playing a hand just because it's your "favorite" is foolish. If you want to become a winning Texas Hold'em player, you need to play each hand correctly based on your position, the hand's strength, the number of players involved in the hand, the size of the pot, and the pot odds.

Believe it or not, I know one player who always, *without fail,* plays 7-2 unsuited at least to the river. For some reason he won with it a few times in a row and has now been convinced that it's worth playing until he at least sees what the flop brings. He's convinced himself it's his lucky hand.

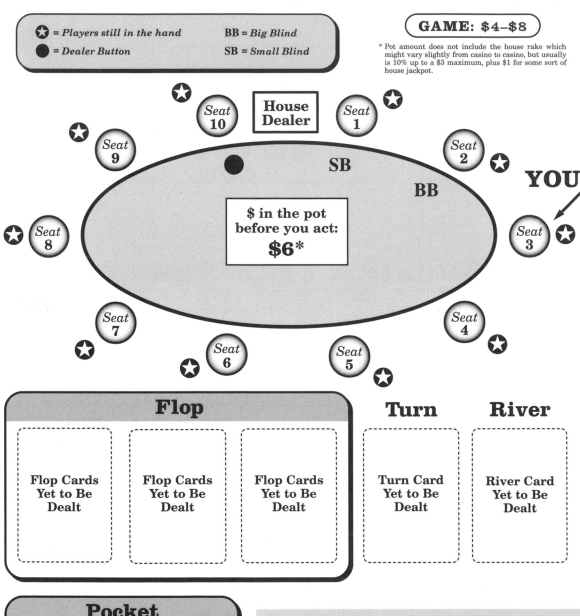

= *Players still in the hand*   BB = *Big Blind*

= *Dealer Button*   SB = *Small Blind*

GAME: $4–$8

* Pot amount does not include the house rake which might vary slightly from casino to casino, but usually is 10% up to a $3 maximum, plus $1 for some sort of house jackpot.

Seat 10   **House Dealer**   Seat 1

Seat 9   Seat 2   **YOU**

SB

BB

Seat 8   **$ in the pot before you act: $6***   Seat 3

Seat 7   Seat 4

Seat 6   Seat 5

Flop

| Flop Cards Yet to Be Dealt | Flop Cards Yet to Be Dealt | Flop Cards Yet to Be Dealt |

Turn

Turn Card Yet to Be Dealt

River

River Card Yet to Be Dealt

Pocket

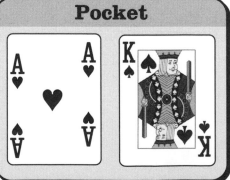

Situation #122

Situations 122–125 all deal with the same hand at the four betting stages.

You have been dealt Ace-King unsuited in your pocket. You are in first position with the other nine players all to act after you. Do you fold, call the $4 big blind bet, or raise to $8, and why?

Starting Hand (Pocket): **A♥ K♠**

This Pocket's Win Rate: **67.0%**

Win Rate Rank: **5 of 169 possible**

Situation #122: Answer

With a win rate of 67 percent, Ace-King unsuited is one of the best pocket hands you can catch in Hold'em (fifth overall out of the 169 possible pocket hands).

Since this is obviously a playable hand, the question is whether to call or raise. There is a fairly large amount of support among many professionals that Ace-King unsuited in first position is a hand that should be raised, and not called. The intent is to thin out the field pre-flop and make for a higher winning percentage, albeit with smaller pots.

Personally, I just call with this hand in low limit games because I like to build larger pots using less of my own money when I have a vulnerable but potentially powerful hand like Ace-King unsuited. This particular decision will ultimately be one of personal choice based on the games you play in and how your usual opponents typically play.

Call the big blind bet and any and all raises if they occur before the flop.

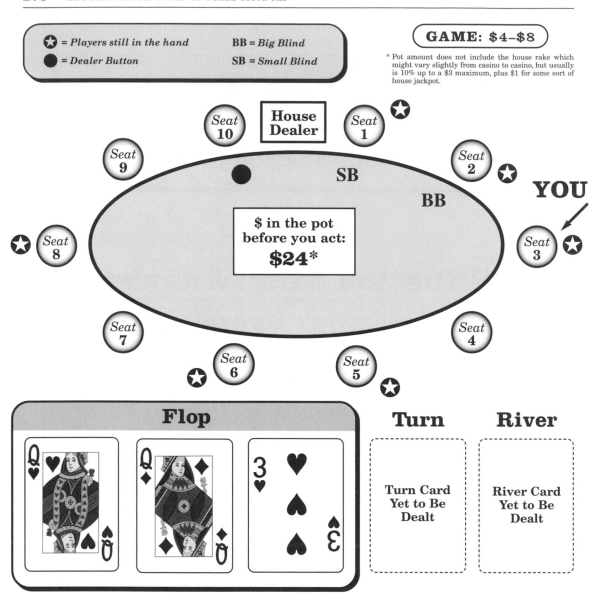

⭐ = *Players still in the hand*   BB = *Big Blind*

⬤ = *Dealer Button*   SB = *Small Blind*

GAME: $4–$8

* Pot amount does not include the house rake which might vary slightly from casino to casino, but usually is 10% up to a $3 maximum, plus $1 for some sort of house jackpot.

Seat 10

House Dealer

Seat 1

Seat 9

Seat 2

SB

BB

YOU

$ in the pot before you act: **$24***

Seat 3

Seat 8

Seat 7

Seat 4

Seat 6

Seat 5

Flop

Turn

River

Turn Card Yet to Be Dealt

River Card Yet to Be Dealt

Pocket

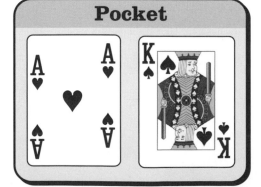

Situation #123

Situations 122–125 all deal with the same hand at the four betting stages.

There were six players who stayed in to see the flop for one bet. After the flop, Seats 1 and 2 both checked. It is now your turn to act. With three players yet to act after you, do you fold in face of the two Queens, check, or bet $4, and why?

Starting Hand (Pocket): **A♥ K♠**

This Pocket's Win Rate: **67.0%**

Win Rate Rank: **5 of 169 possible**

Situation #123: Answer

Since no one has bet before you, you obviously won't fold at this point. The flop only helped your hand in a minor way (the two Hearts). The two Queens are potentially dangerous so you need to proceed with caution. You could bet for information, but then you'd be setting yourself up to be raised, and if everyone called to you, you'd have to consider calling because of the large pot, thereby putting you into the turn for $8 instead of a possible $4.

Also, it's entirely possible no one is holding a Queen in the pocket. If that's the case, your hand isn't that bad. At this point it would be best to check and see what the three players behind you do.

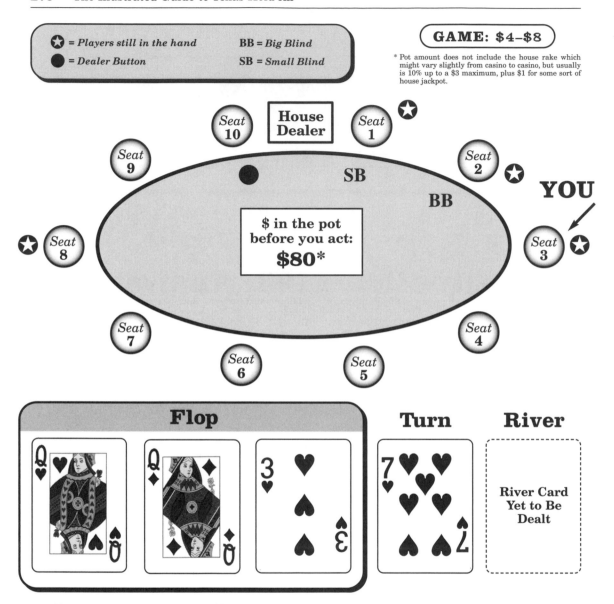

= *Players still in the hand*   BB = *Big Blind*

= *Dealer Button*   SB = *Small Blind*

GAME: $4–$8

* Pot amount does not include the house rake which might vary slightly from casino to casino, but usually is 10% up to a $3 maximum, plus $1 for some sort of house jackpot.

Seat 10

House Dealer

Seat 1

Seat 9

Seat 2

YOU

SB

BB

$ in the pot before you act:
$80*

Seat 8

Seat 3

Seat 7

Seat 4

Seat 6

Seat 5

Flop

Turn   **River**

River Card Yet to Be Dealt

Pocket

Situation #124

Situations 122–125 all deal with the same hand at the four betting stages.

All six players checked after the flop. After the turn, Seat 1 bet $8. Seat 2 and you both called. Seats 5 and 6 both folded. Seat 8 raised to $16. Seats 1 and 2 both called. It is now your turn to act. Do you fold, call the additional $8, or raise to $24, and why?

Starting Hand (Pocket): **A♥ K♠**

This Pocket's Win Rate: **67.0%**

Win Rate Rank: **5 of 169 possible**

Situation #124: Answer

Seat 8 is betting like he either hit his Heart flush or was slow playing three Queens. If he does have three Queens without the full house, or if he hit his Heart flush on the turn, you can still beat him on the river if another Heart comes. The question is, what are the pot odds and are they worth the call?

You are being asked to make a bet of $8 in order to win $80. This is easy to compute: 10-to-1 pot odds. Now, what are the actual odds of hitting that last Heart?

Of the forty-six unseen cards, nine are Hearts. So, 46 - 9 = 37. That makes the formula:

37 ÷ 9 = 4.11-to-1, or roughly 4-to-1

Therefore, your actual odds of hitting a flush are just a bit over 4-to-1 for a payoff of 10-to-1. This is an easy call.

One thing to consider, however, is if the opponent who raised did hit a Heart flush, that would mean there are only seven Hearts available. In that case, the odds of catching another Heart on the river would be about 5.3-to-1. (37 ÷ 7 = 5.29-to-1). Either way, this is still a good call.

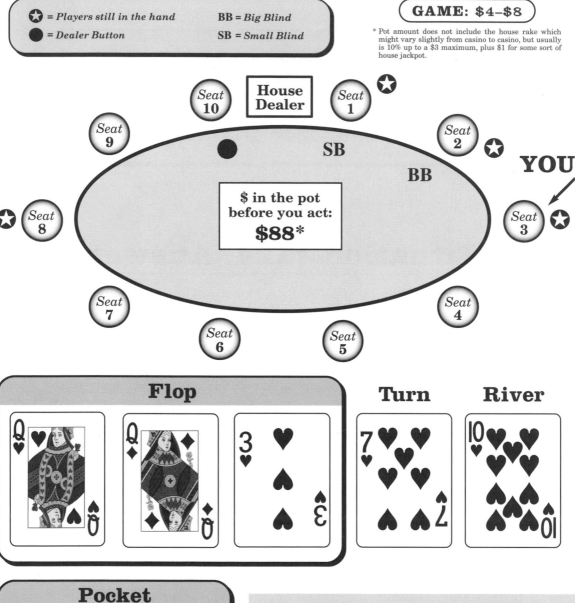

GAME: $4–$8

⭐ = *Players still in the hand*   BB = *Big Blind*

● = *Dealer Button*   SB = *Small Blind*

* Pot amount does not include the house rake which might vary slightly from casino to casino, but usually is 10% up to a $3 maximum, plus $1 for some sort of house jackpot.

House Dealer

Seat 10 Seat 1 Seat 9 Seat 2 Seat 8 Seat 3 Seat 7 Seat 4 Seat 6 Seat 5

SB

BB

YOU

$ in the pot before you act:

$88*

Flop

Turn

River

Pocket

Situation #125

Situations 122–125 all deal with the same hand at the four betting stages.

After you called Seat 8's raise, the river card was dealt. Seats 1 and 2 both checked. It is now your turn to act. With only Seat 8 (the player who raised after the turn) to act behind you, do you check or bet $8, and why?

Starting Hand (Pocket): **A♥ K♠**

This Pocket's Win Rate: **67.0%**

Win Rate Rank: **5 of 169 possible**

Situation #125: Answer

You made the nut flush on the river. The question now is whether or not any of your opponents, especially Seat 8, made a full house. It is unlikely that either Seat 1 or Seat 2 is holding a full house since the whole way they haven't bet like they have strong hands.

That leaves Seat 8. Since he already raised after the turn and before the 10♥ came on the river, we can assume the river card doesn't much matter to him. The only way it would is if he was holding a pocket of Queen-10 or 10-10. Statistically it's possible, but not likely.

A better hand to put him on would be a flush or an overpair (pocket Kings or Aces) which he bet as a semi-bluff when the third Heart came on the turn. Either way, the proper move is to bet now for value with the assumption you have the highest hand. If Seat 8, or either of the other two players, raises you, then you can make the determination as to whether to just call or reraise them. In any event, you will not fold this hand. You have the probable best hand, so make them show they've beaten you if they raise.

★ = *Players still in the hand* BB = *Big Blind*

● = *Dealer Button* SB = *Small Blind*

GAME: $4–$8

* Pot amount does not include the house rake which might vary slightly from casino to casino, but usually is 10% up to a $3 maximum, plus $1 for some sort of house jackpot.

YOU → ★

Seat 9

Seat 10

House Dealer

Seat 1

Seat 2 ★

★

★

$ in the pot before you act: $18*

Seat 8 ★

● Seat 3 ★

SB

BB

Seat 7

Seat 4 ★

★

Seat 6 ★

Seat 5 ★

★

Flop

| Flop Cards Yet to Be Dealt | Flop Cards Yet to Be Dealt | Flop Cards Yet to Be Dealt |

Turn

Turn Card Yet to Be Dealt

River

River Card Yet to Be Dealt

Pocket

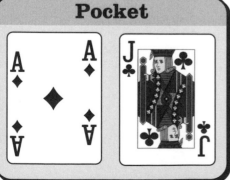

Situation #126

Situations 126–127 both deal with the same hand at the first two betting stages.

You have been dealt Ace-Jack unsuited in your pocket. The first three players to act in front of you all called the big blind bet of $4. It is now your turn to act. With six players yet to act after you, do you fold, call the $4 as well, or raise to $8, and why?

Starting Hand (Pocket): **A♦ J♣**

This Pocket's Win Rate: **48.9%**

Win Rate Rank: **15 of 169 possible**

Situation #126: Answer

Ace-Jack unsuited is a decent calling hand, nothing more. While you can certainly play this hand, it would not be correct to raise because, essentially, you have very little at this point except potential.

Call the bet and, if anyone raises, call that, too, so long as there are at least five other players in the pot (there are three already). This way you'll be getting decent pot odds on a drawing hand to at least see the flop.

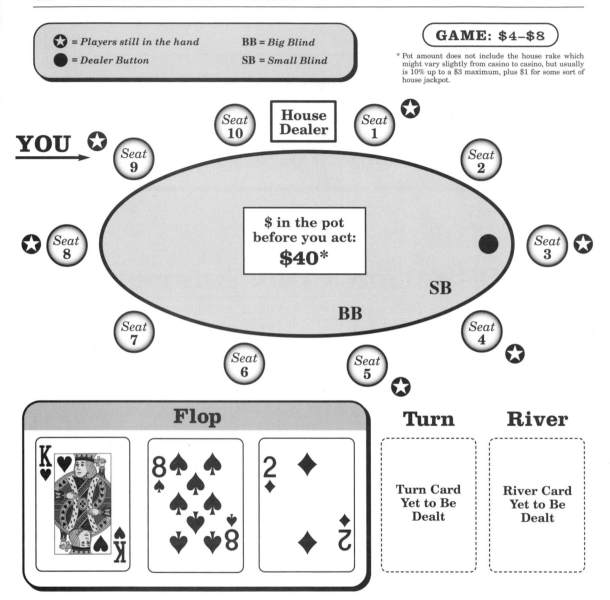

★ = *Players still in the hand*   BB = *Big Blind*

● = *Dealer Button*   SB = *Small Blind*

GAME: $4–$8

*Pot amount does not include the house rake which might vary slightly from casino to casino, but usually is 10% up to a $3 maximum, plus $1 for some sort of house jackpot.

Seat 10

House Dealer

Seat 1 ★

YOU ★

Seat 9

Seat 2

Seat 8 ★

$ in the pot before you act:
$40*

Seat 3 ★

SB

BB

Seat 7

Seat 4

Seat 6

Seat 5 ★

Flop

Turn

River

Turn Card Yet to Be Dealt

River Card Yet to Be Dealt

Pocket

Situation #127

Situations 126–127 both deal with the same hand at the first two betting stages.

Six players stayed in to see the flop for one bet. After the flop, Seat 4 bet $4 and Seat 5 called. Seat 8 then raised to $8. It is now your turn to act. Do you fold, call the $8, or raise to $12, and why?

Starting Hand (Pocket): **A♦ J♣**

This Pocket's Win Rate: **48.9%**

Win Rate Rank: **15 of 169 possible**

Situation #127: Answer

This flop completely missed your hand. Even though there are no pairs on the board, even though it was a **rainbow** flop (three different suits on the flop), and even though you have an overcard (your Ace), you should fold this hand now.

Seat 8 made the decision very easy by raising, but even if he had only called (or even folded), you would still have folded this hand by virtue of the bets by Seats 4 and 5. You've got nothing other than Ace high. You can't make a flush and you need runner-runner (a Queen and a 10) to make a straight. Muck this hand and wait for the next one.

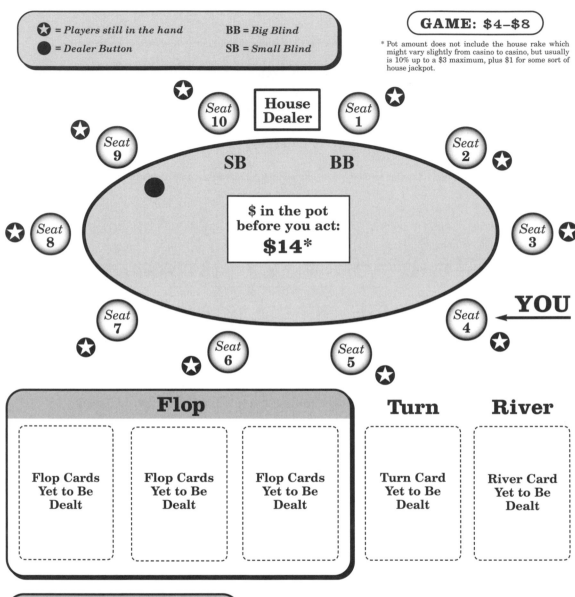

★ = *Players still in the hand*   BB = *Big Blind*

● = *Dealer Button*   SB = *Small Blind*

GAME: $4–$8

* Pot amount does not include the house rake which might vary slightly from casino to casino, but usually is 10% up to a $3 maximum, plus $1 for some sort of house jackpot.

Seat 10   House Dealer   Seat 1

Seat 9   SB   BB   Seat 2

Seat 8   **$ in the pot before you act: $14***   Seat 3

Seat 7   Seat 4   **YOU**

Seat 6   Seat 5

Flop

| Flop Cards Yet to Be Dealt | Flop Cards Yet to Be Dealt | Flop Cards Yet to Be Dealt |

Turn

Turn Card Yet to Be Dealt

River

River Card Yet to Be Dealt

Pocket

A♠   Q♠

Situation #128

Situations 128–131 all deal with the same hand at the first two betting stages.

You have been dealt Ace-Queen suited in your pocket. The first two players to act both called the $4 big blind bet. It is now your turn to act. Do you fold, call the $4 as well, or raise to $8, and why?

Starting Hand (Pocket): **A♠ Q♠**

This Pocket's Win Rate: **64.9%**

Win Rate Rank: **6 of 169 possible**

Situation #128: Answer

Ace-Queen suited is, simply put, a pretty hand to see in your pocket. But in spite of its high win rate of nearly 65 percent, at this point it is still just a calling hand. Remember, you still have seven players to act after you. Certainly, if anyone raises you will call but it's always best to see the flop as cheaply as possible when you have a calling hand.

Calling hands such as this can quickly disappear with the flop. For example, if three red cards come on the flop, your Spades are dead. And if three small or medium cards come up, your big cards are dead. At least if you had a pair of Aces or a pair of Queens you could continue on with many hands after the flop, even if it missed you entirely. With hands such as this, you can't play them if the flop completely misses you.

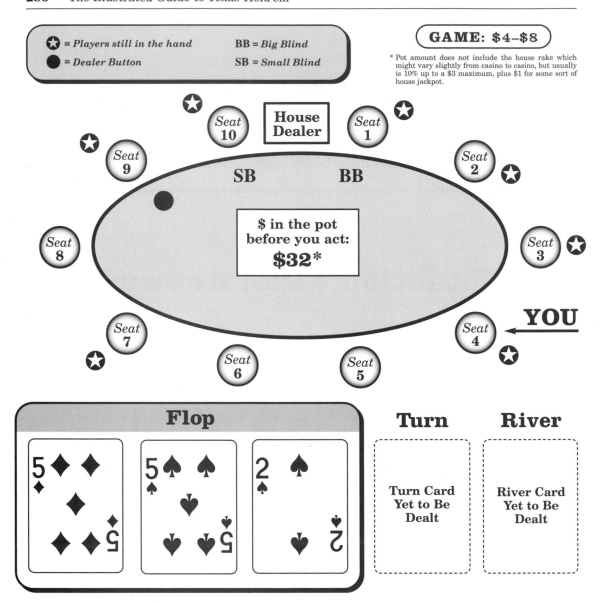

GAME: $4–$8

* Pot amount does not include the house rake which might vary slightly from casino to casino, but usually is 10% up to a $3 maximum, plus $1 for some sort of house jackpot.

⭐ = *Players still in the hand*   BB = *Big Blind*

● = *Dealer Button*   SB = *Small Blind*

House Dealer

Seat 10 · Seat 1 · Seat 2 · Seat 3 · Seat 4 · Seat 5 · Seat 6 · Seat 7 · Seat 8 · Seat 9

SB   BB

$ in the pot before you act:
$32*

YOU

Flop

Turn — Turn Card Yet to Be Dealt

River — River Card Yet to Be Dealt

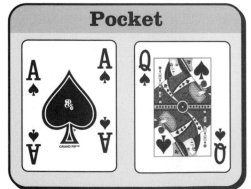

Pocket

Situation #129

Situations 128–131 all deal with the same hand at the first two betting stages.

Seven players stayed in to see the flop for one bet. After the flop, Seats 10, 1, and 2 all checked. Seat 3 bet $4. With two players yet to act after you, do you fold, call the $4, or raise to $8, and why?

Starting Hand (Pocket): **A♠ Q♠**

This Pocket's Win Rate: **64.9%**

Win Rate Rank: **6 of 169 possible**

Situation #129: Answer

The flop hit you quite nicely, giving you four Spades of the nut flush. Of concern, however, are the two 5s on the board. With seven players still active, it's possible someone is holding a 5 in their hand. By just calling Seat 3's bet, you will keep your hand disguised and at the same time encourage other players to stay in as well, thereby building a larger pot.

If you raise Seat 3's bet, you'll likely drive players out of the pot and you want to keep them around as long as possible in case your flush comes on the turn or river, hopefully without the board pairing again.

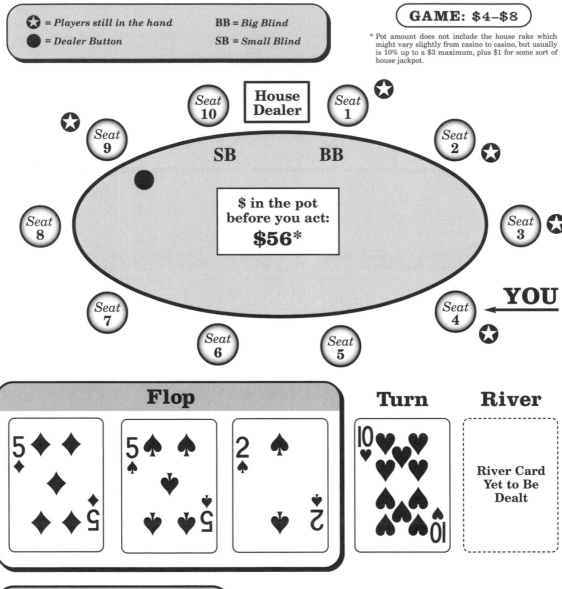

★ = *Players still in the hand*

● = *Dealer Button*

BB = *Big Blind*

SB = *Small Blind*

GAME: $4–$8

* Pot amount does not include the house rake which might vary slightly from casino to casino, but usually is 10% up to a $3 maximum, plus $1 for some sort of house jackpot.

Seat 10

House Dealer

Seat 1 ★

★ Seat 9

Seat 2

SB   BB

Seat 3 ★

Seat 8

$ in the pot before you act: $56*

★ Seat 4 ← YOU

Seat 7

Seat 6

Seat 5

Flop

5♦   5♠   2♠

Turn

10♥

River

River Card Yet to Be Dealt

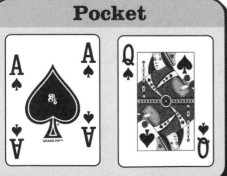

Pocket

A♠   Q♠

Situation #130

Situations 128–131 all deal with the same hand at the first two betting stages.

Five players stayed in to see the turn for one bet. After the turn, Seats 1 and 2 both checked. Seat 3 again was the first to bet, this time $8. It is now your turn to act. With $56 in the pot and only one player yet to act behind you, do you fold, call the $8, or raise to $16, and why?

Starting Hand (Pocket): **A♠ Q♠**

This Pocket's Win Rate: **64.9%**

Win Rate Rank: **6 of 169 possible**

Situation #130: Answer

Other than Seat 3, no one is projecting any power right now. If Seat 3 does have a 5 in his hand, it's likely that he doesn't have anything with it to make a full house (a 2 or a 10). When players stay in with a 5 in their hand, it's *usually* in conjunction with any of the following: another 5, a 4 or 6 of the same suit as the 5 they hold, or an Ace or King of the same suit as the 5 they hold, and none of these (other than the 5s) has showed up on the board.

The turn card totally missed you, so now you have to consider the pot odds for hitting a flush on the river. By now you might have the odds memorized:

37 ÷ 9 = 4.11-to-1 to hit the nut flush

Since the pot odds are 7-to-1 right now, it is proper to make this call.

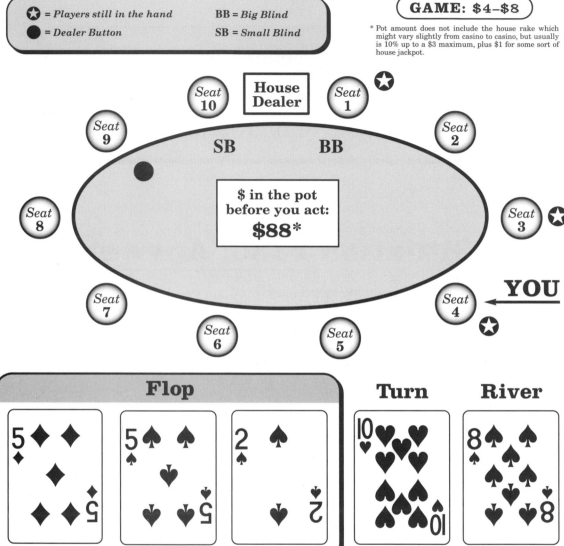

Seat 10   House Dealer   Seat 1 ★

Seat 9   Seat 2

SB   BB

$ in the pot
before you act:

$88*

Seat 8   Seat 3 ★

Seat 7   YOU   Seat 4 ★

Seat 6   Seat 5

Flop

5♦   5♠   2♠

Turn   **River**

10♥   8♠

Pocket

A♠   Q♠

Situation #131

Situations 128–131 all deal with the same hand at the first two betting stages.

Three players stayed in to see the river for one bet. After the river card was dealt, Seat 1 now bet first for the first time, at $8. Seat 3, who had been betting first previously, now just called the $8. Last to act, it is now your turn. Do you fold, call $8 as well, or raise to $16, and why?

Starting Hand (Pocket): **A♠ Q♠**

This Pocket's Win Rate: **64.9%**

Win Rate Rank: **6 of 169 possible**

Situation #131: Answer

You raise to $16. Seat 3, who had been the aggressive bettor until the river, now only called. The only thing that changed, really, was that a third Spade hit the board on the river, thereby making for possible flushes, which Seat 3 now apparently can't beat. Which means he doesn't have the full house.

Since Seat 3 can't beat a flush, what about Seat 1? He was only calling until the river, then bet under the gun when the river card came. He liked the 8♠ on the river. But does he like it because it gives him a flush or because he's holding 8-5 or pocket 8s? If it's a flush, you have him beat. If it's a full house, he has you beat. It would be hard to imagine that someone played 8-5 to begin with, but pocket 8s is not out of the realm of possibility.

Since you have the probable high hand at this point, a raise is in order. If Seat 1 reraises, just call him on the off chance he has the full house.

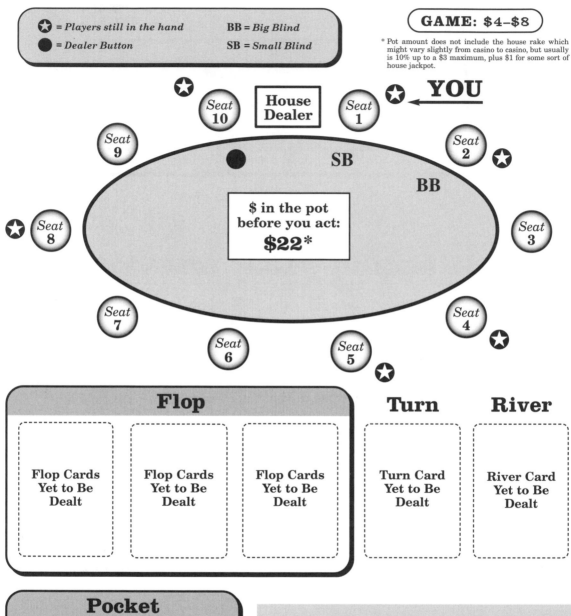

⭐ = *Players still in the hand*

⬤ = *Dealer Button*

BB = *Big Blind*

SB = *Small Blind*

GAME: $4–$8

* Pot amount does not include the house rake which might vary slightly from casino to casino, but usually is 10% up to a $3 maximum, plus $1 for some sort of house jackpot.

YOU

Seat 10 | House Dealer | Seat 1

Seat 9

SB

BB

Seat 2

$ in the pot before you act: **$22***

Seat 8

Seat 3

Seat 7

Seat 4

Seat 6 | Seat 5

Flop

| Flop Cards Yet to Be Dealt | Flop Cards Yet to Be Dealt | Flop Cards Yet to Be Dealt |

Turn

Turn Card Yet to Be Dealt

River

River Card Yet to Be Dealt

Pocket

Situation #132

Situations 132–135 all deal with the same hand at the four betting stages.

You have been dealt King-6 suited in your pocket while in the small blind position. Four players have called the $4 big blind bet in front of you. It is now your turn to act. With $22 in the pot and only the big blind yet to act, do you fold, call the additional $2, or raise to $8, and why?

Starting Hand (Pocket): **K♣ 6♣**

This Pocket's Win Rate: **8.4%**

Win Rate Rank: **58 of 169 possible**

Situation #132: Answer

If you play this hand you are realistically playing for a Club flush. Since the odds of flopping four to a flush when holding two of the same suit in your hand is a shade over 8-to-1, and the pot odds right now are 11-to-1 ($2 bet for $22 pot) it would be a correct call.

One thing that helps to make this a correct call is the fact that you have a King-high flush opportunity. If your two hole cards were, for example, 6-3 suited, it wouldn't be as attractive a call as is King-6.

Prepare yourself for the fact that if you don't get a lot of help on the flop you'll have to fold the hand. You're just playing it now because the pot odds are so great for a $2 call.

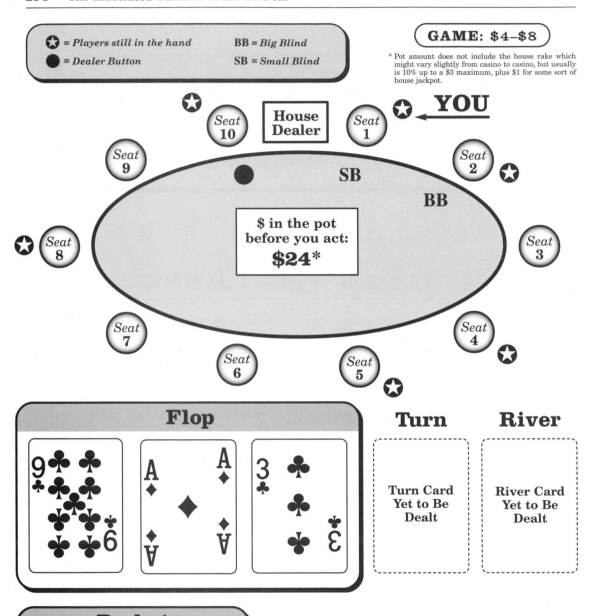

GAME: $4–$8

* Pot amount does not include the house rake which might vary slightly from casino to casino, but usually is 10% up to a $3 maximum, plus $1 for some sort of house jackpot.

YOU

Seat 10 — House Dealer — Seat 1

Seat 9   Seat 2

SB

BB

Seat 8

$ in the pot before you act:
$24*

Seat 3

Seat 7   Seat 4

Seat 6   Seat 5

Flop

9♣   A♦   3♣

Turn

Turn Card Yet to Be Dealt

River

River Card Yet to Be Dealt

Pocket

K♣   6♣

Situation #133

Situations 132–135 all deal with the same hand at the four betting stages.

Six players stayed in to see the flop for one bet. After the flop, you are first to bet. Do you fold, check, or bet $4, and why?

Starting Hand (Pocket): **K♣ 6♣**

This Pocket's Win Rate: **8.4%**

Win Rate Rank: **58 of 169 possible**

Situation #133: Answer

Well, you needed a lot of help on the flop and you got it, so you certainly won't be folding. The question is whether to check or bet. You still do not have a made hand yet, so checking is the sensible way to go. If another player bets, you are still going to call. At this point there is no way you should get out of this hand even if there is a bet and a raise before it gets back to you.

Right now there is $24 in the pot. If there is a bet and several callers before it gets back to you, that means there will be pot odds of at least 9- or 10-to-1 for you on a call that is about 2-to-1 (the odds of catching a flush by the river when you flop four to a flush).

Even if you were to bet at this stage, it would be correct pot odds. However, right now there is no guarantee that you'll hit a flush, and if you don't, this hand is virtually worthless, meaning you'll be putting money into a dead pot for you if you miss.

The correct, safe play is to check, and if someone bets and/or raises, you shouldn't mind calling those bets.

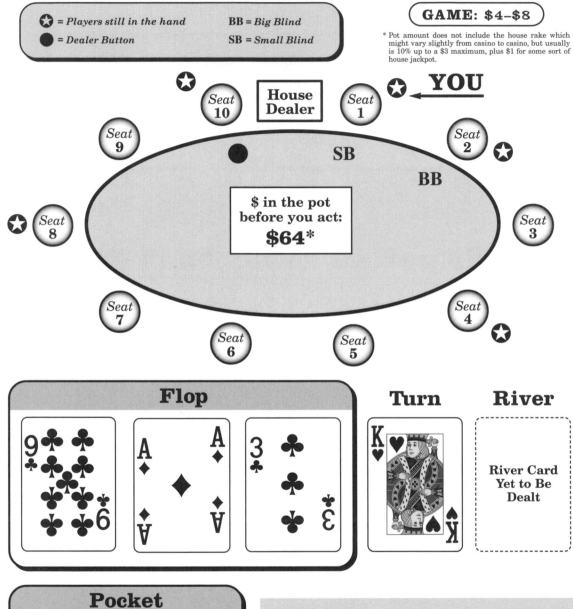

= *Players still in the hand*   BB = *Big Blind*

= *Dealer Button*   SB = *Small Blind*

YOU

Seat 10   House Dealer   Seat 1

Seat 9   Seat 2

SB

BB

$ in the pot before you act: **$64***

Seat 8   Seat 3

Seat 7   Seat 4

Seat 6   Seat 5

Flop

Turn   ## River

River Card Yet to Be Dealt

Pocket

Situation #134

Situations 132–135 all deal with the same hand at the four betting stages.

Five players stayed in for two bets to see the turn. Seat 2 bet and Seat 4 raised. After the turn, you are first to act with four players to act after you. Do you check or bet $8, and why?

Starting Hand (Pocket): **K♣ 6♣**

This Pocket's Win Rate: **8.4%**

Win Rate Rank: **58 of 169 possible**

Situation #134: Answer

This situation has become more clear with the turn card. While you improved your hand, it wasn't what you were hoping for. You now have a pair of Kings with a flush draw.

The problem for you now is that there was a bet and a raise after the flop (when the Ace came on the board). This means that in all likelihood, Seat 2 and/or Seat 4 is holding an Ace.

You still have hope for the Club flush, but your actual pre-turn odds of about 2-to-1 of catching a flush by the river have now risen post-turn to a bit over 4-to-1. This is still an acceptable call, but if you miss the Club flush you will need to hit (in preferred order) a King, 6, or 9 in order to have a reasonable chance to stay in the hand.

★ = *Players still in the hand*   BB = *Big Blind*

● = *Dealer Button*   SB = *Small Blind*

GAME: $4–$8

* Pot amount does not include the house rake which might vary slightly from casino to casino, but usually is 10% up to a $3 maximum, plus $1 for some sort of house jackpot.

Seat 10

House Dealer

Seat 1

★ **YOU** ←

Seat 9

Seat 2 ★

SB

BB

Seat 8 ★

$ in the pot before you act:

$96*

Seat 3

Seat 7

Seat 4 ★

Seat 6

Seat 5

Flop

9♣   A♦ A♦   3♣

Turn

K♥

River

Q♠

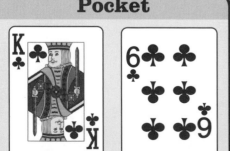

Pocket

K♣   6♣

Situation #135

Situations 132–135 all deal with the same hand at the four betting stages.

Four players stayed in to see the river for one bet. Seat 4 again was the bettor. After the river, you are first to act. Do you fold, check, or bet $8, and why?

Starting Hand (Pocket): **K♣ 6♣**

This Pocket's Win Rate: **8.4%**

Win Rate Rank: **58 of 169 possible**

Situation #135: Answer

Unfortunately, more times than not, you will miss the hand you are drawing for. That was the case in this situation. All you have is a pair of Kings. There is an Ace on the board. Seat 4 has been as aggressive a bettor as the rest of the players have allowed him to be. When Seat 2 bet first after the flop and was raised by Seat 4, that also should give you an indication that Seat 2 has something playable as well.

For now you should check and if any other player bets, then fold, because you are clearly beaten.

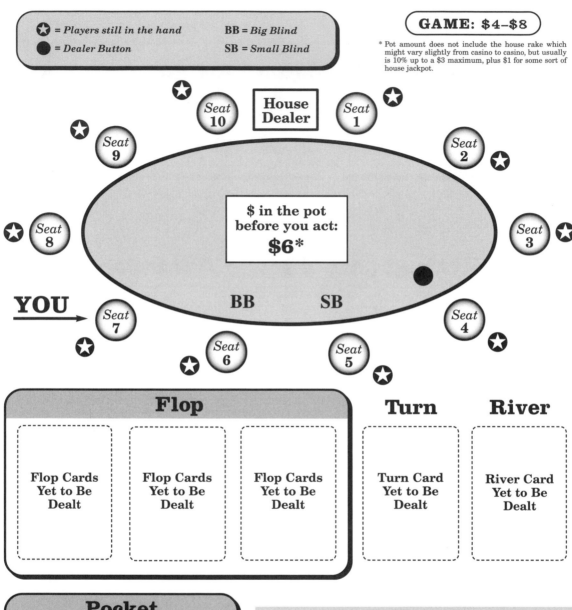

= *Players still in the hand*   BB = *Big Blind*

= *Dealer Button*   SB = *Small Blind*

GAME: $4–$8

* Pot amount does not include the house rake which might vary slightly from casino to casino, but usually is 10% up to a $3 maximum, plus $1 for some sort of house jackpot.

Seat 10

House Dealer

Seat 1

Seat 9

Seat 2

$ in the pot before you act: $6*

Seat 8

Seat 3

YOU →

Seat 7

BB   SB

Seat 4

Seat 6

Seat 5

Flop

| Flop Cards Yet to Be Dealt | Flop Cards Yet to Be Dealt | Flop Cards Yet to Be Dealt |

Turn

Turn Card Yet to Be Dealt

River

River Card Yet to Be Dealt

Pocket

Situation #136

You have been dealt Queen-10 unsuited in your pocket. You are first to act. Do you fold, call the $4 big blind bet, or raise to $8, and why?

Starting Hand (Pocket): **Q♦ 10♠**

This Pocket's Win Rate: **9.3%**

Win Rate Rank: **51 of 169 possible**

Situation #136: Answer

Queen-10 unsuited is not that strong of a hand to begin with, and in first position it is truly a weak hand. With no indication of what everyone else is going to do at this point, it is best to fold this hand.

As a comparison, consider if the two cards were suited instead of unsuited. The win rate would jump from 9.3 percent to 39.4 percent, a more than 400 percent increase in your chances of winning.

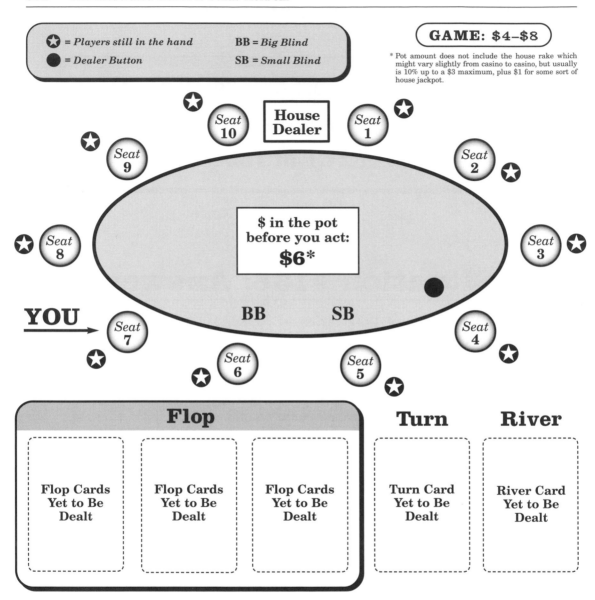

* Pot amount does not include the house rake which might vary slightly from casino to casino, but usually is 10% up to a $3 maximum, plus $1 for some sort of house jackpot.

★ = Players still in the hand   BB = Big Blind

● = Dealer Button   SB = Small Blind

GAME: $4–$8

House Dealer

Seat 10
Seat 1
Seat 9
Seat 2
Seat 8
Seat 3
Seat 7
Seat 4
Seat 6
Seat 5

YOU →

$ in the pot before you act: $6*

BB   **SB**

Flop

| Flop Cards Yet to Be Dealt | Flop Cards Yet to Be Dealt | Flop Cards Yet to Be Dealt |

Turn

Turn Card Yet to Be Dealt

River

River Card Yet to Be Dealt

Pocket

Situation #137

Situations 137–140 all deal with the same hand at the four betting stages.

You have been dealt Queen-10 suited in your pocket. You are first to act. Do you fold, call the $4 big blind bet, or raise to $8, and why?

Starting Hand (Pocket): **Q♥ 10♥**

This Pocket's Win Rate: **39.4%**

Win Rate Rank: **22 of 169 possible**

Situation #137: Answer

As mentioned in the previous situation, Queen-10 is a much better hand when it is suited than when it is unsuited. While it is not a strong enough hand to raise in first position, it is a strong enough hand to call.

If there is a raise later, you will have to make a determination about staying in the hand on a number of variables. Some of these would be: Who made the raise? What kind of player is he; tight and aggressive or wild and loose? How many players are still in the hand? Do you have decent pot odds for playing a drawing hand like this? (You should have a minimum of four other players in the hand to continue on if someone raises.)

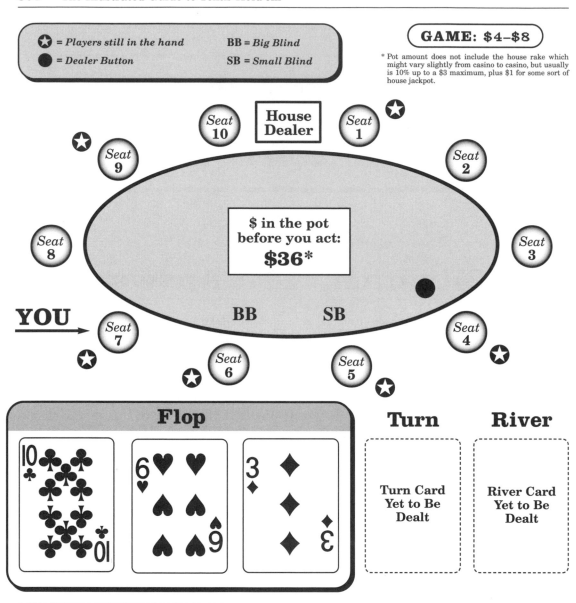

GAME: $4–$8

* Pot amount does not include the house rake which might vary slightly from casino to casino, but usually is 10% up to a $3 maximum, plus $1 for some sort of house jackpot.

House Dealer

Seat 10
Seat 1
Seat 9
Seat 2
Seat 8
Seat 3

$ in the pot before you act: $36*

YOU →

Seat 7
Seat 6
Seat 5
Seat 4

BB   SB

Flop

Turn

Turn Card Yet to Be Dealt

River

River Card Yet to Be Dealt

Pocket

Situation #138

Situations 137–140 all deal with the same hand at the four betting stages.

Six players stayed in to see the flop for one bet. After the flop, Seat 5 bet $4 and Seat 6 raised to $8. It is now your turn to act. With three players yet to act behind you, do you fold, call the $8 bet, or raise to $12, and why?

Starting Hand (Pocket): **Q♥ 10♥**

This Pocket's Win Rate: **39.4%**

Win Rate Rank: **22 of 169 possible**

Situation #138: Answer

Seat 5 obviously caught something on the flop or, when he saw the flop, realized his pocket was pretty good, so he bet. Seat 6, the big blind player, then raised the bet, so he definitely liked the flop.

Now it's your turn. You caught top pair on the flop and you have a decent kicker, so you can't very well throw this hand down yet. In addition to top pair, you have a back-door Queen-high flush draw, a shot at three of a kind, a chance for a full house, and an overcard. Your straight draw went down the tubes, however.

Call the $8 and see what the turn brings.

✪ = *Players still in the hand*   **BB** = *Big Blind*

● = *Dealer Button*   **SB** = *Small Blind*

Seat **10**   **House Dealer**   *Seat* **1**

Seat **9**   *Seat* **2**

$ in the pot before you act:
$104*

Seat **8**   *Seat* **3**

YOU →   *Seat* **7**   **BB**   **SB**   *Seat* **4**

Seat **6**   *Seat* **5**

Flop

10♣   6♥   3♦

Turn

A♥

River

River Card Yet to Be Dealt

Pocket

Q♥   10♥

Situation #139

Situations 137–140 all deal with the same hand at the four betting stages.

Four players stayed in to see the turn for two bets. After the turn, Seat 5 checked and Seat 6 bet $8. You and Seat 9 both called. Seat 5 then raised to $16. Seat 6 just called the check-raise. Do you fold, call the additional $8 as well, or reraise to $24, and why?

Starting Hand (Pocket): **Q♥ 10♥**

This Pocket's Win Rate: **39.4%**

Win Rate Rank: **22 of 169 possible**

Situation #139: Answer

The best hand that any of your opponents can hold right now is three of a kind. The turn card gave you four cards to a Heart flush. You are being asked to make an $8 bet for a chance to win a pot that stands at $104, which translates into 13-to-1 pot odds. The odds of you catching a Heart on the river, as you've learned by now, are just slightly over 4-to-1. This is an easy decision to call the raise.

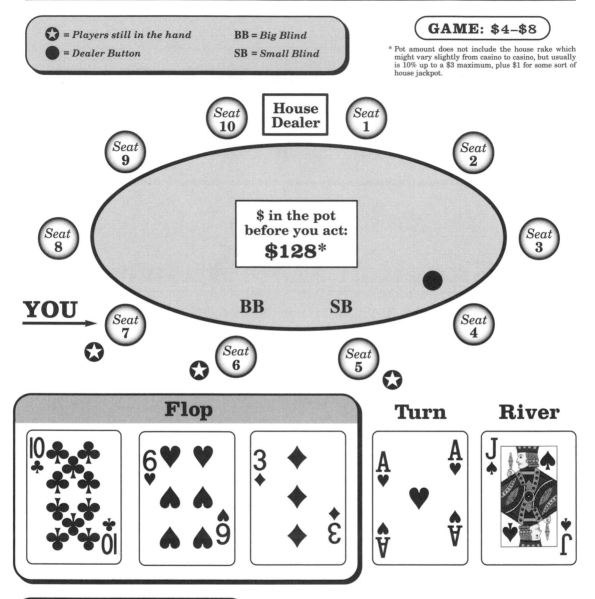

⭐ = *Players still in the hand*   BB = *Big Blind*

⚫ = *Dealer Button*   SB = *Small Blind*

GAME: $4–$8

* Pot amount does not include the house rake which might vary slightly from casino to casino, but usually is 10% up to a $3 maximum, plus $1 for some sort of house jackpot.

Seat 10

House Dealer

Seat 1

Seat 9

Seat 2

$ in the pot before you act:

$128*

Seat 8

Seat 3

YOU ➡

Seat 7

BB   SB

Seat 4

Seat 6

Seat 5

Flop   **Turn**   **River**

Pocket

Situation #140

Situations 137–140 all deal with the same hand at the four betting stages.

Three players stayed in to see the river for two bets. After the flop, Seat 5 bet $8 and Seat 6 called. It is now your turn to act. With no one to act after you, do you fold, call the $8, or raise to $16, and why?

Starting Hand (Pocket): **Q♥ 10♥**

This Pocket's Win Rate: **39.4%**

Win Rate Rank: **22 of 169 possible**

Situation #140: Answer

You ended up with four cards to your Heart flush and four cards to the nut straight. But four cards won't cut it. The only thing you have now is a pair of 10s. It's obvious Seat 5 has something strong and Seat 6 feels he has a hand worth calling Seat 5's bets. You are clearly beaten. Fold the hand, even though it's a large pot.

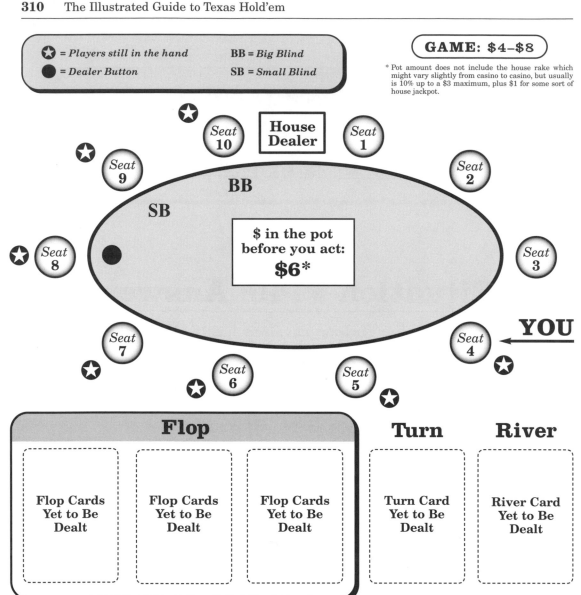

GAME: $4–$8

* Pot amount does not include the house rake which might vary slightly from casino to casino, but usually is 10% up to a $3 maximum, plus $1 for some sort of house jackpot.

Seat 10   House Dealer   Seat 1

BB

SB

Seat 9   Seat 2

$ in the pot before you act:
$6*

Seat 8   Seat 3

YOU

Seat 7   Seat 4

Seat 6   Seat 5

Flop

| Flop Cards Yet to Be Dealt | Flop Cards Yet to Be Dealt | Flop Cards Yet to Be Dealt |

Turn

Turn Card Yet to Be Dealt

River

River Card Yet to Be Dealt

Pocket

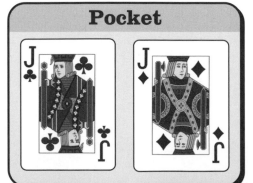

Situation #141

Situations 141–144 all deal with the same hand at the four betting stages.

You have been dealt a pair of Jacks in your pocket. You are fourth to act. All three of the players in front of you have folded. With six players yet to act after you, do you fold, call the $4 big blind bet, or raise to $8, and why?

Starting Hand (Pocket): **J ♣ J♦**

This Pocket's Win Rate: **64.4%**

Win Rate Rank: **7 of 169 possible**

Situation #141: Answer

You were dealt one of the top hands in Hold'em—pocket Jacks. This hand is, however, extremely vulnerable. If anyone pairs a pocket Ace, King, or Queen (assuming they don't have a pair in the pocket already), they have you beat unless you catch a third Jack on the board.

What you need to do is drive out any of the silly calling hands that turn up in low limit Hold'em, like A-7 unsuited, K-4 suited, and Queen-9 unsuited in an effort to keep any of them from hitting a higher pair than yours. One way to drive out hands such as these is to raise from the get go. By raising now, which is what you should do, you might eliminate several of these hands from the game. Many players don't like paying $8 from the beginning on such hands, especially if they know they're likely to be paying a higher price to play throughout the hand.

You can assume that any player who calls your raise has a decent if not strong hand.

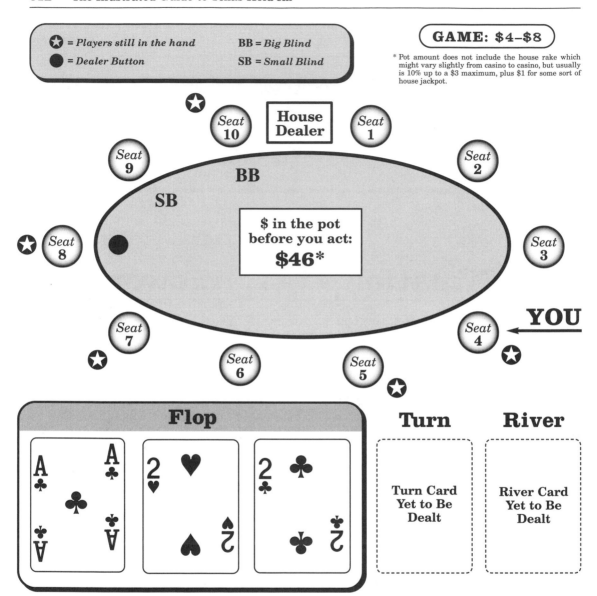

= Players still in the hand   BB = *Big Blind*

= Dealer Button   SB = *Small Blind*

GAME: $4–$8

* Pot amount does not include the house rake which might vary slightly from casino to casino, but usually is 10% up to a $3 maximum, plus $1 for some sort of house jackpot.

Seat 10

House Dealer

Seat 1

Seat 9

Seat 2

BB

SB

$ in the pot before you act:
$46*

Seat 8

Seat 3

Seat 7

Seat 4

YOU

Seat 6

Seat 5

Flop

A♣   2♥   2♣

Turn

Turn Card Yet to Be Dealt

River

River Card Yet to Be Dealt

Pocket

J♣   J♦

Situation #142

Situations 141–144 all deal with the same hand at the four betting stages.

After your raise, you received four callers. After the flop, Seat 10 bet $4. It is now your turn to act. With three players to act after you, do you fold, call the $4 as well, or raise to $8, and why?

Starting Hand (Pocket): **J ♣ J♦**

This Pocket's Win Rate: **64.4%**

Win Rate Rank: **7 of 169 possible**

Situation #142: Answer

The flop missed you completely, with the slight exception of the two Clubs coming which gives you three Clubs to a flush. You have to be particularly careful now. Seat 10, the new first bettor, is in the big blind position. That means he was in for $4 before the flop and when you raised it to $8 it was only $4 more to him. Thus, he might have called with something like Ace-2, or King-2 suited. Since he bet under the gun, he might have hit a genuinely strong hand.

Just the fact that there are two 2s on the board as well as an Ace should give you pause. The card that will really make your hand now is another Jack. What you have to do is calculate whether or not it's worth staying in for. Since there are forty-seven unseen cards, two of which are Jacks, the actual odds are:

(45 ÷ 2) ÷ 2 = 11.25-to-1 actual odds

Now, what are the pot odds? You're being asked to make a $4 bet to win a $46 pot (which will likely grow larger still with three more players yet to act after you). So this means you'll get a return of $46 for a $4 bet, assuming your three Jacks wins the pot.

$46 ÷ $4 = 11.5-to-1 pot odds

Therefore, you can make this call as it is almost exact odds.

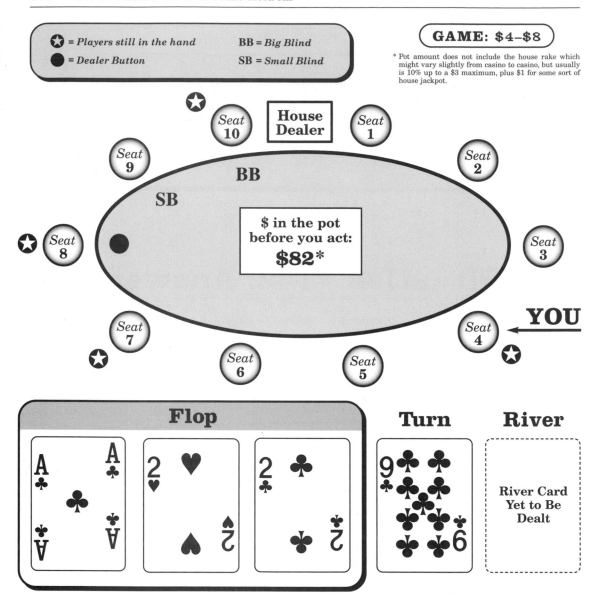

GAME: $4–$8

* Pot amount does not include the house rake which might vary slightly from casino to casino, but usually is 10% up to a $3 maximum, plus $1 for some sort of house jackpot.

Seat 10 · House Dealer · Seat 1

Seat 9 · Seat 2

BB

SB

$ in the pot before you act:

$82*

Seat 8 · Seat 3

Seat 7 · **YOU** → Seat 4

Seat 6 · Seat 5

Flop

A♣ 2♥ 2♣

Turn

9♣

River

River Card Yet to Be Dealt

Pocket

J♣ J♦

Situation #143

Situations 141–144 all deal with the same hand at the four betting stages.

Four players including you stayed in to see the turn for one bet. After the turn, Seat 10 and you both checked. Seat 7 then bet $8 and was called by both Seats 8 and 10. It is now your turn to act. Do you fold, call the $8, or raise to $16, and why?

Starting Hand (Pocket): **J ♣ J♦**

This Pocket's Win Rate: **64.4%**

Win Rate Rank: **7 of 169 possible**

Situation #143: Answer

The turn card helped you significantly, giving you a Club flush draw. This increases your number of outs on the river by nine (the outstanding Clubs). You now have four chances for a full house (the two Jacks and the two 2s) and nine chances for a Club flush. This doesn't necessarily mean you'll win if you get any of these cards, but you will drastically improve your hand if you hit any of them.

If you do get a 2 on the river, keep in mind that any Ace out there in anyone's hand will beat you. If a Jack comes on the river, you will have the best probable hand (only pocket 2s or pocket Aces will beat your Jack-high full house). If a Club comes on the river, you will have a good hand, but anyone holding the King or Queen of Clubs in their hand will have you beat. Remember, Seat 7 now became the new first bettor after the 9♣ came on the turn.

Call the bet and see what the river brings.

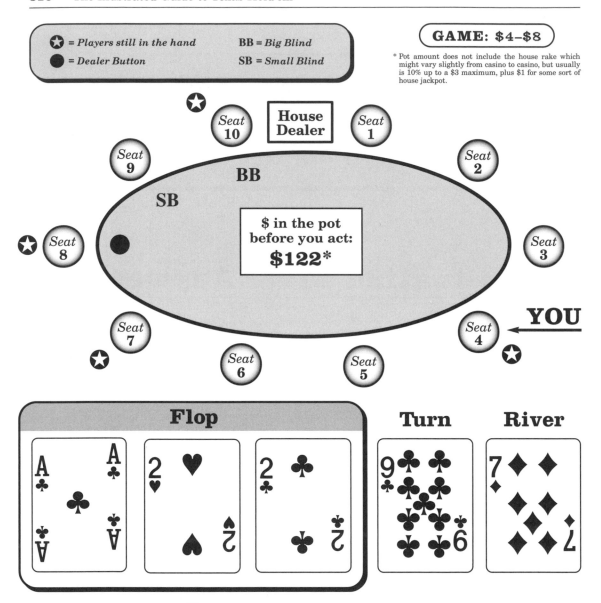

★ = *Players still in the hand*   BB = *Big Blind*

● = *Dealer Button*   SB = *Small Blind*

GAME: $4–$8

* Pot amount does not include the house rake which might vary slightly from casino to casino, but usually is 10% up to a $3 maximum, plus $1 for some sort of house jackpot.

Seat 10

House Dealer

Seat 1

Seat 9

Seat 2

BB

SB

$ in the pot before you act: **$122***

Seat 8

Seat 3

YOU

Seat 7

Seat 4

Seat 6

Seat 5

Flop

Turn   **River**

Pocket

Situation #144

Situations 141–144 all deal with the same hand at the four betting stages.

All four players stayed in to see the river for one bet. After the river card was revealed, Seat 10 and you both checked. Seat 7 then bet $8, Seat 8 called, and Seat 10 check-raised to $16. It is now your turn to act. Do you fold, call the $16, or raise to $24, and why?

Starting Hand (Pocket): **J ♣ J♦**

This Pocket's Win Rate: **64.4%**

Win Rate Rank: **7 of 169 possible**

Situation #144: Answer

You missed both the full house and the Club flush, leaving you with two pair. Seat 7 is betting first again, Seat 8 is calling, and Seat 10 is check-raising. Seats 7 and 10 both have obvious hands of strength at this point, and who can tell what Seat 8 is holding. The two 2s on the board probably don't help you (and hurt you if anyone holds a 2 in their hand). With the Ace on the board you can rest assured someone (or two) is holding an Ace in their hand.

You had a lot of outs before and after the turn, but missed them all. Fold the hand in the face of obvious defeat.

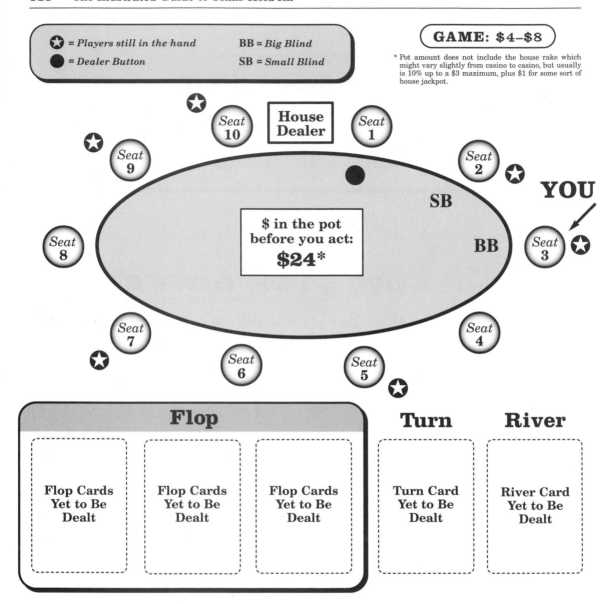

House Dealer

Seat 10 • Seat 1 • Seat 2 • Seat 9 • Seat 8 • Seat 7 • Seat 6 • Seat 5 • Seat 4 • Seat 3

SB

BB

YOU

$ in the pot before you act:
$24*

Flop

Flop Cards Yet to Be Dealt	Flop Cards Yet to Be Dealt	Flop Cards Yet to Be Dealt

Turn

Turn Card Yet to Be Dealt

River

River Card Yet to Be Dealt

Pocket

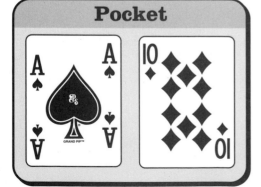

Situation #145

Situations 145–146 both deal with the same hand at the first two betting stages.

You have been dealt a pocket hand of Ace-10 unsuited while in the big blind position. There have been five callers in front of you. You are now the last to act. Do you fold, call as well, or raise the bet to $8, and why?

Starting Hand (Pocket): **A♠ 10♦**

This Pocket's Win Rate: **34.4%**

Win Rate Rank: **25 of 169 possible**

Situation #145: Answer

Ace-10 unsuited is a fairly decent calling hand, nothing more. This is a hand that you want to play as cheaply as possible if you do play it at all. If that sounds like less than a ringing endorsement, that's because it is. Ace-10 unsuited is somewhat deceptive in its strength. It's almost like you don't know whether you'd rather play it against an opponent heads up or against a field of five or six opponents.

This hand you were in because you were in the big blind, although you would have also called this hand in either the small blind or late position for one bet.

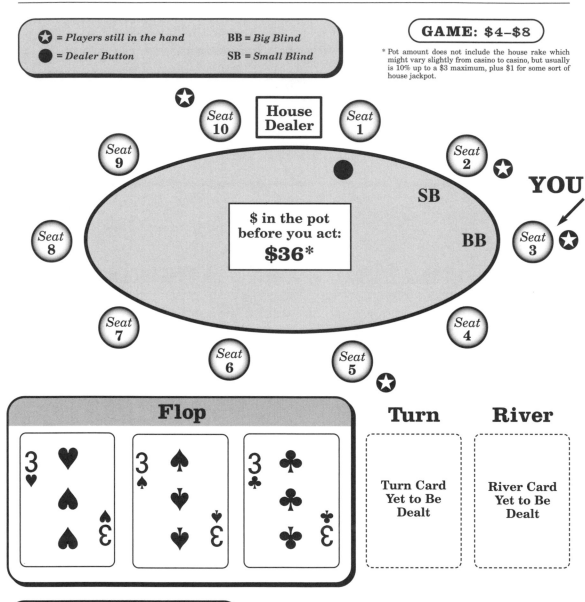

GAME: $4–$8

* Pot amount does not include the house rake which might vary slightly from casino to casino, but usually is 10% up to a $3 maximum, plus $1 for some sort of house jackpot.

Seat 10 · House Dealer · Seat 1

Seat 9

Seat 2 ★

YOU

SB

$ in the pot before you act:
$36*

BB

Seat 3 ★

Seat 8

Seat 7

Seat 4

Seat 6

Seat 5 ★

Flop

3♥ · 3♠ · 3♣

Turn
Turn Card Yet to Be Dealt

River
River Card Yet to Be Dealt

Pocket

A♠ · 10♦

Situation #146

Situations 145–146 both deal with the same hand at the first two betting stages.

Six players stayed in for one bet to see the flop. After the flop, Seat 2 and you both checked. Seat 5 bet $4. Seats 7 and 9 folded. Seats 10 and 2 both called. It is now your turn to act. With no one to act after you, do you fold, call the $4 bet, or raise to $8, and why?

Starting Hand (Pocket): **A♠ 10♦**

This Pocket's Win Rate: **34.4%**

Win Rate Rank: **25 of 169 possible**

Situation #146: Answer

Oftentimes when a flop like this comes up, the first bettor is betting more for information than based on the fact that he has the fourth card to the quads. I would almost be more concerned about Seats 10 or 2 than I would by Seat 5, even though Seat 5 was the bettor.

Another concern, besides the obvious 3, is a pocket pair, which you don't have. As you've learned earlier in this book, the odds of pairing up one of your hole cards on the turn or river is approximately 11-to-1. The pot odds right now are 9-to-1 if you call, so that is a bit of a disadvantage for you.

Your only hope here, probably, is to hit either an Ace or a 10 on the turn or river, but the odds are definitely against you. And even hitting a 10 may not be enough because an opponent could hold or hit a higher pair. This doesn't even take into account an opponent slow playing a 3, which renders everything else moot. Because you essentially have to chase what you need to win, you should fold this hand.

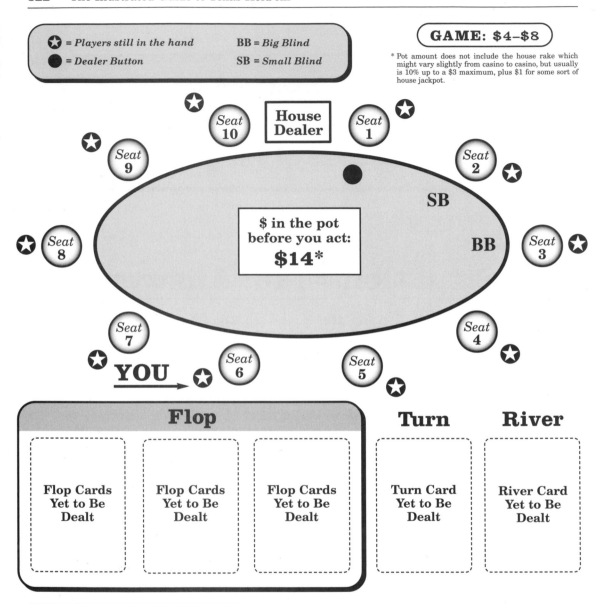

= *Players still in the hand*   BB = *Big Blind*

= *Dealer Button*   SB = *Small Blind*

GAME: $4–$8

* Pot amount does not include the house rake which might vary slightly from casino to casino, but usually is 10% up to a $3 maximum, plus $1 for some sort of house jackpot.

Seat 10

House Dealer

Seat 1

Seat 9

Seat 2

SB

$ in the pot before you act: **$14***

BB

Seat 8

Seat 3

Seat 7

Seat 4

YOU ➡

Seat 6

Seat 5

Flop

| Flop Cards Yet to Be Dealt | Flop Cards Yet to Be Dealt | Flop Cards Yet to Be Dealt |

Turn

Turn Card Yet to Be Dealt

River

River Card Yet to Be Dealt

Pocket

Situation #147

You have been dealt Queen-8 suited in your pocket. You are third to act. The first two players to act have both called the big blind bet. It is now your turn to act. Do you fold, call the $4, or raise to $8, and why?

Starting Hand (Pocket): **Q♣ 8♣**

This Pocket's Win Rate: **4.2%**

Win Rate Rank: **69 of 169 possible**

Situation #147: Answer

As you can see from the chart above, Queen-8 suited is not a very good hand. Don't be deceived by the suited aspect of the hand. If you don't hit three clubs on the board, you're left with a long shot straight possibility, needing a Jack-10-9 fitted in between your Queen and 8.

If you don't make the long shot flush or straight, you're left with trying to pair up Queens and 8s. Another long shot. On top of all these negative propositions, you're in early position. This hand only wins once in twenty-five times. Do you really want to play hands such as this? Fold this hand now before you fritter away your money.

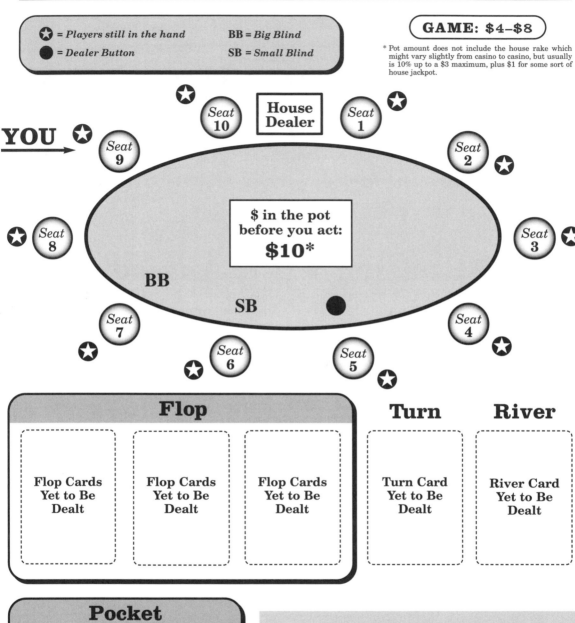

⭐ = *Players still in the hand*   BB = *Big Blind*

⚫ = *Dealer Button*   SB = *Small Blind*

$ in the pot before you act: **$10***

Flop

Flop Cards Yet to Be Dealt

Flop Cards Yet to Be Dealt

Flop Cards Yet to Be Dealt

Turn

Turn Card Yet to Be Dealt

River

River Card Yet to Be Dealt

Pocket

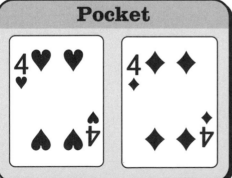

Situation #148

You have been dealt a pair of 4s in your pocket. You are second to bet. The first player to act called the big blind bet. Do you fold, call the $4, or raise to $8, and why?

Starting Hand (Pocket): **4♥ 4♦**

This Pocket's Win Rate: **8.3%**

Win Rate Rank: **61 of 169 possible**

Situation #148: Answer

Pocket 4s in early position is a poor hand. Your only outs, essentially, are the other two 4s. And even if you hit one, you still have to worry about everyone else holding a pair catching their three of a kind, which is likely higher than your 4s.

If you flop something like 3-5-6, for an open-ended straight shot, you have to worry about someone having played something higher, like 7-8 suited, whose straight, if they hit it, will be higher than yours.

If you do play this hand, what are you going to do if and when you get raised a bet or two before it ever gets back to you? Then you're in a poor hand two or three bets. And if everyone folds except for Seats 7, 8, and you, you're still at a disadvantage because Seat 8 obviously has some sort of a big hand and you'll be going heads up or shorthanded with a weak hand.

Plain and simple, you need to fold small pairs in early position.

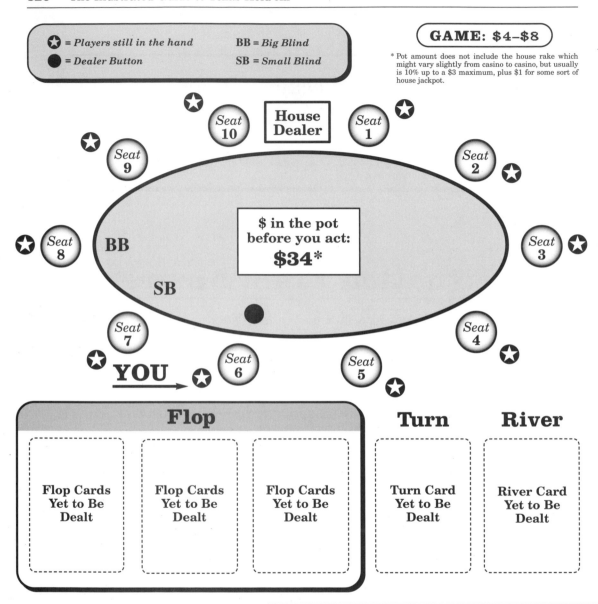

★ = *Players still in the hand*   BB = *Big Blind*

● = *Dealer Button*   SB = *Small Blind*

GAME: $4–$8

* Pot amount does not include the house rake which might vary slightly from casino to casino, but usually is 10% up to a $3 maximum, plus $1 for some sort of house jackpot.

Seat 10 — House Dealer — Seat 1

Seat 9 — Seat 2

Seat 8 — BB — Seat 3

$ in the pot before you act:
$34*

SB

Seat 7 — Seat 4

YOU → Seat 6 — Seat 5

Flop

| Flop Cards Yet to Be Dealt | Flop Cards Yet to Be Dealt | Flop Cards Yet to Be Dealt |

Turn

Turn Card Yet to Be Dealt

River

River Card Yet to Be Dealt

Pocket

9♦   3♦

Situation #149

Situations 149–150 both deal with the same hand at the first two betting stages.

It has been announced by the house that they are closing and this is the last hand to be dealt for the night. You have been dealt a pocket hand of 9-3 suited while on the button. You are eighth to act. The first seven players have all called in front of you. With the two blinds to act after you, do you fold, call the bet as well, or raise to $8, and why?

Starting Hand (Pocket): **9♦ 3♦**

This Pocket's Win Rate: **0.3%**

Win Rate Rank: **153 of 169 possible**

Situation #149: Answer

As you can see from the chart above, 9-3 suited is a terrible hand. However, with everyone in the pot in front of you, and likely both players behind you, if you call this bet, the pot odds of this family pot will be 9-to-1 out of the gate. This will give you a good start in case you hit a miracle flop, which is just about what you have to have with a hand like this.

Call this bet and hope for three Diamonds, or two 9s or 3s, one of each, or something like 10-8-7, which will give you an open-ended straight draw. Go into this hand knowing this is a long shot and if you don't hit it very, very strong on the flop, be prepared to fold.

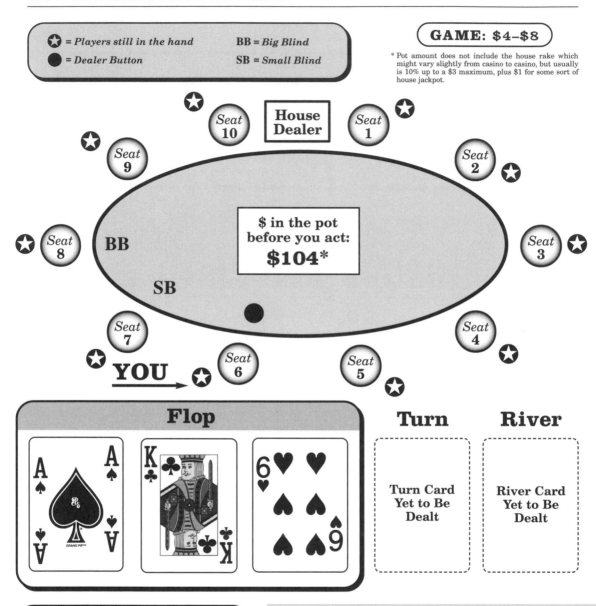

★ = Players still in the hand   BB = Big Blind

● = Dealer Button   SB = Small Blind

GAME: $4–$8

* Pot amount does not include the house rake which might vary slightly from casino to casino, but usually is 10% up to a $3 maximum, plus $1 for some sort of house jackpot.

Seat 10   House Dealer   Seat 1

Seat 9

Seat 2

BB

$ in the pot before you act: **$104***

Seat 8

Seat 3

SB

Seat 7

Seat 4

YOU →   Seat 6   Seat 5

Flop

Turn

Turn Card Yet to Be Dealt

River

River Card Yet to Be Dealt

Pocket

Situation #150

Situations 149–150 both deal with the same hand at the first two betting stages.

All ten players stayed in for one bet to see the flop. After the flop, Seat 7 bet $4, Seat 8 raised to $8, and Seats 9, 10 and 1 all called the raise. Seats 2 and 3 folded. Seat 4 raised to $12 and Seat 5 capped the betting at $16, making for a whopping $104 pot. You are last to act and it is your turn. Do you fold or call the $16 bet, and why?

Starting Hand (Pocket): **9♦ 3♦**

This Pocket's Win Rate: **0.3%**

Win Rate Rank: **153 of 169 possible**

Situation #150: Answer

In spite of how "whopping" the pot is, the flop missed your hand about as much as it was possible to miss it. You have no chance for a flush or straight. You have no pairs. There are two overcards to your top card. There's nothing you can do to change this sow's ear of a hand into a silk purse worth playing.

You can't let the fact that the pot is huge with lots of potential for getting even larger persuade you to stay in a hand that has virtually no chance of winning. Your only remote hope might be if two 9s came on the turn and river, and the odds of that happening are more than 2,000-to-1.

Also, don't let your desire for action on one last hand for the night be the deciding factor of keeping you in on a poor hand. Realize that your session is over before the hand is. Fold it and go home, confident in the knowledge that you played good poker, even to the end.

The Terminology of Texas Hold'em

Ace The highest or lowest card in the deck. When played as the lowest, it is used to make a 5-high straight, as in A-2-3-4-5 of mixed suits.

Ace high A no-pair hand in which the highest card held is an Ace.

Aces full A **full house** made up of three Aces and a smaller pair.

Ace-high straight A **straight** consisting of A-K-Q-J-10 of mixed suits.

Aces over Two pair, the higher of which are Aces.

Aces up See **Aces over**.

act To bet, **call**, **fold**, or **raise** in turn at the appropriate time. When it's your turn to play, the dealer (or another player) might say to you, "It's your turn to *act*."

action 1) Similar to **act**. When it's your turn to play, someone might say, "It's your *action*." 2) A term used to describe the liveliness (or lack thereof) of a game. If there are a lot of bets and raises, someone might say, "There's a lot of *action* in this game tonight." Conversely, if it's a slow game without a lot of betting, you might hear, "There's not much *action* tonight." 3) That portion of a pot that a player qualifies for. For example, if on the **river** player A bets $16 and player B calls the bet for $16, and then you go **all in** for your remaining $5, then a **side pot** is created for $22 for players A and B. You are said to only have *action* for the first $5 each of you placed into the pot.

active hand A hand which is still in contention for a pot.

active player A player who is still in contention for a pot.

add-on 1) One last optional chip buy offered to all players in a re-buy tournament, usually with no minimum chip requirement, and usually at a specified time. 2) In live play, when a player's current chip count is less than the minimum **buy-in** and he purchases additional chips that are less than the minimum buy-in amount but brings his new total to more than the minimum buy-in is considered to have purchased an *add-on*.

advertise The intentional showing of one's cards in order to set up the other players at the table for a planned future action. Typically a player who is advertising will turn over a hand in which he bluffed his opponent(s) out of a pot in order to make them think he bluffs a lot, hoping then to trap them with a good hand the next time. Less typically, a player will show his good cards in order to make his opponents think he only plays good cards, thereby setting them up to be bluffed later on.

aggressive This term relates to a style of play that is represented by much betting, **raising**, and reraising. This should not be construed as the same thing as **loose** play. Some very good players who don't play a lot of hands will, when they get good hands, bet, raise, and reraise aggressively.

ahead Having more chips than you started with. If you bought in for $100 and after two hour's play your stack was at $135, then you would be $35 *ahead*.

air ball A card that is of no help to you. See **blank**.

all black Having a **Club** or **Spade** **flush**.

all in Placing all of one's chips into the pot on one bet. In tournament play, this can represent a huge amount of chips, as you might witness on television. In live play, this represents a final bet, **call**, or **raise** of one's remaining chip(s), typically representing less chips than one's opponents have at the table.

all red Having a **Diamond** or **Heart** **flush**.

ammunition A slang term for chips.

announce Declare, as in one's hand.

announced bet A verbal declaration by a player of his intended bet which is binding if made in turn.

ante One or more chips put into the pot by each player before the cards are dealt and which do not constitute part of a player's bet, like a blind. While *antes* are used in all major tournaments, they are not usually used in a live limit Texas Hold'em game.

backdoor When a player **catches** two cards on the **turn** and **river** that gives him a hand that he only had two or three cards of on the **flop**, and typically either didn't expect to catch, or wasn't originally trying to catch. Examples: catching the last two cards of a **straight**, **flush**, or **four of a kind**.

backdoor flush Catching two cards on the **turn** and **river** for a **flush**.

backdoor straight Catching two cards on the **turn** and **river** for a **straight**.

backer Someone who financially backs another player in either a live game or a tournament.

backs The reverse sides of the cards, as opposed to the **faces**, or fronts of the cards that show the **ranks** and **suits**.

back-to-back Catching two of the same cards in a row, as in, "I caught *back-to-back* Aces."

bad beat When a **strong hand** is beaten by a **long shot** hand, especially when the holder of the eventual winning hand should not have been in the pot to begin with (at least if playing correctly, or according to the disgruntled loser).

bad beat jackpot Typically a large house **jackpot** that is awarded when a particularly high hand of minimum qualifications is beaten by an even higher hand of minimum qualifications. Although it varies from poker room to poker room, the typical *bad beat* would consist of a **full house** of at least Aces over 10s being beaten by **four of a kind** or better. Usually the house rules require that both **pocket** or **hole** cards must play. The usual breakdown of the jackpot would be to award 50 percent of the jackpot to the loser of the *bad beat,* 25 percent to the winner of the *bad beat,* with the remaining 25 percent being divided equally among the players at the table who were dealt in the hand.

bad beat story The sad tale of someone who suffered a *bad beat* on a hand, usually a big pot. Typically no one else at the table wants to hear the story.

balanced games The philosophy employed in some poker rooms of keeping tables with the same betting limits balanced with the same number of players rather than unequal numbers. For example, in a poker room with two active $3-$6 games going on, rather than have one table with nine players and one with five, the house will seat seven players at each game.

bankroll The money a player has available to gamble with.

bar To officially ban someone from playing in an establishment.

beat the board To have a hand that beats the five **community** cards displayed on the table, as in, "I can *beat the board.*"

behind Having less chips than you started with. If you bought in for $100 and, after two hour's play you had $30, then you would be $70 *behind.*

bet for value To bet a hand with the intention of getting **called** by one or more lesser hands, as opposed to making a bet in order to get others to **fold**.

bet into To make a bet before another player, often one who potentially holds a better hand, as in, "You only had a pair and you *bet into* a straight draw?"

bet on the come To make a bet hoping that the card(s) you need will eventually come.

bet out of turn To make a bet before it's one's turn to do so. In most poker rooms betting out of turn is not binding and the player is required to take his bet back. Betting out of turn is often an honest mistake, either because the player is new or because the player couldn't see the cards of one or more players between himself and the last player to have acted. Sometimes, however, it is a ploy utilized by savvy players to influence the action of other players in the hand. Some poker establishments consider such a bet unethical which might result in either a penalty or barring from play.

bet the limit To bet the maximum amount allowed.

bet the pot To make a bet equal to the size of the pot in a **no-limit** or **pot-limit** game.

betting level The limit currently being played at in a tournament. The betting levels increase at appointed times, or rounds. For example, a tournament may start off with **blinds** of $10-$20 but after fifteen minutes they will increase to $20-$40. After another fifteen minutes the blinds might go to $40-$80, and so on.

betting limit In a limit Texas Hold'em game, there are four rounds of betting and each round has a structured, required betting limit. For example, in a $4-$8 game, after the two **pocket** cards are dealt there is a round of betting. All bets and **raises** must be in increments of $4. After the **flop**, there is another round of betting, again at required $4 increments. After the **turn**, another round of betting takes place, this time in $8 increments. And after the final card is turned up, a final round of betting takes place, again at the required $8 increments.

betting round In **limit** Texas Hold'em there are four betting rounds, one each after the dealing of the **pocket** cards, the **flop**, the **turn**, and the **river**.

bicycle Slang term for a 5-high **straight** in which the Ace is played as the low card. Also called a *wheel*.

big bet In **limit** Texas Hold'em, there are two limits of betting, one **small** and one *big*. For example, in a $4-$8 game, the $4 betting level would be considered a small bet and the $8 level would be considered a *big* bet.

big blind In a typical Hold'em game, the big blind (see also **large blind**) represents the largest mandatory **blind** required on each hand. The required *big blind* rotates around the table from player to player. The blind structure can vary from casino to casino. In a $4-$8 game, for example, the *big blind* would typically be $4, or the amount of a full small bet. Sometimes three blinds are used. In this case, there might be two **small blinds** of $2 and one *big blind* of $4. If there are only two blinds being used, then the small blind is the player one seat to the left of the **dealer button** and the *big blind* is one seat to the left of the small blind. Blinds are utilized to get the betting action going.

big hand A strong, powerful hand.

big player A player who plays in big-limit games.

big slick The name given to a player's **pocket** hand when he holds an Ace and a King.

black Meaning **Clubs** or **Spades**. If, for example, there are three **Hearts** on the **board** with just the **river** yet to be dealt, and a player holds a hand (such as **three of a kind**) that he believes will beat anything currently out there but will lose if a fourth Heart comes up (thereby probably giving an opponent a flush) you might hear the player say, "Bring *black!*"

black chip A $100 chip at most casinos.

blank A card that adds no value to a hand. For example, let's say you hold a Queen and a Jack unsuited. The **flop** comes up King-10-3 of different suits. With no chance of a **flush**, you're now hoping for either an Ace or a 9 for a **straight**. If a 4 comes on the **turn**, that is said to be a *blank* as it is no help to you at all. Also called an **air ball**.

blind Either as a **small**, **middle**, or **big** blind, this is money that is required to be put into the pot before the cards are dealt and which becomes part of a player's bet should he decide to stay in the hand. If the player decides he doesn't like his hand, he may forfeit his *blind*. In Texas Hold'em, *blinds* are mandatory, the amount of which can vary from casino to casino, and will vary from level to level.

blind bet A bet made without looking at one's cards.

blind game A game which utilizes **blinds** (like Texas Hold'em).

blind off In a tournament, when a player either hasn't shown up yet or is gone from the table when it's his turn to post a **blind**, his chips are placed into the pot by the dealer to cover his blind(s). If the player never shows up, his chips will ultimately be *blinded off.*

blind raise A **raise** in which the player to the left of the **big blind** raises before receiving any cards.

bluff To make a bet with a weak hand hoping the remaining players in the hand will **fold** their hands. Sometimes a good player will *bluff* on a hand actually hoping he's called in order to show his hand as **advertising**, thereby setting up the other players at the table for a later hand in which he won't be *bluffing.*

board 1) In Hold'em, the *board* represents the **community** cards turned up on the table. The *board* consists of five cards: the **flop**, the **turn**, and the **river**. 2) The sign-up *board* used by the poker room to make a list of waiting players who either want to play or active players who want to change tables or seats. Most poker rooms have an actual blackboard or large dry erase board on which to make their lists. The *board* will also usually list the games currently being played and their limits as well as jackpot amounts.

board man The person employed by the casino to operate the **board** and who will call out the waiting players' names when they have a seat in a game.

boat Slang term for a **full house**. See also **full boat.**

bone Slang term for a $1 chip.

book The mystical set of rules that supposedly apply to the proper play of poker. While there may be certain obvious smart plays in Hold'em, there is no actual "book" that is all encompassing.

boost To **raise**. A player might say, "*Boost* it up."

bottom pair A **pair** that is represented by one of your **pocket** cards and the lowest card of the **flop**. For example, if you have a K-6 in your pocket and the flop comes up A-J-6, you have flopped *bottom pair.*

bounty A premium paid in some tournaments for busting another player out of the tournament.

bounty tournament A tournament in which **bounties** are utilized.

box 1) The house dealer's location at the table. 2) The actual **chip rack** that the dealer operates out of while at the table. If the dealer is actually dealing, he is said to be in the *box.*

boxed card A card turned the wrong way in a deck. Upon discovery, this will usually lead to a reshuffle.

break 1) To win all of another player's chips, either forcing him out of the game or to buy more chips. 2) To *break* down a stack of chips into commonly used increments for ease of counting.

break even To end a **session** not having won or lost any money.

bring it Oftentimes said by a player who is hoping the dealer brings the one card he needs, especially on the **river**.

bully Said of a player who is running over the game by betting **aggressively** whether or not he has the best cards. Sometimes said affectionately among friends at the table.

bump it Slang term for a **raise**. A player might be heard to say, "*Bump* it up."

buried A term for losing heavily. A player might say, "I'm *buried* three hundred."

burn To take the top card of the deck out of play, usually by placing it face down on the table in the *burn* pile. In Hold'em, a card is burned before each round of cards are dealt.

bust 1) To break a player out of a game. 2) To go broke yourself in a game. 3) To draw to a hand and miss. 4) A worthless hand.

busted flush To miss on a **flush** draw.

busted straight To miss on a **straight** draw.

bust out To lose all one's chips and be forced out of the game or tournament.

button 1) The actual dealer button used in a house dealt game that is placed in front of the player who is in the acting dealer position. It is usually a large white plastic disc with the word "DEALER" stamped in black on both sides. 2) The player represented by the button. A player might ask, "Who's the *button?*" or "Where's the *button?*"

buy 1) To purchase chips. 2) To **bluff** and win a pot simply by betting. Another player might ask, "Did you *buy* that pot?"

buy-in 1) The minimum amount required to get into a game. In many casinos, the minimum *buy-in* is ten times the **small blind**. For example, if you are looking to join a $3-$6 game, the minimum *buy-in* would usually be $30. 2) The cost of entering a tournament.

cage The cashier's area, usually behind glass or bars in which the cage person will buy and sell casino chips. At the end of a playing session, this is usually where you will take your chips to cash them in before leaving the casino.

call To match a bet made before you. You would say "*call,*" or, "I *call.*"

called hand A hand that someone bet and someone else **called**.

caller Someone who **calls** another player's bet or **raise**.

calling hand A hand with which a player feels he must **call** under almost any circumstances, even if he feels his opponent has already made his hand.

calling station A term used to describe a player who rarely **raises** but seems to **call** every bet, even with weak hands. Such a player should never be **bluffed**.

can't beat the board Said of a hand that can't beat the five **community** cards on the **board**. Thus, the player is playing the hand on the board.

cap To put in the maximum number of bets allowed in a round. Usually said, "*Cap* it."

capped A dealer might say, "It's been *capped,*" meaning that the maximum number of bets and **raises** in a round has been reached.

capper The chip or other item used to cover one's cards to protect them from accidentally being **mucked**, either by the dealer accidentally scooping them up or when another player's discarded cards touch an unprotected hand.

cappuccino A slang term used by some dealers to indicate that the betting has been **capped**.

card down What is announced by the dealer to attract the attention of the **floor person** to apprise him that a card has fallen to the floor. Usually the dealer or other players are not allowed to pick up the card. Whether or not the card that fell to the floor is still in play is subject to the individual card room's policies.

card room *sometimes cardroom* 1) The section of a casino where poker is played. 2) An establishment where poker is played. 3) The room inside a club where poker is played.

card sense An acute awareness of what is going on in the entire game, not just one's own hand, and the ability to adapt one's play to the ever-changing game situation.

card shark An expert or professional card player. Not to be misconstrued as a card cheater.

card sharp A card cheater.

cards speak The rule that says that no matter what a player may say about his hand, the cards themselves speak for what the hand actually is.

cash in To leave the game and *cash in* one's chips with the cashier.

cash out See **cash in**.

casino An establishment, usually larger and more opulent, devoted to gambling games of all kinds.

casino cage The cashier's **cage** where players go to buy and sell casino chips and conduct all matters financial.

catch To receive a card, usually in the context of making a good hand. "Nice *catch*," you might hear an opponent say.

center pot Another term for main pot.
chance Odds, as in, "You had a one in four *chance* of making that hand."

change list A list kept by the **floor person**, usually on the **board**, of which players have requested seat or table changes.

chase To bet recklessly, usually when losing, in order to get even. One is said to be *chasing* cards when undertaking this poor strategy.

cheat To play dishonestly. If caught cheating in a licensed poker establishment you will be barred from playing there again and might even face criminal charges. If caught cheating in a private game you might be physically assaulted.

check 1) To make no bet but still retain your cards. If someone bets after you, you will then either have to **fold** your hand, **call** the bet, or **raise** the bet if the betting limits permit. 2) The technical term for a casino chip.

check blind To check your hand before receiving or looking at your cards. Also called *check in the blind*.

check in the dark Another term for **check blind**.

check rack A rack that holds one hundred casino checks or chips. A rack of one hundred $1 checks, which are usually white chips, is called a *rack of white*. A rack of one hundred $5 checks, which are usually red, is called a *rack of red*.

check-raise To **check**, usually with a good hand, and then, when someone bets and it gets back to you, to **raise**.

chips The common term for casino checks.

chip rack Another term for **check rack**.

chop the blinds When, after all the other players have folded before them, the two **blinds** each take their blind bets back. They are said to be *chopping it up.*

chop the pot When two (usually) players split a pot equally.

cinch An unbeatable hand. Also called a *cinch hand.*

cinch player A player who only plays the **nuts**.

circle A pot boundary. In some casinos there is an actual line drawn around the table. If a player's bet crosses that line it is committed to the pot. In casinos without an actual line, the dealer can determine if a bet is actually committed or not, depending on where the player places his bet or potential bet.

clear the rail A request by either a player or the dealer for all uninvolved persons hanging around a poker table to step back to a designated distance away from the table.

clip joint A casino that either uses crooked dealers or works in confederation with crooked gamblers to fleece unsuspecting players.

close Also called *close to the vest.* A conservative player, as in, "He plays it *close.*"

Club flush A hand with five cards, all Clubs.

Clubs One of the four suits of cards, the symbol of which is the shamrock: ♣ Clubs are black in the traditional deck, green in the four-color deck. A single card in the Clubs suit is called a *Club.*

cold No good cards coming out. If a particular player isn't catching any good cards, he is said to be *cold.* If no one seems to be catching any good cards, the deck is said to be cold.

cold call To **call** a bet and one or more **raises** without yet having any money in the pot.

color change To exchange **checks** of one color for checks of another color. Typically this occurs when a player is leaving the table and exchanges a lot of lesser value chips for a fewer number of higher value chips.

color up See **color change**.

come This means to bet and stay in a hand with the hope and/or expectation of getting the card you want in order to win the hand. A common example in Hold'em is when you hold two cards of one suit in your **pocket** and **flop** two more of the same suit. You then either bet or **call on the come** the next two rounds with the expectation that the fifth card of your suit is going to come.

come back at To reraise.

come in on the blind To sit down and join a game at the exact moment it is your turn to put in the **big blind**.

come over the top To raise a **raise**.

community card One of the five **board** cards that all players can make use of with their two **pocket** cards in the making of their best five-card hand.

community pot See **family pot**.

complete the bet When a player goes **all in** with less than the amount of the required bet, the next player can *complete the bet* by bringing it up to the limit. In a $4-$8 game, for example, if on the last round one player goes all in with his last $3, another player may *complete the bet* by putting the whole $8 in the pot. Under standard poker rules, a player may only *complete the bet* if the all-in player bets less than half of the specific bet. If the all-in player bets more than half a bet, the next player must either **call** that amount or **raise** a full bet.

concealed hand A hand that, because of the way it was played, was concealed from being a good hand. This happens sometimes when three or more players are involved in a hand and two of them are actively raising each other. The player with the *concealed* good hand just keeps calling, letting the other two players do the work of building a pot he is likely to win. For example, if a player holds 8-8 in the **pocket** and the **flop** comes up A-K-8, he now holds a set of 8s, likely the best hand. Then, if the **turn** and **river** come up something like 5-5, he now has a full house, 8s over 5s, and can only be beaten by pocket Aces, pocket Kings, or pocket 5s, none of which are impossible, but none of which are statistically likely.

connectors Usually refers to two unsuited **pocket** cards in sequence, such as 9-10.

conservative player Description of a **tight** player who doesn't bet unless he has a good hand, and usually the best hand.

corner seat Either of two seats next to the house dealer in a house-dealt game. Also called *Seat 1* (the first seat to the dealer's left) and *Seat 10* (the seat to the dealer's immediate right).

count down The act of the dealer counting down a player's chips to arrive at his total so that another player, contemplating a **call**, can make the decision to call or not. Usually associated with a no-limit game.

cowboy Slang term for a King.

crank it up To start a poker game in a card room.

crimp A bend in a card. Sometimes it's accidental, but sometimes it's done intentionally by a card cheat in order for him to spot it from a distance when it's dealt out. This is one reason card decks are replaced quite often in casinos.

cut Also called *cutting the deck*. To separate the deck into two packets after they've been shuffled and place the former bottom packet on top before dealing the cards.

dark Without looking at your cards. To bet in the *dark* is to bet without looking at your cards. To call in the *dark* is to call without looking, and to raise in the *dark* is to raise without looking at your cards.

dead card Any card not in play or a card which, according to rules of play, cannot be played in a hand, such as a card which falls to the floor.

dead game Term used to describe a game without much **action**.

dead hand A reference to a hand which, for a variety of reasons, might be declared legally unplayable, such as when it is touched by another player's discarded hand.

dead man's hand Two pair, Aces and 8s. So called because this was the hand Wild Bill Hickok was alleged to have been holding when he was shot in the back by Jack McCall in a Deadwood, South Dakota, saloon in 1876.

dead money 1) Money put into a pot by a player or players who subsequently **fold** their hands and therefore cannot win. 2) A term used to designate players of lesser ability who are unlikely to win in a game or tournament.

deal To distribute the cards to the players.

dealer The person who physically deals the cards to the players.

dealer button The large round plastic disc that is placed in front of the player who is designated as the acting dealer.

deal in To be included in a specific hand. A player might tell a dealer to *"deal me in,"* as he gets out of his chair to get a cup of coffee or perform some other quick errand. He wants to let the dealer know that he'll be back in his seat before it's his turn to act. Also, a dealer may ask a player if he wants to be *dealt in* after missing his **blinds**, in which case the player would have to post the blind(s) he missed while gone from the table.

deal out To skip a player during the deal, usually because he's gone from the table or has announced he's leaving the table for a short while.

decision The resolution of a dispute, usually by the poker room's floor person.

deck The complete pack of fifty-two cards used in a Texas Hold'em poker game. The Jokers are not used.

deck change Changing the deck in the game. Sometimes a dealer will ask the floor person to change the deck due to damage to one or more cards in the deck. It is also not unusual to hear a player ask for a deck change, either because he's noticed something physically wrong with some of the cards or he's just having a bad run of luck and feels a new deck will change his luck for the better.

declaration The verbal announcement at showdown of one's hand. For example, a player might say, "I have a King-high flush."

declare To make a **declaration**.

denomination A card's rank, such as Jack or 7.

deuce The 2 card.

deuces full A **full house** consisting of three 2s and another pair.

dewey Another name for the 2 card.

Diamond flush A hand with five cards, all Diamonds.

Diamonds One of the four suits of cards, the symbol of which is shaped like the rhombus: ♦ Diamonds are red in the traditional deck, blue in the four-color deck. A single card in the Diamonds suit is called a *Diamond*.

dimestore A term used to describe a **pocket** hand of 5-10 (five and dime).

discard To throw one's hand away.

discard pile The place on the table where the dealer puts all of the cards that have thrown away, or **discarded**, by the players.

discards All of the thrown-away cards, which are sometimes combined with the undealt cards at the end of a deal.

Dolly Parton A term used to describe a pocket hand of 9-5, so called after the movie *9 to 5*.

donate To throw one's chips into the pot not really expecting to win. The player might say, "Okay, I'll *donate*," or "Here's my *donation*."

double gutter or **double gut shot** A hand with two **holes** in it that if either are filled will give the holder a **straight**. For example, a hand of 7-9-10-J-K has two holes in it, the 8 and the Queen. If the player catches either of these two cards he makes a straight.

double bluff A bluff that is performed by betting, being raised, and by reraising.

double up Said of a player who goes all in during a tournament and wins an equal amount from an opponent who calls his bet. He is said to have *doubled up* his chip stack.

down Behind, or losing. A player might say, "I'm *down* two hundred."

down to the felt An all-in bet or busted out of a game.

Doyle Brunson A term for a **pocket** hand of 10-2. So called because professional poker player Doyle Brunson twice won the World Series of Poker (1975 and 1976) with those two **hole** cards.

drag 1) To remove the house cut from a pot before the dealer pushes the pot to the winner. 2) The act of a player scooping in a winning pot.

draw In Hold'em, a hand that is not yet complete, such as a **straight** or **flush** *draw,* but if made complete on the **turn** or the **river** will likely beat one's opponent(s).

draw dead Drawing to a hand that cannot win even if made and not usually recognized as such by the player hoping to hit the draw. For example, if you hold A-J and the flop comes up 6-5-5, you're hoping to draw another Diamond on the **turn** or **river** for a **flush**. But if another player holds a pair of 6s, a pair of 5s, or a 6-5, you're *drawing dead* because he already has either a **full house** or **four of a kind**, either of which will beat your Ace-high flush.

draw for the button When the dealer, at the start of a game, deals one card, face up, to each player. The high card gets the dealer button to start the game.

drawing hand In Hold'em, with four cards to a **flush** or **straight** with one or two cards yet to be dealt, you are said to have a *drawing hand*.

draw out To beat an opponent by drawing a winning card on the **turn** or **river**. A player might say, "I had him beat on the **flop** but he *drew out* on me."

draw to To have a hand that you are hoping to make on the **turn** or **river**. If, for example, you have two Diamonds in the pocket and catch two more on the **flop**, you are *drawing to* a flush.

drink pot An agreement between two or more players that whichever of them wins the next pot will buy a round of drinks for all involved in the agreement.

drop The amount taken from each pot by the dealer and (usually) physically dropped into a box located underneath a slot on the poker table next to the dealer's chip tray. The drop amount funds the house's expenses for running the game. Anything left over is the house's profit.

drop box A box which is usually connected to the underside of a poker table and slides in place into which the dealer will drop the house **rake** from a pot or the collections from the players who pay by time.

drum A term used to describe a **tight** player, as in, "He plays tighter than a *drum*."

duck Another name for the 2 card.

dust The term used to describe the action a dealer takes when he either claps his hands together or rubs his palms together before turning his palms upward so the security cameras can see his hands are empty and that he is not stealing chips.

early position Usually considered to be the first three positions to **act** in a Hold'em game.

easy money 1) An inexperienced or poor player 2) money won from such a player.

edge The advantage that one player has over another in a poker game.

eights full A **full house** with three 8s and another pair. Also called *eights over* or *eights up*

eighty-sixed To be barred from an establishment, as in, "He's been *eighty-sixed*."

end bet A final round of betting in some Hold'em games in which a higher amount (usually double the big bet) is allowed to be bet and raised.

even To be even, as in not winning or losing. A player might say, "I'm *even* for the night," or "If I win this pot I'll be *even* for the night."

expectation 1) In the long run, the average expected profit or loss from a particular bet 2) the average expected win rate of a particular hand 3) the average number of times you expect to hit the hand you're drawing for.

exposed card Any card which is turned face up on the table, either intentionally such as when the **board** cards are dealt, or unintentionally as when a player **discards** his hand and accidentally or purposely flips his cards up.

face The front side of a card which depicts the **rank** and **suit** of the card.

face card Any King, Queen, or Jack. Also called *picture cards* or *painted cards*.

family pot A pot in which all players at the table are participating. Also called a **community pot**.

fan To spread the cards out on the table face up, usually to inspect that all cards are present in a new deck being used for the first time.

fast game A game that either moves along quickly or one with a lot of betting and raising.

fatten the pot To put more chips in the pot. Also called *sweeten* the pot.

favorite The hand or player that has the best chance of winning.

feed the pot Putting money in the pot, especially when done foolishly. Also called *feeding the kitty*.

feeler bet A small bet made to see if anyone else will **call** or **raise**. A bet made to gain information.

felt The cloth surface that covers a poker table.

fifth street The fifth and final **board** card in Hold'em.

filled up 1) To make a **full house** 2) To make a specified hand. A player might say, "I *filled up* my flush."

final table In a tournament consisting of multiple tables, as players are eliminated the remaining players are combined on lesser and lesser tables until only one table of players remains. This is called the *final table*. In most tournaments of size, anyone making the *final table* can usually expect to place in the prize money.

first Ace At the start of a new game, the dealer will deal all players one card to see who starts with the dealer button. If two players each draw an Ace, the first Ace wins.

fish A term used to describe a loose or poor player who usually loses.

fives full A **full house** consisting of three 5s and another pair. Also called *fives over* and *fives up*.

fixed limit In Hold'em, the betting increments are *fixed limit*, meaning the players have no option on how much they wager. The bet and raise limits are *fixed*.

flash To inadvertently expose one of your **hole** cards.

flat call To just **call** another player's bet when you could (and maybe should) have **raised** because you have a good hand. Also called a *smooth call*.

floor 1) The proximate area of the poker tables. 2) The floor person in charge of the dealers, players, and tables on a given shift. If a dealer has a question, or if a dispute between two players arises, the dealer might say, "Floor!" meaning she wants the floor-person to come to her table. Also called *floorman* and *floor person*.

flop In Hold'em, the first three **community cards** turned face up on the table by the dealer. The *flop* comes immediately after the betting is completed after the **pocket** cards are dealt. After the three-card *flop,* another round of betting takes place before the dealer brings a fourth up card. If, for example, you hold two 7s in your pocket and the three-card *flop* brings another 7, you are said to have "*flopped* a set of 7s."

flush Five cards of the same suit but not in consecutive sequential order. A *flush* outranks a **straight** and is just below a **full house**. A *flush* is typically called by its highest card, such as "Queen-high *flush.*"

fold To throw one's cards away and no longer be involved in a hand.

fold out of turn The act of folding before it's one's turn to do so. Not only is this practice against the rules, it is heavily frowned up in poker rooms because it could affect the play of others at the table.

forced blind A mandatory **blind** that is required to be put into the pot, on a rotating basis, before the cards are dealt to stimulate the betting in a hand.

forced-move game Also called a *must-move game*. When a casino or card room has more than one table playing the same limit game, there is usually one table that is considered the main game. The other tables are known as feeder tables, in which players can be forced to move to the main game when a seat comes open in order to keep the main game full. This is different from a balanced game in which an equal number of players are kept at each table and players are not allowed to move to another table unless someone at another table volunteers to switch with them.

four-card flush To hold four cards to a **flush**.

four-card straight To hold four consecutively ranked cards of various suits to a **straight**.

four-color deck As opposed to the traditional deck which uses only red and black for the suits, a four-color deck employs black for Spades, red for Hearts, blue for Diamonds, and green for Clubs.

four-flush Four cards to a **flush**.

four of a kind Also called *quads*. Four of a kind means four cards of the same rank, such as four Kings or four 6s. Four of a kind ranks above a **full house** and below a **straight flush**.

fours full A **full house** consisting of three 4s and another pair. Also called *fours over* and *fours up*.

four spot A 4 card.

fourth street In Hold'em, the fourth **community card** dealt face up on the table. Also called the **turn** card. After this card is another round of betting before the fifth and final **board** card is brought by the dealer.

free card When no one active in a hand bets after the **flop** or the **turn**, then the next card is brought by the dealer without costing the players any money, in essence a "free card."

free-roll tournament A Hold'em tournament which costs the player nothing to play, the prize money being put up by the house. Usually players must qualify to play in the tournament by some predetermined house policy, such as number of hours played in the previous week, month, quarter, or year. Oftentimes players with more hours played are awarded more chips at the beginning of the tournament.

freeze-out tournament A tournament in which players cannot re-buy. Once they've lost all their chips, they're out. Prizes are awarded based on the order of elimination.

front Having a position at the table that is to another player's left, meaning you **act** after the other player. You are said to be "in *front* of the other player."

full bet A bet that is as large as the current limit. For example, in a $4-$8 game, on the **river** $8 is a full bet. Anything less, such as a player who goes all in for his remaining $3, is not a *full bet*. Card rooms vary on their rules as to whether or not a partial bet can be raised or not.

full boat Another term for **full house**.

full buy A buy-in equal to or greater than the minimum amount required to join a game.

full house A poker hand consisting of three cards of one rank and two cards of another rank, such as three Queens and two 10s. This would be called a *full house, Queens over 10s,* or maybe *Queens full of 10s*. A *full house* ranks just above a **flush** and just below **four of a kind**.

full table A poker table in which every available seat is occupied. A *full table* consists of either nine, ten, or eleven players, depending on the card room.

gamble To play loosely or even recklessly. Among poker players, this is a specific term applied to the play of a loose player, or one who is not playing by "the book." It does not have the same meaning as the traditional understanding of the word.

game The specific kind of poker game being played. For example, when you first arrive at a card room and ask the floor person what games are going on, he might say, "We have both a $3-$6 game and a $10-$20 game going on right now."

gap A missing card in a hand, usually when referring to **straight**. For example, if you hold a 7-8-9-J, the *gap* is where the 10 should be.

gapper Also called **one-gapper**. This refers to one's **pocket** hand when the cards are separated by just one rank in the middle, such as 6-4, or K-J.

garbage 1) The **discard** pile. 2) A poor hand.

get a hand cracked To have one's hand beaten, usually late in the hand and usually when one's opponent was **drawing** against the odds.

get out To **fold** a hand.

get well To win a big pot that puts you even or ahead.

give away A poker tell; to reveal your hand by some manner or obvious play.

go all in See **all in**.

good hand A legitimate, playable hand.

good game A game in which you expect to win a lot of money, usually because you're better than all the players in the game.

green chip A $25 casino check.

grift To cheat.

grifter A cheater or swindler.

grinder A player who grinds out his wins (or a living) at poker by only

playing when getting the correct odds on his hands, or when it is at his advantage to do so.

grind out To win at poker gradually, but consistently. Sometimes said disparagingly of a **conservative**, winning player who never wins big but also rarely plays risky hands.

gut shot The card that fills an inside **straight** draw. For example, if you hold a 10-9-8-6 of mixed suits, and draw a 7 on the **turn** or **river**, you have made a *gut shot* straight.

half kill A game in which the betting limits increase 50 percent when one player wins two or more consecutive pots. For example, if a player wins two pots in a row in a $4-$8 game, the betting increases to $6-$12 until that player fails to win a pot, at which point the betting returns to $4-$8. The dealer will place a *kill* or *half kill* button in front of the player responsible for the *half-kill* situation until he fails to win a pot at which point the dealer will return the button to his tray. In a *half-kill* $4-$8 game, the player winning the *half-kill* button must place a $6 bet into the pot, so he is automatically in the hand unless another player raises to $12. The player on the *kill* button may then either **call** or **fold**, in which case he forfeits his $6 *half-kill* bet.

hand One deal around the table in which all players involved are dealt two **pocket** cards which, when used in combination with the five **community cards** to form one's best five cards, comprise a player's hand.

heads up A situation when only two players are left competing for a pot. They are said to be going *heads up*.

Hearts One of the four suits of cards,

the symbol of which is shaped like a heart: ♥ Hearts are red in both the traditional deck and the four-color deck. A single card in the Hearts suit is called a *Heart*.

heater Hot streak.

help To improve one's hand. A player awaiting the **turn** or **river** cards might be heard to say, "I need some *help*."

high card The card that determines the winner at the showdown between two hands with no **pairs** or better, or when two **flushes** or **straights** are being compared. In these situations, the hand with the higher card wins the pot. If the two hands are exactly tied, then the pot is split.

hit To make a hand by receiving a card you need.

Hold'em Officially known as Texas Hold'em. A form of poker that originated in the American Southwest, spread to the Nevada casinos, and eventually became the nearly universal form of poker played around the world. Two cards are dealt face down to each player at the table and five **community cards** are dealt face up in the middle of the table. Each player's hand is represented by the best possible five cards of the seven. There are four rounds of betting, the first after the two down cards are dealt, the second after the simultaneous three-card **flop**, the third after the fourth up card, and the last after the fifth up card. After all betting is complete, players still active in the hand turn their two down cards over and the dealer declares a winner.

holding The cards in your hand. A player might ask, "What are you *holding*?"

hole Also called **hole cards.** The term

used to describe the two down cards each player is dealt at the beginning of the hand. Also called the **pocket**. You might hear a dealer say, "You didn't qualify for the jackpot because both *hole* cards didn't play."

honest or **keep you honest.** The act of calling another player's bet even though you feel you are beat just so you can see their hand to see if they are bluffing or not. The calling player might say, "Okay, I'll call. Someone's got to *keep you honest.*"

hot Catching good cards; winning a lot of pots.

house 1) Another term for an establishment such as a casino or card room. 2) A shorter term for a **full house**.

house cut The portion of each pot that a dealer removes and places into the **drop box** before paying the winner of the pot. The *house cut* pays for the establishment's expenses and provides its profit. See also **rake**.

house rules Rules that are specific to a particular establishment. Usually the establishment's complete list of *house rules* is posted for public viewing somewhere in the establishment.

hustler Someone who makes his living playing cards. He might do so ethically or unfairly.

idiot end of a straight The low end of a straight which can or does lose to a higher straight. For example, if your two **pocket** cards are 7-8 and the **flop** is a 9-10-J, you have the *idiot end of the straight* because anyone holding 8-Q or Q-K has you beat. And even if they only hold the Queen, if a King comes up on the **turn** or **river** they'll make their straight and beat you. You have to proceed very cautiously when holding the low end of a straight. Also called the *ignorant end*.

implied odds The calculated ratio of what you should win on a particular hand to what the current bet is costing you. This also includes what money is likely to be bet in subsequent rounds.

improve To make one's hand better, especially by catching the one particular card you are hoping for.

in for The amount of action a player in a hand is entitled to. This usually comes into play when **side pots** are involved. A player who went **all in** for less than other players is only *in for* that portion of the pot, usually the main pot. He is not *in for* the side pots because he has no monetary stake in them.

inside straight Four cards to a **straight** with one **hole** in it, such as a 9-10-J-K of various suits. This will become a straight upon catching a Queen and filling the hole. Also called a **gut shot straight**.

in the air The term used to describe the dealing of the cards. At the start of a tournament, you might hear the floor person say, "Okay, dealers, let's put them *in the air*."

in the blind Being in one of the two or three **blind** positions of a hand.

in the dark Betting, **calling**, or **raising** without seeing one's cards. You might hear a player say, "I'm raising *in the dark*."

in the money Having lasted long enough in a tournament to receive some of the prize money.

in turn The act of playing in order, when it is one's turn to do so.

isolate To bet in such a way, usually aggressively, in order to drive opponents out of a pot so as to isolate yourself against one particular player, usually a poor player, thereby increasing your odds of winning.

Jack The face card that ranks just above the 10 and below the Queen.

jack it up To **raise**. You might hear a player say, when raising, "Okay, let's *jack it up*."

jackpot Any of a variety of extra cash prizes awarded by the establishment to a player who attains, usually, a specified high hand. Jackpots vary from house to house so it's always best, when playing in a new establishment, to ascertain what the jackpot hands are so you don't accidentally discard a jackpot winner without collecting the prize. Some common types of jackpots are the bad beat, Monte Carlo style, high hands for the day, etc. The jackpots are usually player funded by a dollar taken out of each pot and dropped into a slot in the table into a second drop box (besides the house rake drop box). The establishment is responsible for keeping this jackpot money on account so that it can be paid out any time it's won by a player.

Jacks full A **full house** consisting of three Jacks and another pair. Also called *Jacks over* and *Jacks up*.

Joker The fifty-third and fifty-fourth cards in the deck which are not used in Hold'em.

keep someone honest To **call** them even though you believe you're going to lose just to see if they were **bluffing** on their bet or not.

kicker The highest unpaired card in your hand. Many times the *kicker* will determine who wins the hand. For example, if you have A-J in the **pocket** and your sole opponent at the showdown has A-10, and the **community cards** are A-K-8-4-2 and neither of you made a **flush**, then you will win. You both have a pair of Aces with a King, but you have a Jack-8 and your opponent has a 10-8 for your last two cards. Your Jack is better than his 10, thus, your *kicker* was better than his. This is also called having your opponent *outkicked*.

kicker trouble Getting into a hand with a low second card, such as when you play an Ace-4. Since most low limit Hold'em players will play Ace Anything, if you play an Ace-4 you're likely to lose since more **kicker** cards will beat your 4 than your 4 will beat (only a 3 or 2). A player who gets himself into such a position might be heard to say, "I've got *kicker trouble*," once the community cards come out and they're all higher than his kicker.

kill The act of deliberately making a hand **dead** by the dealer so that there will be no argument as to whether or not the hand was live. For example, if Player A bets on the **river** and Player B **calls**, Player A will then toss his hand away because he knows he was **bluffing** and cannot beat Player B. Player C, who was not in the hand but has the right in most card rooms to request to see any called hand, then requests to see Player A's cards. The dealer will then take Player A's cards, tap them against the **discard** pile (thus *killing* the hand), and turn them over for everyone to see.

kill pot Betting limits which are double the normal limits. In some card rooms, when a player wins two consecutive hands the pot becomes a *kill pot*. In a $4-$8 game, for example, after a player wins two pots in a row the dealer will place a *kill* button in front of

that player and the betting limits now become $8-$16 until that player fails to win a pot. The player must place an $8 bet into the pot. This does not remove the obligation of the players in the **blinds** to post their normal $2-$4 blinds. The purpose of the *kill pot* is to stimulate higher betting activity. See also **half kill**.

King The face card that ranks just above the Queen and just below the Ace.

Kings full A **full house** consisting of three Kings and another pair. Also called *Kings over* and *Kings up*.

kitty Another name for the **pot**.

lady Another name for the Queen.

large blind Another name for the big **blind**.

last position The last position to **act** in a particular round. This is a very powerful position in Hold'em because it allows you to gain information by seeing what everyone else does before you.

last to act The player who **acts** last in a particular round. This is, generally speaking, the best position to be in.

late position In Hold'em, when the table is full, *late position* is generally considered to be one of the last three positions to **act** at the table.

laydown To **fold** one's hand. This term is often used as a compliment as in, "Good *laydown*," because it implies that the person who folded probably folded a good hand that most players would have called with but realized he was beaten by a better, unseen hand.

lie To **bluff**. Lying is an integral part of poker, whether subtle or blatant.

limit The amount of the betting increments in Hold'em. In a $4-$8 game, the increments, or *limits,* are $4 the first two betting rounds and $8 the last two betting rounds.

limit game What the vast majority of casino Hold'em games are. Whether a game is $3-$6, $4-$8, $10-$20, or $100-$200, it is still structured by betting limits. The rest, such as most of the games you see on television, are no-limit games.

limp in 1) To get into a pot cheaply because no one raised. 2) To **call** reluctantly, usually with a mediocre or poor hand and because no one **raised** the bet which would have forced you to **fold** a hand that was less than desirable.

line Sometimes actual, sometimes imaginary, this is a pot boundary that determines whether or not a player's bet is committed to the pot. In casinos without an actual line, the dealer uses his or her own judgment as to whether or not a bet is actually committed, depending on where the player places his bet or potential bet.

little blind Also called the **small blind**, this half (or other less-than-full) bet is placed as a bet by the first player to the dealer's left at the beginning of each hand. The *little blind* (and all blinds) rotate after each hand so that all players are in the blinds an equal share of the time.

live A live, actual game in which real actual dollar-valued chips are being bet as opposed to a tournament. Also called a *ring game*. When you go to a casino or card room, you will be playing in a *live* game.

live hand A hand that is still eligible to win the pot.

long shot A hand that has little chance of winning.

look To **call** a bet.

loose game A game filled with **loose players**.

loose-passive game A game with lots of **action** but little raising.

loose player A player who plays almost any hand that has even a prayer of winning. The opposite of a **tight player**.

loser A losing player.

low limit game A poker game played for small amounts of money. The lower stakes Hold'em games you'll find in casinos and card rooms will be along the lines of $1-$2, $2-$4, $3-$6, and $4-$8.

luck A pure illusion that bad players think is responsible for their losing and which good players realize will only determine the outcome of their play in the short run.

made hand A complete hand, such as a **straight**, **flush**, or **full house**.

main game In a casino with more than one poker table of the same limit, the main game is the one the house keeps filled up as long as possible, even feeding it players from the other tables when seats come open.

main pot The pot that all players have a stake in when a **side pot** has become necessary due to a player or players going **all in** for less than full bets.

make To **catch** the specific card you need to complete your hand. For example, a player holding four Spades would need to catch another Spade in order to *make* his **flush**.

make up the blind To post whatever **blind** money is necessary after having missed a hand that included one of your blinds.

marked cards Cards that have been marked or altered in some way by a cheater in order to tell their rank when held by other players.

marker An IOU, usually held by the casino, which represents money owed by a player and against which the player plays.

mechanic A **card sharp**, usually a dealer, who cheats by manipulating the cards.

middle Another name for the main pot when there is a **side pot** involved in a hand.

middle blind The second **blind** in a three-blind game, coming after the small blind and before the big blind.

middle pair When a player has paired one of his two **pocket** cards with the second highest card on the board. For example, if you have 9-8 in your pocket and the **flop** comes up K-8-3, you are said to have flopped *middle pair*.

middle position In a nine-handed Hold'em game, *middle position* is generally considered the fourth, fifth, and sixth seats to act in a hand. If it's a ten-handed game, then the seventh player to act is also in *middle position*.

misdeal Any of a number of situations that arise causing the dealer to redeal the cards before any **action** has been taken. Many times this happens when a dealer notices he has accidentally skipped a player, or has given a player three cards, or notices that he began dealing without one of the players having returned his cards from the previous hand, etc.

miss To not draw a needed card.

missed blind To be absent from the table when it was your **blind**, such as during a bathroom or meal break.

miss the flop A situation said to occur when the three-card **flop** completely fails to improve your hand.

money plays An announcement, usually by the dealer, that a player's cash money on the table will cover any bets he makes until the floor person brings the player chips equal to the cash money so that he can participate in the game. This situation may occur when a new player first sits down at a table or when a player already in the game busts out and requests more chips.

monster Also called *monster hand*. A very high hand.

motion The act of betting. Some establishments have a house rule that states that if you make a *motion* toward the pot with chips in your hand like you are betting, it constitutes the intention of betting and will be binding.

move all in To go **all in** with your remaining chips.

muck 1) The **discards** or **discard pile**. 2) To **fold** one's hand. You might hear a player ask about another player, "Is he still in the hand?" to which the dealer might reply, "No, he *mucked* his hand," or, "No, he tossed them in the *muck*."

multiway pot A pot involving more than two players.

must-move game A Hold'em game that requires players to move to a different game in order that the house can keep as many tables full as possible.

nice hand A frequent comment, usually meant as a compliment but occasionally sarcastically, heard at the table, most of the time directed by the loser of a hand to the winner of the hand.

nines full A **full house** consisting of three 9s and another pair. Also called *nines over* and *nines up*.

no limit The other form of Hold'em poker besides **limit** poker. In no limit Hold'em, a player may bet any or all of his chips at any time, unlike limit Hold'em in which a player may only bet according to the structured limits.

nuts Also called *the nuts,* and, if a **flush** or **straight** is involved, *nut flush* or *nut straight*. The *nuts* is the highest possible hand, at any point in the hand, given the **community cards** displayed. It is unbeatable. For example, if you have two Aces before the **flop**, then you have the *nuts* since no hand (at that point, anyway) can beat two Aces. If the flop then comes K-J-4 of mixed suits, then any player holding two Kings would have the *nuts* since the best possible hand at that point would be three of a kind. As another example, if the five community cards displayed were A-Q-J-8-3 of mixed suits (meaning no flush possible), then a player holding K-10 would have the *nuts* because an Ace-high straight would be the best possible hand.

odds The probability of something occurring or not occurring, as in the **catching** of a needed card, usually expressed in numerical form, one number to another, such as 4-to-1.

offsuit A term used to describe your two **pocket** cards when they are of different suits. Also called **unsuited**.

on Describes whose turn it is. Example, if the dealer says, "Dennis,

it's *on* you," that means it is Dennis's turn to act.

on a heater On a hot streak.

on a rush In the middle of a hot streak.

one-card draw A hand that needs one card to become complete, such as a **straight** or **flush**.

one-gapper Also called **gapper**. This refers to one's **pocket** hand when the cards are separated by just one rank in the middle, such as 6-4, or K-J.

one pair A poker hand that contains only one pair.

on the board 1) The face-up **community cards** in Hold'em. 2) To have your name listed on the poker room's board as wanting a seat in a particular game. It is common for players to be listed as wanting to play in more than one game, such as $3-$6 and $4-$8, and then take a seat in whichever game opens up first.

on the button The player who has the **dealer button** in front of him. This is a powerful position because it allows the player to be the last to **act** in the last three betting rounds of a Hold'em hand.

on the come The act of betting on a hand that isn't yet made, as when a player bets when he has only four cards to a **flush** or **straight** after the **flop** with the expectation (hope!) of making the straight or flush. Such a player is said to be betting *on the come,* or what is yet to come.

on the end To **catch** a needed card on the **river**.

on the side In reference to a bet that goes into the **side pot** as opposed to the main pot because an opponent still in the hand doesn't have enough money to match the bet.

on tilt Description of a player who starts to play recklessly and more poorly than usual because he's become upset. This typically occurs when a player has lost a number of hands in a row, usually due more to bad luck than to his own bad play.

open-ended straight Holding four consecutive cards to a **straight**, such as 9-10-J-Q. Hitting either an 8 or a King will give you a straight. Also said to be a straight that is *open on both ends*. Also called an *open-ender.*

open seat A vacant seat at a poker table.

option 1) The opportunity of the player in the big **blind** to **raise** the bet if no other player has raised before the **action** gets back to him. 2) In a **kill** game, the opportunity of the person who killed the pot to raise the bet if no one else raised before him. He has this *option* to raise even if he is the first to act.

oral declaration When a player verbally announces his intention on his turn before actually placing the chips in the pot. Such a declaration is considered binding.

out 1) Not participating in a hand. 2) **Folding** a hand. You might hear a player say, "I'm out."

out of turn The act of a player who bets, **raises**, or **folds** when it is not his turn to do so. In most establishments acting *out of turn* is not binding.

outs The total number of cards that could yet come to improve one's hand.

overcall To **call** a bet after one or more other players have already called the bet.

overcard A card on the **board** that is higher than either of your **pocket** cards. If, for example, your pocket consists of a pair of 8s and the board shows K-J-7-5-2, then there are two *overcards* to your pair, the King and the Jack. Any opponent holding either a King or a Jack has you beaten. This is why it is dangerous to bet or **call** in an overcard situation.

overpair A **pocket** pair that is higher than any card on the **flop**. For example, if you hold a pair of 10s and the flop is 8-7-3, you hold an *overpair.*

overs button A button placed in front of any player at the table who is willing to play for a higher limit than the regular game. Playing *overs* is not required. As few as two players at the table may agree to play *overs.*

over the top A **raise**, generally when done on top of a previous raise.

paint A face card. Also called *painted card.*

pair Two cards of the same rank, such as two 6s, or two Kings.

pass Loosely construed, to **check**.

pat hand A hand that needs no other cards for improvement. Usually made on the first five cards dealt.

pay off To **call** a final bet in order to see the other player's cards just to make sure he wasn't **bluffing**, usually with the belief that you're already beaten. A player might say, as he's calling the bet, "Okay, I'll *pay you off.*"

percentage call A **call** in which a player is the decided underdog in the hand but does so because he is receiving such good money odds for making the call. In other words, the pot is so big in relation to what he's being asked to bet, he's making the smart play in doing so.

player Any participant in the poker game.

play the board A situation in Hold'em when a player's **hole** cards are not used and the player's best hand is formed from the five **community cards**. If two players end up *playing the board* (not an uncommon occurrence), the pot is split.

pocket The first two cards dealt face down to each player in a Hold'em game.

pocket pair Two cards of the same rank dealt to the player's **pocket**. A *pocket pair* can be especially powerful when a third card of the same rank comes on the **flop** for two reasons. First, because it gives the player **three of a kind**, which is a strong hand. Second, because the hand is well hidden from your opponents because two of the three cards are hidden away, face down.

pocket rockets A slang term for holding two Aces in one's **pocket** hand.

poker A card game in which players try to make the best five-card hand possible and place bets against other players projecting that they indeed have the best hand possible, try and convince them they have the best hand possible, or attempt to drive them out or bluff them out with wagers in order to win the communal pot.

poker face To maintain a consistent, unchanging facial expression during the game so that opponents are not able to tell whether you've got a good hand or bad hand, hit the card you were after or missed it, or are making a serious bet or are bluffing.

poker hand The five cards that a player ultimately ends up playing when contesting for a pot.

poker table In Hold'em, the poker table is oblong in shape and usually seats nine or ten players plus a dealer.

position Where a player sits in relation to all the other players in the game in the context of where the **dealer button** is.

position bet A bet made more on the strength on one's position in the betting scheme rather than on the strength of one's hand. For example, if everyone in the hand **checked** after the **flop** and after the **turn**, if the player who is first to **act** makes a bet after the **river** card comes even though it doesn't help his hand, he is said to be making a *position bet* because he thinks everyone else has weak hands as well based on the previous two rounds of checking, and will **fold** if there's a bet.

post If a player misses his **blinds** for some reason, he can either wait until the blinds come around to him again and join the game, or, if he wants to join in again immediately after returning to the table, he can *post* the amount of his missed blinds. In effect, he's just making up for what he missed while he was away from the table.

pot The chips in play on a given hand. The pot is located in the middle of the table in front of the dealer and is formed when the dealer scoops in the bets of all players and places them together in a pile.

Pot A! Sometimes said by a player who wins their first pot of the night.

pot limit Hold'em A form of Hold'em in which the maximum betting limit is always equal to the size of the pot.

pot odds A term you'll hear used by the better players, *pot odds* is the ratio of the size of the pot compared to the size of the bet a player must **call** to stay in the hand. For example, if the pot contains $30 and you are asked to make a $6 call, then the pot odds are 5-to-1. If the odds on making the hand you need to win are 10-to-1, then you are not getting the correct *pot odds* and you should **fold** the hand.

pre-flop The situation or the bet before the **flop** is dealt.

protect 1) As in *to protect your hand,* this means to cover your two pocket cards with a chip or some other object so that the dealer doesn't accidentally scoop them in. Also, to prevent another player's **discards** from touching your cards which, under Hold'em rules, requires that your hand be declared **dead**. 2) A strategy of aggressive betting by a player other than you that helps you win the main pot when you're **all in** because it drives out other bettors not willing to contest the aggressive bettor for the **side pot**. This other player, then, has *protected* your hand. 3) A strategy of aggressive betting that drives other players out of a pot because they are unwilling to match higher bets on a drawing hand.

puck Another name for the **button**.

pump To **raise**. Also said *pump it up.*

put Also called *put you on it*. This is when you make an educated guess as to what another player is holding. You might hear a player say, "I *put you on* a pair of Kings."

put the clock on A request by a player to the dealer to turn the stopwatch on a notoriously slow player. Once so notified, the slow player has one minute to **act**. If he fails to do so, his hand is considered to pass, or fold if the situation calls for it.

quads Holding **four of a kind**.

Queen A face card that ranks just above the Jack and just below the King.

Queen high When you hold no **pairs** or better and your highest card is a Queen.

Queen-high flush A **flush** in which the Queen is your highest card in that suit.

Queen-high straight A **straight** consisting of a Q-J-10-9-8 of mixed suits.

Queens full A **full house** consisting of three Queens and another pair. Also called *Queens over* and *Queens up.*

quorum The minimum number of players required to start a game. This varies from casino to casino, but is generally six.

rabbit hunt To search through the undealt cards after a hand is over to see what you would have drawn had you not **folded**. Most card rooms frown on such a request by a player and in many it's not allowed. Only poor or beginning players make such a silly request.

race off In a Hold'em tournament when the betting levels have increased to the point where lower denomination chips are no longer used, a *race off* occurs. In this scenario, all players place their soon-to-be excluded lower denomination chips in front of them. The dealer will break them down and exchange as many as possible for higher denominations. The few remaining chips that do not comprise enough to make for another higher denomination chip are left in front of the player. The dealer will then deal one card to the players for each chip they have in front of them. In most casinos, whichever player gets the highest card wins all the small chips, which are then exchanged for the higher denomination chips which are about to be used in the next betting level.

rack A chip rack, typically that holds five rows of twenty chips each.

rag A poor hand.

rail An actual or imaginary barrier that is used to separate the players from onlookers and those waiting to play.

rainbow The term used to describe a **flop** which reveals cards of three different suits.

raise 1) To increase the bet to the next permitted level. 2) The amount of the increase.

rake 1) The percentage of the pot that the dealer removes and puts into his **drop box**. The *rake* accounts for house expenses, profits, and the jackpots. 2) The act of taking the *rake*.

rank The denomination of a card. The fourteen ranks, in order, from high to low: Ace (when played as high card), King, Queen, Jack, 10, 9, 8, 7, 6, 5, 4, 3, 2, and Ace (when played as low card).

rap The physical act of rapping ones knuckles (or tapping one's fingers) on the table to indicate your intent to check.

read To come to a conclusion about another player's hand based on his actions, remarks, betting patterns, or other **tells**.

reach for one's chips To make a move toward one's chips, presumably in preparation for making a bet. This often has the effect of causing other players who had **checked** previously to **fold**; they only needed to see you go for your chips before throwing away their hands.

re-buy In Hold'em tournaments where it is allowed, the purchase of chips after going **bust** or nearly bust.

red Hearts or Diamonds. You might hear the player say, "Bring red!"

redeal To deal again, usually because of a misdeal.

release To **fold** a hand.

represent To bet in such a way as to indicate a particular hand. When you see a **raise** before the **flop**, the bettor is usually representing a powerful hand, such as **pocket** Aces, Kings, or Queens, or maybe an Ace-King suited. Watch his subsequent betting because if an Ace comes on the **river** and he **checks,** it might be because he holds something like pocket 10s or 9s, for example, and now a pair of Aces beats him.

reraise To **raise** a raise.

riffle To shuffle the cards.

ring game Any non-tournament game.

river The fifth and last **community card** placed face up on the **board** by the dealer. There is a round of betting after the *river* card is dealt.

rock An extremely **tight** player who takes few chances. When he bets, he has something.

roll Winning streak.

round Once around the table in which everyone has had the opportunity to be on the **button** and in the **blinds**.

rounder A slang term for a poker player.

royal Short for a **royal flush**.

royal flush The highest hand in Hold'em. This hand consists of an A-K-Q-J-10 of the same suit. How rare is the hand? Statistically speaking, if you hit a *royal flush* today, then played poker forty hours a week thereafter, it would be about eleven years until you got your next one, assuming it came exactly at the time statistical probabilities say it should.

runner A **flush** or **straight** card that arrives on the **turn** or **river** after holding only three cards of that particular hand after the **flop**.

runner-runner **Flush** or **straight** cards that hit on both the **turn** and the **river** when you held only three of that particular hand after the **flop**. It is particularly galling to a player to have a hand seemingly won only to lose to a player who hits *runner-runner* to beat him, especially if the river card fills a **gutshot straight**.

run over the game To bet in an aggressive and intimidating manner toward the other players.

rush A winning streak in which a player will win several hands in a row.

sandbag To **pass** or check a good hand with the intention of **raising** later. Similar to **check-raising**.

sandbagger One who **sandbags**. Sometimes met with disapproval by other players.

satellite tournament A tournament whose prize is oftentimes a paid entry into a larger tournament. In 2003, Chris Moneymaker won his $10,000 seat into the World Series of Poker by winning a satellite tournament for which he'd paid about $40. He eventually won the World Series and its $2.5 million first prize. The 2004 champion, Gary Raymer, who won the $5 million first prize, won his seat by winning a $180 satellite.

scramble Prior to shuffling the cards, a dealer will turn all the cards upside down on the table and fan them out over a large area. He will then thoroughly mix the cards before collecting them up and shuffling.

seat A chair at a poker table.

seat change Sometimes players will change seats, either because they think the other seat is luckier, their seat is unlucky, the lighting is better, or they just have a favorite seat position at a table. To request a seat change, a player should tell the dealer who should then make sure that the seat change request is written on the board. This eliminates disputes later as to who is entitled to which open seat.

seat position The seat next to the dealer's left is seat #1. Going clockwise from there, the seats are numbered up to 9, 10, or 11, depending on how many chairs the establishment chooses to have.

second pair A pair that consists of one of your **hole** cards and the second-highest card on the **flop**. Same as **middle pair**.

see A called bet.

semi-bluff A bet made on a hand that is likely not the best hand at the table when the bet is made, but which has definite possibilities of improving when subsequent **community cards** are dealt out. If everyone else **folds**, then the bet succeeded as a **bluff**. If it doesn't, it might still improve.

send it A remark said by an ungracious winner at the showdown when he wins the pot.

session A period of playing poker that begins from the time a player first sits down at the table until the time he cashes in his chips and leaves the game.

set Three of a kind. A set is achieved when holding a **pocket** pair and having another card of the same rank coming on the **flop**, **turn**, or **river**.

set over set One player's **set** as compared to another player's set.

setup A box containing two decks of cards. Either a dealer or a player might request a new setup. The dealer would request it of the floor person if she felt there was a defective card, for example, and a player sometimes requests it of a dealer if he feels his luck is running badly.

sevens full A **full house** consisting of three 7s and another pair. Also called *sevens up* or *sevens over*.

shill A player who is playing for the house to help get a game started or keep a shaky game going. Actual shills do not keep any of their winnings. They are paid an hourly wage and play with house money.

short buy A **buy-in** of less than the usual minimum buy-in. Sometimes the house will allow this to keep action going in a shaky game. At other times, when there is a waiting list of players,

short buys either will not be allowed or only one *short buy* will be allowed between full buys.

short handed A game with less than the normal amount of players. Some card rooms will not offer *short-handed* games. In those that do, some players will not play in *short handed* Hold'em games because it doesn't allow them to get the correct odds on many types of bets.

short stacked Low on chips.

show To show one's cards on the **showdown**.

show both cards At the **showdown**, sometimes a player will only turn up one of their two **hole** cards. The dealer will then tell the player to "*show both cards,*" since the rules require it and the dealer is not permitted to touch a player's live hand.

showdown The point in the hand when, after all betting activity has taken place, all players turn their two **pocket** cards face up and compare them to everyone else's to determine who has the best hand.

show one, show all The unwritten rule in almost all poker rooms that says if a player shows his cards privately to one player, that all other players have a right to see the cards if challenged by a player in the game.

shuffle To mix the cards before dealing them.

side pot. Often referred to as *on the side*. A secondary pot that is created when one or more players still active in the hand have run out of chips while others remain who have enough chips to continue to bet. The additional bets go into the *side pot*.

sign-up board See **board**.

sixes full A **full house** consisting of three 6s and another pair. Also called *sixes over* and *sixes up*.

small bet The lower betting limit in a double-limit Hold'em game. For example, in a $4-$8 game, $4 is the *small bet*.

small blind Another name for the **little blind**.

smooth call To **call** with the intention of **raising** if anyone else raises. A form of slow playing one's hand similar to **check raising**.

snap off To win a hand you were behind on by **drawing** a needed card on the **river**. Or if you were on the losing end of such a situation, you might say, "My Aces were good until they were *snapped off* on the river by that third 4."

soft break The exchanging of cash for part chips, part money. For example, a player may give the dealer a $100 bill and ask for $40 cash and $60 worth of chips.

Spades One of the four suits of cards, the symbol of which is shaped like an inverted valentine with a stem: ♠ Spades are black in both the traditional deck and the four-color deck. A single card in the Spades suit is called a *Spade*.

splash the pot To throw one's chips into the pot rather than placing them in front of you, thereby mixing your chips in with those already in the pot. *Splashing the pot* is highly unethical as it makes it difficult or even impossible for the dealer or other players to tell how much you put into the pot. Some establishments will even remove a player who *splashes the pot* as it can be used as a form of cheating.

split pot A tied pot that is divided equally among all players with the same hand.

spread 1) To start a poker game. You might hear a floor person say, "We're just about to *spread* a $4-$8 game." 2) To fan out the cards of a new deck in front of the players to give them a chance to see that all fifty-two cards are in the deck.

square the table A request by either the dealer or a player to have the chairs at the table aligned properly so that all players are equally spaced at the table. Typically called for when one or more players are being crowded.

stack 1) All of one's chips. 2) A stack of twenty chips. 3) To arrange one's chips in neat piles after scooping in a pot.

starting hand A player's first two cards in Hold'em, also called **pocket** or **hole** cards.

steal a pot To win a pot by **bluffing**.

steal the blinds To win only the two **blinds** by making a **bluff** bet, usually in late position.

steam To be **on tilt**.

stiff the dealer Failing to tip the dealer after winning a pot.

straight A poker hand which consists of five cards of consecutive rank of mixed suits. A *straight* ranks just above **three of a kind** and just below a **flush**.

straight draw A poker hand that contains four cards to a **straight**.

straight flush A poker hand which consists of five cards of consecutive rank all of the same suit. A *straight* *flush* ranks above **four of a kind**. An Ace-high *straight flush* is also known as a **royal flush**.

string bet A bet which is either illegal or can be challenged as illegal by another player because all of the chips were not put into the pot at the same time.

strong hand A hand that has a high likelihood of winning.

structured-limit game Limit Texas Hold'em is a structured-limit game because the betting levels and limits are proscribed. There is no deviation of betting limits allowed in limit Hold'em.

stuck Amount one has lost. You might hear a player say, "I'm *stuck* two hundred."

sucker A loser or poor player.

suck out To draw out on an opponent.

suit One of the four groups of cards: Clubs ♣, Diamonds ♦, Hearts ♥, or Spades ♠.

suited Holding two **pocket** cards of the same suit.

suited connectors Holding two **pocket** cards of the same suit and consecutive in rank.

sweeten the pot To **raise**.

table change A request by a player to move to another table.

table charge 1) The portion taken out of each pot for house expenses and profit. Also called the **rake**. 2) In some casinos, players pay an hourly *table charge* instead of participating in a rake game. Sometimes referred to as *time* or *time collection*.

tell A mannerism that another player can pick up on that gives away your hand.

tens full A **full house** consisting of three 10s and another pair. Also called *tens over* and *tens up*.

Texas Hold'em The official name of Hold'em.

three of a kind A poker hand consisting of three cards all of the same rank, such as three Jacks. *Three of a kind* ranks just above **two pair** and just below a **straight**.

threes full A **full house** consisting of three 3s and another pair. Also called *threes over* and *threes up*.

tight Playing very conservatively.

tilt See **on tilt**.

time charge A fee charged by the establishment for the privilege of playing in the establishment, which provides the premises, licenses, cards, other players, etc.

toke A tip.

top pair A pair made by matching one of your **hole** cards with the highest **community card** on the board.

tournament chips Chips with no actual cash value and used only in tournaments.

trap To catch one or more players by playing your hand in such a way as to disguise its strength, usually by **checking**, underbetting, or **check-raising**.

tray The dealer's chip rack.

trey The 3 card.

trips Three of a kind. Shortened from the word triplets. *Trips* are usually considered to be made when holding one of the cards in your **pocket** and making two more on the **board**. Similar to a **set,** which is made when holding two of the cards in your pocket and making the third card on the board.

turn The *turn* card, which is the fourth card dealt face up on the **board**. After the *turn*, the betting level increases to twice the limit of the first two rounds.

two bets The first **raise** after a bet.

two pair A poker hand consisting of two cards of one rank and two cards of another rank. *Two pair* ranks just above **one pair** and just below **three of a kind**.

twos full A **full house** consisting of three 2s and another pair. Also called *twos over* and *twos up*.

uncalled bet A bet that is made by one player and not called by any other player, thereby giving the pot to the player who made the bet.

underbet To make a smaller bet than one might normally make, or to **call** instead of **raising**, in order to entice another player into raising for the purpose of reraising him later when one holds a powerful hand. One of the strategies used in **trapping** other players.

underpair To hold a **pocket** pair whose rank is lower than any of the three cards on the **flop**. For example, if you hold two 6s in your pocket and the **board** flops K-J-9, you hold an *underpair*.

under the gun The first player to **act** in a hand.

unlimited re-buys A tournament in which players who **bust out** are allowed to take an unlimited number of re-buys during a certain time period.

unsuited A term used to describe your two **pocket** cards when they are of different suits. Also called **offsuit**.

upcard In Hold'em, the five **community cards** are *upcards*–cards dealt face up.

upstairs To **raise**. Can be said, "Take it *upstairs*."

up to The person whose turn it is to bet. For example, if the **action** gets to a player who's not paying attention, after a few seconds that dealer might say to the player, "It's *up to* you."

value Getting paid off for a good hand. Also called *full value*.

value bet To bet for full **value** of one's hand.

varying one's play To occasionally play differently than you normally do so as to throw off opponents who think they know your style.

verbal bet An oral bet, which is binding if made in turn in most, but not all, card rooms.

verbal declaration An oral declaration of one's hand.

wager A bet.

wait To **check**.

weak hand A poker hand with a low probability of winning.

wheel A 5-high **straight** when the Ace is played as the low card.

white A $1 chip in most casinos. A stack of white is $20 and a rack of white is $100.

winning hand The best hand at **showdown**.

wired Holding a pair, usually as one card in the **pocket** and one on the **flop**, but occasionally used as a term for a pocket pair. You might hear a player say, "I had *wired* Kings but lost on the **river** to a set of 5s."

World Series of Poker Oftentimes written as WSOP. The game's grandest tournament was held at Binion's Horseshoe Casino in Las Vegas in late spring of each year through 2004, but has moved from downtown to the strip at the Rio starting in 2005. The tournament actually consists of numerous smaller tournaments featuring all kinds of poker, capped off by a No Limit Texas Hold'em tournament with a $10,000 buy-in. With the explosion of Hold'em worldwide, first place prize money grew to $5 million in 2004, up from $2.5 million in 2003, and from $1 million just a few years before that. The winner of each of the World Series events also gets a coveted gold bracelet.